PERCEVAL'S NARRATIVE

A PATIENT'S ACCOUNT OF HIS PSYCHOSIS

1830–1832

EDITED BY

GREGORY BATESON

WILLIAM MORROW & COMPANY, INC.
NEW YORK   1974

Perceval's Narrative was originally
published in two volumes, 1838 and
1840, under a different title (see
frontispiece). This edition contains
all of the first volume and much of
the second.

First Morrow Paperback Editions Printing 1974.

Perceval's Narrative was originally published in two volumes,
1838 and 1840, under the title *A Narrative of the Treatment
Experienced by a Gentleman, During a State of Mental Derangement; Designed to Explain the Causes and the Nature of Insanity, and to Expose the Injudicious Conduct Pursued Towards
Many Unfortunate Sufferers Under That Calamity.* This edition
contains all of the first volume and much of the second.

A Morrow Paperback Edition published by arrangement with
Stanford University Press.

Printed in the United States of America.
1 2 3 4 5 78 77 76 75 74

Library of Congress Catalog Card Number 74-14420

ISBN 0-688-07883-4 (pbk.)

INTRODUCTION

ON THE AFTERNOON of Monday, May 11, 1812, a certain John Bellingham, a businessman, armed with two pistols, entered the House of Commons and waited for the then Prime Minister, Spencer Perceval. When the Prime Minister arrived Bellingham shot him and killed him. This event is Bellingham's only claim to fame and is certainly the most conspicuous item in what remains in human memory of the life of Spencer Perceval.

A few days later Bellingham was hanged, and the House of Commons voted an indemnity of 50,000 pounds to the surviving family of the deceased Prime Minister.

Before this the family had apparently been in somewhat straitened circumstances. There were six sons and six daughters and there are hints that the Prime Minister was pressed in his political and legal career by the needs of these "twelve ravenous Percevals." Be that as it may, the indemnity granted by Government undoubtedly altered their circumstances very considerably and made it possible, when the fifth son, John Perceval, became insane, to place him in what were undoubtedly some of the best lunatic asylums in the country. We are told that it cost 300 guineas to incarcerate him for fourteen months, much against his will, in the asylum of Dr. Fox at Brisslington near Bristol.

It appears further that, after his recovery, his share of the indemnity made him so independent that he could write and publish—against his family's wishes—his *Narrative*. This consisted of two books, in which he makes contributions to our knowledge of schizophrenia, which entitle him to fame of a very different order from that achieved by his stuffy but ambitious father.

In recent years a number of autobiographical books have been published dealing with the writers' experiences during psychosis, but in general the value of these works is as specimens of psychotic or postpsychotic utterance rather than as scientific contributions in their own right. John Perceval achieved something more. Parts of his narrative, especially those parts that he wrote in hospital, are marred by his need to justify his bitterness, but he went further. In his compulsive struggle to make sense of his psychotic experiences, he discovered what we would today call the Freudian Unconscious and related this system of phenomena to what Freud later called the "psychopathology of everyday life" [p. 259]. He even observed the creative processes that occur during perception—those processes by which we make after-images or attribute imaginary forms to ink blots or to clouds in the sky—and he went on from this to realize that his own hallucinations might be phenomena of this sort.

His theoretical position is perhaps midway between that of Freud and that of William Blake. What Blake called the Creative Imagination Perceval assigns to some inner action of the Almighty. His language is often that of theology, where his thoughts are those of a scientist.

He says: ". . . the mind acts by beautiful and delicate machinery, which is disorganized in all men by sin and violence—by perverseness" [p. 291].

As his editor, working over what John Perceval wrote 120 years ago, I shall attempt two tasks: to summarize the information about John Perceval's life, and to call the reader's attention to some of Perceval's discoveries and to features of his story that have relevance and importance for modern psychiatry.

THE AUTHOR'S LIFE

John Thomas Perceval was the fifth son, among the twelve children of Spencer Perceval, the Prime Minister. He was born in 1803, and was therefore nine years old when his father was killed in the House of Commons. When he was eleven his mother married again, her second husband being Lieutenant Colonel Sir Henry Carr, K.C.B. There were no children by this second marriage, and indeed the only reference to Sir Henry Carr in Perceval's books is his occasional use of the name in letters to his mother. When angry, he addresses her, not as "Dear Mother," but as "Dear Lady Carr."

His boyhood seems to have been conventional. He entered the army and first served as an officer with a regiment of cavalry. Later he held the rank of Captain in the 1st Foot Guards. He saw overseas service in Portugal without combat.

Throughout this military period of his life, he was severely disturbed by religious conflict. His father had been a rabid anti-Catholic and an avid student of prophetic Scriptures, and now the son came under the influence of evangelical doctrines.

Early in 1830, he sold his commission and went briefly to the University of Oxford. From there he traveled to Scotland in June 1830 to inquire into the Row Miracles. This was an outburst of an extreme evangelical cult whose members were later called Irvingites. The devotees of the sect spoke with tongues in an unintelligible gibberish which they partly believed to be the language of the Pelew Islands. They were also much concerned with the problems of sincerity and with the need to speak both from the heart and in a spiritually given utterance.

Perceval was much impressed by the Irvingite doctrines, but it is evident that, even in this setting where gibberish was acceptable, Mary Campbell and other leaders of the group at Row felt that Perceval's behavior was too erratic.

He went from Row to Dublin, and recounts that he then had relations with a prostitute and believed himself to have contracted syphilis. From this he made a rapid recovery, which he attributed partly to medical and partly to miraculous intervention. He narrates with retrospective humor the characteristically schizophrenic dilemma in which he then found himself—whether to trust in God for the completion of his cure or to take the medicine which his doctor had ordered: he took half the prescribed dose.

Within a few days he was behaving in an actively disordered manner and was placed under restraint on December 16, 1830, in the room of the inn where he was staying. His oldest brother, Spencer, fetched him from Dublin and placed him in the asylum run by the Drs. Fox at Brisslington near Bristol in January 1831. He remained in this institution until May 1832, when he was moved to the asylum of Mr. C. Newington at Ticehurst in Sussex. He seems to have remained in this second institution until the beginning of 1834.

In 1834 he married Anna Gardner, by whom he had four daughters, the first born in 1836.

In 1835 he was in Paris writing his first book, which was published in 1838.

In 1840 the second book was published.

He later edited a book of verse, "Poems by a Prisoner in Bethlehem" by Arthur Legent Pearce. This was published in 1851.

I have almost no information about the remainder of his life. In 1859 he gave evidence to the Select Committee for Lunacy on behalf of an organization called the "Alleged Lunatics Friends Society." He also wrote occasional letters to *The Times* on the subject of lunacy laws, still defending the unfortunate people whose hardships he had experienced.

He died in 1876.

PERCEVAL'S INSIGHTS

Perceval asserts again and again that the patient knows more about the nature of insanity than either the general public or the "lunatic doctors" and he sees himself as having the serious purpose of communicating to the world what insanity is like and how the insane should be treated. What he has to say on the subject is first and foremost this: that it is the task or duty of the physician or of those who love the patient to *understand*. The patient's utterance is not to be brushed off as crazy nor is his behavior to be penalized with cold tubs or manacles.

This thesis is perhaps most clearly stated on the occasion when his oldest brother, Spencer, came to fetch him from Dublin:

When my brother first appeared by my bed-side, "I have hopes now," said I, "I shall be understood and respected;" for he had written to me that he believed the reported miracles at Row. When, however, I first told him, "I am desired to say so and so," "I am desired to do this, or that"—he replied to me, in an ill-judged tone of levity, and as if speaking to a child; ridiculing the idea. My hopes of being comprehended were blighted, and my heart turned from him [p. 52].

It is of course easy for the mental patient to argue that if only somebody else had done something different, he would not be in his present state; and it may be doubted whether, if Spencer had been both accepting and critical, John would have listened to him. But other material indicates that John's later recovery was facilitated whenever he encountered primary acceptance accompanied by doubt or criticism.

He says articulately in regard to his voices: "I perished from an habitual error of mind, . . . that of fearing to doubt, and of taking the guilt of doubt upon my conscience" [p. 37].

Perceval writes here, as often, with hindsight wisdom, as though it were only necessary to discover the uses of doubt in order to escape from a complex network of delusions. He ignores the facts of his own experience: that the courage to doubt his voices and his delusions grew in him slowly and painfully, and that the delusions themselves contributed to the process of this growth. Fearing to doubt, he falls into literal belief in his delusions and in what his voices tell him. But these messages are, after all, exaggerated caricatures of his own distorted Puritanism and guilt. By their very nature his delusions contain, in an inverted or concealed form, the very doubts that he is afraid to entertain in a more conscious shape. These same delusions lead him to those experiences that are their *reductio ad absurdum,* and it is, among other things, these repeated experiences of the ridiculous that finally drive him sane.

The phrase "taking the guilt of doubt upon my conscience" is a strange one, and we may well ask what precisely Perceval regarded as his "habitual error." Perceval goes on to assert that doubt, being involuntary, is not appropriate grist for the conscience. "To reject persuasion wilfully is one crime; but to declare wilfully that we believe what we doubt, or presumptuously that our doubts are wilful, is another" [p. 37]. He was, above all, a Protestant and concerned to extend rather than restrict the domain of the individual conscience. His error, as I read it, was a failure of responsibility. He ought not to have glutted his pride and weighted his conscience by branding doubt as "guilty." Rather, he should have accepted doubt as a function of the individual mind to be responsibly exercised. He ought to have taken the *responsibility* for doubt upon his conscience.

The whole of what Perceval has to say about the treatment that he *wishes* he had received turns upon this notion of responsibility. His brother Spencer should have given that acceptance which would have made the patient responsible for belief or doubt regarding the delusions. Merely to deny or to mock at the delusory material only subtracts from the patient's self-esteem. It asserts that he is incapable of the necessary wisdom and motivates him to a further caricaturing of his own imputed weakness.

The black-and-white universe of the paranoid may appear very certain, but it is not founded on certainty. Rather, it is compensatory. It is a denial of those accumulated inner fears and weaknesses which long and bitter experience of being put in the wrong has built up. Perceval says nothing of what his parents and siblings did to him to reinforce these feelings of weakness and unworthiness, but he narrates in some detail how he was treated by his hallucinatory voices. At the beginning of his psychosis in Dublin, he narrates:

I was tormented by the commands óf what I imagined was the Holy Spirit, to say other things, which as often as I attempted, I was fearfully rebuked for beginning in my own voice, and not in a voice given to me. These contradictory commands were the cause, now, as before, of the incoherency of my behaviour, and these imaginations formed the chief causes of my ultimate total derangement. For I was commanded to speak, on pain of dreadful torments, of provoking the wrath of the Holy Spirit, and of incurring the guilt of the grossest ingratitude; and at the same moment, whenever I attempted to speak, I was harshly and contumeliously rebuked for not using the utterance of a spirit sent to me; and when again I attempted, I still went wrong, and when I pleaded internally that I knew not what I was to do, I was accused of falsehood and deceit; and of being really unwilling to do what I was commanded. I then lost patience, and proceeded to say what I was desired pell-mell, determined to show that it was not fear or want of will that prevented me. But when I did this, I felt as formerly the pain in the nerves of my palate and throat on speaking, which convinced me that I was not only rebelling against God, but against nature; and I relapsed into an agonizing sense of hopelessness and of ingratitude [pp. 32–33].

Here the voices present him with the false thesis that there exist alternatives of action among which he might choose one course of which the voices would approve. He makes his choices and tries to obey, but is always blamed at some more abstract level —e.g., for lack of sincerity. He is placed by the voices in what has been called a "double bind" such that even if he does the right thing he is blamed for doing it for the wrong reasons.

And his final word, "ingratitude," suggests that this pattern of unconscious expectation—that every course will lead to rejection—has probably been early instilled by the behavior of parents and siblings.

Later the voices shift their ground:

At another time, my spirits began singing to me in this strain. "You are in a lunatic asylum, if you will"—"if not, you are in," &c. &c. "That is Samuel Hobbs if you will—if not, it is Herminet Herbert," &c. &c. &c. But I had been so long deceived by my spirits that now I did not believe them when they spoke truth. However, by listening and finding that the patients called him Samuel Hobbs, and by other accidents, I discovered at last that I was yet on earth, in natural, although very painful, circumstances in a madhouse. My delusions being thus very much abolished, I soon after got liberty of limb during the day-time [p. 146].

Here the voices are doing what Perceval wished his brother had done—accepting the fact of the delusion and reinforcing the doubt. They are also presenting real alternatives between which the patient can and must choose, while indicating their willingness to accept either choice. Perceval remarks that it was very unpleasant to have the voices do this, but he is honest enough to perceive that every time they do it he makes a step toward recovery.

Here then Perceval presents, in two diagrammatic thumbnail sketches, the recipes, first for inducing his insanity and then for curing it.

But the matter is not so simple. The therapist cannot just go on the wards and sing to the schizophrenic patients little ditties which will offer them alternatives instead of double binds. The therapist is (usually) not an hallucinated voice, and, in any case, what Perceval's voices do for him—what he has them do—is first to administer the pathogenic recipe and only later the curative. It is the combination of the two recipes that constitutes the total psychotic experience through which the patient must go in order to recover.

This is one of the most interesting characteristics of the strange condition known as schizophrenia: that the disease, if it be one, seems sometimes to have curative properties. What Perceval tells us has been more generally recognized in recent years. We are today familiar with the fact that many of the so-called symptoms of organic disease are the efforts that the body makes to correct some deeper pathology, and we are familiar with the fact that dreams, with or without interpretation, may contribute to the process of psychotherapy. There is even evidence that indicates that to be deprived of dreaming leads to psychic stress.

The dynamics of the curative nightmare are, however, quite obscure.

It is one thing to see the symptom as a part of a defense mechanism; it is quite another to conceive that the body or the mind contains, in some form, such wisdom that it can create that *attack* upon itself that will lead to a later resolution of the pathology.

Perceval's voices tear him down till he is nothing but a passive slob of "ingratitude." But they are *his* voices and he has them do this to him. Later he has them shift their ground and do to him something that is the converse of what they did earlier—they present him with alternatives. But this too is painful. Again, in the process of getting well he achieves the appropriate attack upon himself.

By mysterious unconscious processes, then, Perceval was able to orchestrate his own psychic experience to enforce his own passage through psychosis, but this does not mean that it would have been at all simple for his brother Spencer, or for the doctors, to interact with Perceval in a way that would speed up the process. What he tells us about the asylums in which he was confined is, however, worth examining from this point of view. Were they effective?

From the diatribes of a single patient in 1830, it is not possible to assess whether his treatment was more or less humane—or more or less effective—than that which a similar patient might encounter in an expensive institution in 1961. It is evident, however, that the mental hospitals of that day were already trapped in the dilemmas that beset such places today. Perceval's voices were able to provide him with gross and painful caricatures of double-bind experience, but the hospitals could only simulate this experience out of clumsiness and hypocrisy. Then as now, the principal modes of treatment were such as to reduce the patient's sense of his own worth and responsibility. To the strait jackets, the cold tubs, and the isolation rooms of those days, modern institutional psychiatry has added the shock therapies and the tranquilizing drugs, but the principles of treatment are not much changed. Even in 1830, there was a strong desire on the part of the staff to keep the ward quiet, and even then there was a tendency to tell the patient as little as possible about decisions that concerned him and still less about the reasons for these decisions. All in all, much was done to increase the patient's sense of isolation and unworthiness, and he was provided with plenty of unexplained and painful experiences around which he could build delusional explanations.

Perceval, as he began to realize the nature of the system that surrounded and controlled him, became enraged. He saw clearly the hypocrisy, the ignorance, and the venal motives of the practitioners, and, no doubt, this rage and this insight contributed much to his recovery.

But, even then, the patients' rage was met with an increased intensity of treatment, and, then as now, patients noticed that these intensified treatments resembled punishment.

Perceval's voices were grotesquely punitive and, with a caricature of injustice, reduced him to feelings of utter ingratitude; the doctors and the asylum staff attempted no less, but without caricature. The failure of the system is evident in Dr. Fox's letter [pp. 206–8], and Perceval is not slow to perceive the sanctimonious and self-contradictory character of this document. He sums the matter up: "Even now that suspicion still affects me, whether I am to consider that Dr. Fox was acting wittingly, or that from the habitual and unchecked practice of imposture he knew not what spirit he was of" [p. 207].

It thus appears that the system of treatment, while attempting to reduce the patients to self-repudiation, could not do so in a manner that would speed their passage through psychosis. The practitioners, whether trapped in good intentions or in the need to appear to have good intentions, were bound to a rigid system of conduct—a system even more rigid than the exaggerated evangelicism of Perceval's voices. The latter, after all, could shift their ground and tone according to the needs of the patient.

At this point a digression is necessary. Every recovered schizophrenic presents the problem—how and why did recovery occur?

And this problem is seen as especially urgent when the recovery is achieved with a minimum of medical interference. What is called "spontaneous remission" is regarded as a mystery.

Perceval's narrative and some of the other autobiographical accounts of schizophrenics* propose a rather different view of the psychotic process. It would appear that once precipitated into psychosis the patient has a course to run. He is, as it were, embarked upon a voyage of discovery which is only completed by his return to the normal world, to which he comes back with insights different from those of the inhabitants who never embarked on such a voyage. Once begun, a schizophrenic episode would appear to have as definite a course as an initiation ceremony—a death and rebirth—into which the novice may have been precipitated by his family life or by adventitious circumstance, but which in its course is largely steered by endogenous process.

In terms of this picture, spontaneous remission is no problem. This is only the final and natural outcome of the total process. What needs to be explained is the failure of many who embark upon this voyage to return from it. Do these encounter circumstances either in family life or in institutional care so grossly maladaptive that even the richest and best organized hallucinatory experience cannot save them?

Let us consider what sort of man Perceval was and to what extent he is justified in claiming that he had completely recovered when he was writing the first book in Paris in 1835 and the chapters about his recovery in the second book. How sane is the anger of a man who must repetitiously justify his anger? How sane is a man whose final word to the world is the statement that he still intends to sue his mother for complicity with the Doctors Fox? How sane is a man who must assert his intention to escape from a lunatic asylum before he makes the actual attempt? How sane is a man who says: "I found that no patient could escape from his confinement in a truly sound state of mind, without lying against his conscience, or admitting the doctrine, that deception and duplicity are consistent with a sound conscience" [p. 125].

* Barbara O'Brien, *Operators and Things* (Arlington Books, 1958).

All of these questions are interrelated and together give us a picture of a man, ridden by anger on the one hand and by over-scrupulosity on the other. These characteristics form a mutually promoting couple. The greater the anger, the more need to re-strain it by scrupulous examination of its justification; and the stronger the logical proof of justification, the greater the anger. This is a man singularly uncomfortable to live with. He would have been easier to live with had he been a little less upright and a little less angry—all in all, a little less rigid.

But the rigidity and the underlying violence of his character also provide the dynamics, whereby he is compelled to undertake the gigantic effort to make sense of his delusions and thereby to achieve his "recovery." He owed his recovery to those same per-sonal idiosyncrasies that had cast him into insanity. He indeed says this, though in a theological idiom: ". . . thus the Almighty condescended to heal by the imagination that which, by tricks on the imagination, he had wounded, broken and destroyed" [p. 308].

Another question which we may appropriately ask about his recovery concerns the shifts and shadings of his belief in his hal-lucinatory voices. He recounts how he had taken the voices liter-ally at the beginning of his illness. Later he discovers what is now generally recognized, namely, that the utterances of a schizophren-ic and his delusions are to be taken as metaphoric rather than literal: "The spirit speaks poetically but the man understands it literally" [p. 271]. He even engages in humorous—perhaps hebe-phrenic—interchanges with his voices. He speaks of "a spirit of humour, which made me try to deceive my spirits" [p. 113].

He discovers also that his voices are remarkably unreliable—that what they promise does not happen; and he recognizes that every such contradictory experience, while unpleasant, contributes to his recovery.

He discovers the power of his imagination to create perceptions and images, either in the ear or in the eye, and this relieves much of his anxiety regarding the phenomena of hallucination.

But in spite of all these discoveries, his voices are still in some sense real to him. Speaking of the acts that he performed in obedience to them he says: "I now know that scarcely one of the things I said, or one of the things I did, was I intended to perform" [p. 265].

The voices are still real, they still intend certain meanings; it was he that was in error in his understanding of them. This may be insanity, but it is not far from orthodox theology nor far from orthodox psychoanalytic theory in which the patient must learn a new way of understanding his dreams.

He has returned to the normal world but with a new perception of it.

We now ask what system of circumstances may have been responsible for forcing Perceval to embark upon this extraordinary voyage and what circumstances may have hindered its progress.

The second of these questions is already partly answered by Perceval's comments upon the doctors and their institutions. They may have helped him by promoting rage, but they also hindered him by their inflexible need to appear virtuous and wise.

If these were hindering and even exacerbating circumstances during the progress of the psychosis, it is reasonable to look for similar circumstances in Perceval's relations with his family to see whether these might not have been precipitating or conditional causes.

He gives us no picture of his boyhood, so that all we have to go on is the sequence of steps through which he came to perceive his own role vis-à-vis his mother and his brothers.

In the Preface to his second book he states:

. . . he hopes to teach the wretched and affectionate relations of a deranged person, what may be his necessities, and how to conduct themselves toward him, so that they may avoid the errors which were unfortunately committed by the author's own family.

But he is not able to give clear recipes for how the relatives should behave. What is available in the narrative is a voluminous statement of how he felt and expressed himself toward his mother and toward his oldest brother, Spencer, during the period of his psychosis and recovery. Several times he identifies his family with the doctors and plans to sue both for their treatment of him. At other times he writes to his family letters which he hopes the doctors will see:

I could not always overcome my exasperation. But even then I was frequently influenced by a spirit of bravado and defiance of the doctors, to whom I knew my letters were subjected for inspection; I was determined, if they declared that my anger at being confined, and at my treatment, was a proof of my madness, that they should have evidence enough of it [p. 211].

Such perverse behavior, deliberately provoking the outside world to do its damnedest, is characteristic of so many schizophrenics that their motto would seem to be "If things are not as I want them, I will prove it."

He continues this discussion of the reasons for his sarcasm and violence with an extraordinary piece of insight:

Even a deeper motive lay hid under all this violence of expression; and this may perhaps by many be deemed an insane motive: I knew that, of all the torments to which the mind is subject, there is none so shocking, so horrid to be endured as that of remorse for having injured or neglected those who deserved our esteem and consideration. I felt for my sisters, my brothers, and my mother: I knew they could not endure to look upon what they had done towards me, to whom they were once so attached, if they rightly understood it; that they could know no relief from the agony of that repentance which comes too late, gnawing the very vitals, but in believing me partly unworthy of their affection; and therefore I often gave the reins to my pen, that they might hereafter be able to justify themselves, saying he has forfeited our respect, he has thrown aside the regard due to his parentage and to his kindred—he has deserved our contempt, and merited our abandonment of him [pp. 211–12].

Perceval here puts his finger on a central theme of the relationship between the psychotic and those closest to him. In almost every such family, it is possible to recognize that the psychotic individual has the functions of a necessary sacrifice. He must by his schizophrenic behavior conceal or justify those actions of the other members which evoked—and still evoke—his schizophrenia.

One side of this picture is familiar. The rejected child is commonly unable to accept the fact of rejection without giving the parent ample justification for it. To perceive that he was rejected unjustly would intolerably devalue the parent in the child's eyes. From this perception, he must therefore protect himself:

> I also found it a relief to my mind, to be able to say that there was some excuse for my relations' conduct towards me; for that which I found most insufferable, was the sense or the idea that I was treated with complete injustice, and without any cause of offense [p. 214].

Such complex reversals of motive are exceedingly difficult for the parents to meet. They cannot perceive their own perfidy except as justified by the patient's behavior, and the patient will not let them perceive how his behavior is related to his view of what they have done and are now doing. The tyranny of "good intentions" must endlessly be served while the patient achieves an ironic sainthood, sacrificing himself in foolish or self-destructive actions until at last he is justified in quoting the Saviour's prayer: "Father, forgive them, they know not what they do.—Amen" [p. 209].

This prayer is after all appropriate when we remember that the schizophrenic has devoted years to preventing his parents from seeing their own actions except within the frame of his misbehavior.

In sum, it appears that there is a strong formal analogy between the trap in which the doctors find themselves and that of the relatives of the schizophrenic. In each case there is an appearance of unyielding hypocrisy. There is, however, this difference, that the patient's love for his parents enforces upon him a deep secrecy regarding the sacrificial nature of his behavior. This secrecy is so strong in most schizophrenics as to be of the nature of a repression. The patient himself cannot entertain consciously the idea that these are his motives. And Perceval makes a big stride toward sanity when he accepts this insight.

It is reasonable to picture the young Perceval before his psychosis as a very rigid, disciplined, and careful young man with grotesque standards of honesty and a habit of distrusting passion. Consciously, he probably believed that honesty could only be achieved through an exact carefulness. Unconsciously this exact carefulness had the function of concealing the gross discrepancies and lacunae in his relationship with his family. Before the psychosis his exactitude was his self-sacrificing mode. During psychosis, he passes through the phase of bitterness, where the violence takes the place of the former precision.

We may suppose that this code of concealment and sacrifice was in many ways uncomfortable and that his groping after evangelical religion was both a quest for some escape and a clinging to whatever would support his careful uprightness. All this was a build-up of conditional causes; the actual precipitating cause may well have been his adventure with the Irvingites. Here he faced a new challenge, the thesis that he ought as a religious man to combine sincerity with spontaneity and that he contained within himself an immanent supernatural force which he should allow to speak even nonsense through his mouth.

These doctrines, which presented themselves under the guise of religion and which therefore were an acceptable variant on the dogmas of his childhood, were, however, an ironic converse of all that childhood discipline which he needed to conceal what was basically wrong in his previous way of life.

It is interesting to follow his sexual history. The excitements of Row were immediately followed by his adventure with the prostitute in Dublin. For this he was punished by a real or imaginary venereal infection. He then plunged into psychosis and, as it seems, experienced two periods when his visions took on sexual forms of great beauty. The first of these periods he had to repudiate as evil, the second he was able to accept as a miraculous gift of the Almighty, and almost immediately following his release from Newington's asylum he married.

To evaluate a psychosis is perhaps impossible. Conventionally, schizophrenia is regarded as a disease, and, in terms of this hypothesis, both the conditions necessary for it and the precipitating causes which bring on the attack must be regarded as disastrous. But it would appear that Perceval was a better, happier, and more imaginative man after his psychotic experience, and in this introductory essay I have suggested that the psychosis is more like some vast and painful initiatory ceremony conducted by the self. From this point of view, it is perhaps still reasonable to regard the conditional causes with horror. The precipitating causes can only be welcomed.

> We shall not cease from exploration
> And the end of all our exploring
> Will be to arrive where we started
> And know the place for the first time.
>   T. S. ELIOT, "Little Gidding"*

BIBLIOGRAPHIC NOTE

The title page of John Perceval's second book is reproduced as frontispiece to the present volume. The title page of the first is in a somewhat different type face but the wording is the same except for the omission of the author's name. The date of the first book is 1838.

In content, the two books are almost entirely different. The first consists of a brief biography of the author up to the time of his confinement in Dr. Fox's asylum, followed by an extensive account of his fourteen months in that asylum. It terminates with the farewell speech of Dr. Fox, "Good bye, Mr. ——, I wish I could give you hopes of your recovery."

The author tells us that the whole of the first book was written in Paris in 1835 after his confinement under Mr. Newington. He had left behind in England many documents and a diary which he had written at Dr. Fox's, and wrote the account from memory. This anonymous first volume ends with a postscript: "The Letters promised in an appendix at the end of the volume have been suppressed on the ground of delicacy by the advice of my Publisher."

The second book starts with a long invective Preface, which is omitted in the present volume.

The Preface is followed by a confused two-page Introduction (here omitted) which he indicates was written in 1834, but in which he refers to the writing of the first book in Paris in 1835 and to its publication (1838).

---

* From *Four Quartets*, copyright, 1943, by T. S. Eliot; reprinted by permission of Harcourt, Brace & World, Inc.

There follow four chapters which are a preliminary draft, written in Newington's asylum in 1832, of the material which Perceval later expanded to form the first book.

The second book continues with the reproduction of a number of letters and documents written at Dr. Fox's—presumably the letters referred to as suppressed at the end of the first book. These are followed by an account of his troubles with Dr. Newington and his attempts to get the attention of the magistrates whose duty it was to supervise the treatment of the insane.

This book also contains three magnificent chapters on the steps of his recovery.

In reducing these two books to a single volume I have tried to give the reader everything pertinent to an understanding of John Perceval, his psychosis, and his narration of the steps by which he believed that his recovery was achieved. I have also included almost all the material relevant to his relations with his family.

There are, however, many pages devoted to bitter protest against his family and against the institutions in which he was confined. That these protests were in many ways justified I have no doubt, and indeed a majority of those confined today in mental hospitals must with equal justification think similar bitter thoughts. The problem of how best to deal with the psychotic is still unsolved at the institutional level. But Perceval's justifications of his bitterness become repetitive, and a sufficient sample of this material is already included with the narrative chapters.

In detail the present volume is constructed as follows:

1. It contains the whole of Perceval's first book.

2. It omits the whole of his 26-page Preface and the two-page Introduction to the second book.

3. Chapters I–III and the beginning of Chapter IV are omitted, so that in the present version the second book begins with the presentation of the letters written while he was at Dr. Fox's, which letters he says that he suppressed when he published the first book "on the ground of delicacy by the advice of my Publisher." These letters become Chapter XXVIII of the present volume.

4. Chapters V and VI are omitted as being contentious and repetitive.

5. The first three pages of Chapter VII have been omitted; the remainder is retained and becomes Chapter XXIX in the present volume.

6. Chapter VIII is retained and becomes Chapter XXX.

7. Chapter IX is omitted.

8. Chapter X becomes Chapter XXXI.
Chapter XI becomes Chapter XXXII.
Chapter XII becomes Chapter XXXIII.
Chapter XIII becomes Chapter XXXIV.
Chapter XIV becomes Chapter XXXV.
Chapter XV becomes Chapter XXXVI.
Chapter XVI becomes Chapter XXXVII.

9. Chapters XVII and XVIII describing Perceval's ineffectual appeals to the magistrates are here omitted, except for Perceval's letter in which he inquires about the possibility of resuming his career at Oxford. This letter becomes Chapter XXXVIII.

PERCEVAL'S NARRATIVE

"By detailing and explaining his sufferings, and his complaints, and his difficulties—he hopes to teach the wretched and affectionate relations of a deranged person, what may be his necessities, and how to conduct themselves toward him, so that they may avoid the errors which were unfortunately committed by the author's own family."

—*Author's Preface to 1840 edition.*

CHAPTER I

In the year 1830, I was unfortunately deprived of the use of reason. This calamity befel me about Christmas. I was then in Dublin. The Almighty allowed my mind to become a ruin under sickness—delusions of a religious nature, and treatment contrary to nature. My soul survived that ruin. As I was a victim at first, in part to the ignorance or want of thought of my physician, so I was consigned afterwards to the control of other medical men, whose habitual cruelty, and worse than ignorance—*charlatanism*—became the severest part of my most severe scourge. I suffered great cruelties, accompanied with much wrong and insult; first, during my confinement, when in a state of childish imbecility in the year 1831; secondly, during my recovery from that state, between November, 1831, and May, 1832; thirdly, during the remainder of the year 1832, and the year 1833, when I considered myself to be of sane mind. Having been under the care of four lunatic doctors, whose systems of treatment differ widely from each other—having conversed with two others, and having lived in company with Lunatics, observing their manners, and reflecting on my own, I deem that alone sufficient excuse for setting forth my griefs and theirs, before men of understanding, to whom I desire to be supposed addressing myself, and for obtruding upon them more of my personal history than might otherwise be prudent or becoming. Because I wish to stir up an intelligent and active sympathy, in behalf of the most wretched, the most oppressed, the only helpless of mankind, by proving with how much needless tyranny they are treated—and this in mockery—by men who pretend indeed their cure, but who are, in reality, their tormentors and destroyers.

I open my mouth for the dumb; and let it be recollected, that I write in defence of youth and old age, of female delicacy, modesty, and tenderness, not only of man and of manhood—surrendered up in weakness to indecent exposure, disgusting outrage, or uncalled for violence—that I write for the few who are objects of suspicion and alarm,—to society, who too much engrossed in business or in pleasure to exercise reflection, are equally capable of treating these objects of their dread and insolence, with lunatic cruelty, and the insanest mismanagement; being deprived, like them, of understanding, by exaggerated and unreasonable fear, but not like them by illness, of the guilt of their misconduct. The subject to which I direct attention, is also one on which, my readers, according to man's wont, the wisest of you are hasty to decide in action, or to hazard an opinion in proportion even to your ignorance.

In the name of humanity, then, in the name of modesty, in the name of wisdom, I intreat you to place yourselves in the position of those whose sufferings I describe, before you attempt to discuss what course is to be pursued towards them. Feel for them; try to defend them. Be their friends,—argue not hostilely. Feeling the ignorance to be in one sense real, which all of you confess on your lips, listen to one who can instruct you. Bring the ears and the minds of children, children as you are, or pretend to be, in knowledge—not believing without questioning, but questioning that you may believe.

CHAPTER II

I was born of parents powerful, honourable, and happy, till a cruel blow deprived my mother of a husband, and her family of a father. He was a minister of state; and my relations rank among the aristocracy and wealth of my country. I was educated in the bosom of peace and plenty, in principles of delicacy and decorum, in modest and temperate habits, and in the observance of, and real veneration for, the religion of my country.

At the age of seventeen, I left the public school, at which I had passed seven years, not without credit, to study with a private tutor, and the next year, the inclination I had formed in childhood for a military life still predominating, my family procured me a commission in a regiment of cavalry; two troops of that regiment being shortly after reduced, I was placed on half-pay, and allowed next year to exchange into the Guards. I owed both my commissions to the kindness of the Duke of York, and to the attention of his secretary, Sir Herbert Taylor, who were glad to show their respect for the memory of my father. I had been nursed in the lap of ease, and scrupulous morality; I now entered the school of polite and gentlemanly behaviour.

I passed my life in the Guards quiet and unobserved. I had, as at school, three or four friends, and no very extensive general acquaintance. If I was remarkable in society for any thing, it was for occasional absence of mind, and for my gravity and silence when the levity of my companions transgressed the bounds of decorum, and made light of religion, or offended against morality. I was firm also in resisting all attempts to drive me by ridicule into intemperance. In private I had severe conflict of mind upon the truth and nature of the Christian religion, accompanied with acute agony at my own inconsistency of conduct and sentiment with the principles of duty and feeling taught by Jesus and His apostles; and mingled with astonishment at the whirlpool of dissipation, and contradiction in society around me. After several years' inward suffering and perplexity, question and examination, I found at last, for a time, peace, and joy, and triumph, as I imagined, in the doctrines usually styled "evangelical." Till then the sacrifice of Jesus Christ, instead of being a message of gladness, had always been to me one of increasing woe and shame; as a sinner, to whom it made the law more binding, the offences against the law more ungrateful—the heinousness of crime deeper, in proportion to my conception of the boundless love of Almighty God. Then I understood that the law was done away in Christ, and liberty given to the mind, so that the soul might choose gratefully what it could not be driven to by fear. In the year 1829, my conduct first became decided and extreme, through the active principle instilled by the doctrines I have named; and in the spring of the year 1830, influenced chiefly by this new principle of action, I obtained permission to sell my commission in the Guards.

Since, however, many reasons combined to determine this resolution, I will mention them briefly. Not unconscious that they may excite the ridicule of many, nor that a few may accuse me of vanity in the detail, as well as in what I have already written. But my object is, without affecting more candour than is necessary, and without pretending to excuse or to blame, to show in my own instance the kind of disposition that was exposed to treatment of too sad a nature. For in arguing on the treatment of lunatics, mankind usually, though confessing ignorance, set out with the conceit that ill-treatment (or, to use the well-disguised language of the physicians, "wholesome restraint," or "wholesome correction") is necessary; and proceed as if this conceit were a principle established on evidence, instead of wickedly admitted through the very ignorance they avow. Next, in hearing the complaints of lunatics, they are prone to the suspicion, that the evil conduct of the complainant brought both his calamity and his persecutions upon him; and not that mild and civil, and even childlike, as well as childish natures, are submitted to cruel tortures from profane hands—through the supineness of society in abandoning individuals, without knowledge of the disease or discrimination, into the hands of men of little education, and of low origin, implicitly relying on their pretensions, yet as men dealing only practically with such patients.

CHAPTER III

In the first place, the evangelical opinions I had embraced, containing, as I imagined, the light of everlasting truth, given me freely through the election of God the Father, for the sake of the obedience, and sacrifice of Jesus Christ, and to the end that His own glory might be made manifest, in changing a vile and weak creature into the likeness of Divine holiness, excited in me gratitude and fear: gratitude for the gift given me, and for that election; and fear of the wrath of God, if I disobeyed the end for which it was given. That which had been done for me, I thought it my duty to preach to others, and to explain the doctrines, whereby I had been saved. Moved by these arguments, I spoke and acted in open confession of my faith, a line of conduct not very agreeable to the army, even if called for, and judicious. Being then in Dublin, I attached myself to a society for reading the Scriptures to the Irish poor; I attended the regimental schools; I read the service to a detachment I commanded, as the men had not seats provided for them in church;—I tried to establish a reading-room for the soldiers of my battalion;—I procured religious and other books for the sick in hospital, and being afterwards quartered in town, hearing that two battalions of guards and the recruits, through the neglect of the Chaplain and indifference of the commanding officers, had been for a long time upon one pretence or another without opportunity of attending Divine service at all, by privately applying to a clergyman in Westminster, and to an officer of one battalion of like sentiments to my own, we procured seats for the men in a large chapel, belonging to the Church of

England. I had obtained the like permission from a clergyman of the established church for the other battalion, when I found that this conduct excited suspicion and offence. Both Colonel and Chaplains showed some symptoms of chagrin—they charged me with having sent the men to a dissenting minister. My conduct in reading the service to the detachment I for a time commanded near Dublin, in circulating religious books, and in other respects, drew on me also private animadversions, although in no instance did I transgress military discipline; in the first case, I acted only in obedience to the regulations of the army. Now, though not sure that I was doing quite right, I felt inclined to do more;—for I outfaced slander and cavil thus, that even if I were in the extreme, it was but fair that one should be in the extreme in the cause of Christ, when so many were running recklessly a course of gaiety and dissoluteness. But as I really esteemed my superior officer, who was both kind, intelligent, and actively beneficent; and as I loved good discipline, I judged it prudent to withdraw from a scene of constant conflict with my own conscience, where I was tempted to act unwisely, and where I might be led into quarrel with those whom I loved and respected, through conduct I might afterwards sincerely repent of.

In the next place, I was led by a passage in the New Testament, exhorting the Christian to choose *liberty* rather than slavery. I conceived this advice applicable to a situation like my own, where I was so much confined in the liberty of speech and conversation with the private soldier, by the strict discipline of the service. After that, I reflected on my natural disposition, talents, and acquirements. I was fond of quiet, seclusion, and study; unused to boisterous sports, untried in situations requiring promptitude and decision. I had a long time mistrusted my courage, and presence of mind, and had feared, that in the hour of trial, I might do discredit to the regiment and to my own name. In 1827, in Portugal, I had seen a bloodless campaign, excepting the assassination of one or two of the men and outrages upon the officers, unatoned for. Though the scene was novel and the country beautiful, my mind was fatigued by the long marches between the towns—to do nothing. I disliked idleness, accompanied by suspense of mind, separation from all means of regular study, and the absence of the attractions of female society. One night we had encamped, and I came to the resolution that my life might be a very romantic one, but that it was far from being agreeable. I was cheerful and contented, and glad that we had a fine night, but I judged coolly, and with reason, that a better cause than that of kings and constitutions, the instruments after all, and the embodyings of the spirit of Satan, was required to justify the sacrifice of happiness and comfort to one, who needed not to gain his *living* by cutting his neighbour's throat. I felt too, in the end, that we had been made fools and tools of. My tastes, therefore, were little suited to a military life, and my talents and acquirements not much more. I had already too much religion, to enjoy thoughtless dissipation, and too much reflection, to be the blind instrument of power; though I had been a long time in the army, and had devoted part of that time to acquire an insight into the principles of the profession, and a knowledge of languages, in hopes of being of service to my country; yet my attention had been chiefly absorbed by points of evidence and doctrine connected with religion, and I found myself at last, better adapted to confute a Papist or an infidel, without committing myself, than to manœuvre a battalion, or even to direct a company.

Religion therefore and propriety thus dictating to me, affection also had its weight. My youngest brother held a commission as captain in a regiment of cavalry, and was endowed with many qualities which fit a man to be a soldier. I regretted that I had placed myself in his way, and I hoped by removing myself from the army, that the interest of my family would be united to further his advancement when an opportunity might offer.

I next took a view of politics. At that time the Duke of Wellington had just succeeded Mr. Canning, and I had been disgusted and exasperated by what I still consider the betrayal of Portugal into the hands of Don Miguel, for continental purposes. My last attachment to the Tory party, and to the pride of being an Englishman, were then severed. I had thought my country upright, noble, and generous, and that party honest and honourable. I now despised the one, and began to hate and fear the other. Holding his conduct to have been dishonourable in respect of Portugal, I was not surprised at the Duke's change of policy in yielding the Roman Catholic question to the Irish Papists, but I was alarmed by the tone of his government, opposing the desire of the nation for reform, after that fatal blow to our Protestant institutions, and I conceived it but too possible that he might have the idea of putting down the will of the people by the bayonet; and if that struggle come, thought I, I should like to be free to choose my side, if it be agreeable to the will of God that I should interfere at all.

I was also strongly persuaded that the time of the end was at hand, and that God was about to visit the nations with His plagues, His promises having been rejected; and finding in Scripture an exhortation to His people to come out in those days from the profane, and to flee to the mountains, &c., &c., I reflected whether the words had not a practical, as well as a figurative application, and I deemed it right to place myself at liberty to act as I might be enlightened.

So, seeking liberty, I fell into confinement; seeking to serve the Almighty, I disgraced His worship and my own name. During the period that I was under personal restraint, my brother left the army, the Duke of Wellington and his colleagues resigned, and were succeeded by a Whig administration; and when the cholera visited my country, I was preserved from it. "It came not nigh my dwelling." My own mind also had undergone a complete change in its views of the Christian faith, principle, and duty, and God knows my courage was submitted to severe trial.

CHAPTER IV

Now, my readers, come with me to Oxford. I have stated that I imagined I had found peace and triumph in the doctrines of the evangelical preachers. I add, and it follows of course, joy unutterable and full of glory. At first this was the case. In Dublin, where the light of these doctrines first broke in upon me with force sufficient to give decision to my conduct I found in society individuals of congenial thought; and here my own conduct was one series of devotion to supposed religious duties and to religious enquiry. I felt endued with a new nature, and with power to overcome all those habits, which had most vexed me during my life. In boldness of conduct—and of speech—in activity—in diligence, and in purity of mind, I conceived I saw the fruits of a new life, the evidences of the gifts of the Holy Spirit. My mind and conduct were for the first time consistent with each other; but when I returned to England, where I stood alone, amongst society, and amongst officers, gentlemanly and moderate, but indifferent to spiritual truths, and inclined to turn *religion* or too much religion into ridicule, I felt first puzzled, then undecided, then mistrustful of myself, then mistrustful of my call to be a disciple of Christ Jesus,—I became lukewarm,—I became inconsistent—I fell into sin—I expected to have been kept from sin by the Holy Spirit —*that* was my idea of salvation—*that* I understood was the gift promised to me in the gospel. Now at times, I feared that I was a castaway—at times, I threw away all fear, in bold, but contrite reliance on the pledged word of the Almighty, for on that alone I fancied I had *relied*; therefore when I left the army, I desired in my own mind to retire to study at Dublin, which I called *my cradle in the Spirit,* because there I might unite society with study, and be corroborated in practice by the example of the zealous churchmen in that city. Religion is not amongst them a matter of form and ceremony, it is *the motive and end of their life.* My duty to my mother, however, and my attachment to England, determined me to choose an English university, and a hope of acquiring habits of *regularity,* made me fix on Oxford. I was pleased with my choice. The order, the quiet, the cleanliness, the beautiful simplicity of character I met with there—the majesty, the elegance, the antiquity of the buildings, the variety of their architecture, their solidity, their preservation, with all the means of study, repose, and reflection, enchanted me. I only regretted that I had not retired from a military life earlier. I only wanted, as I thought, a wife to add to my tranquillity. The evangelical doctrines I put faith in having at that time very few preachers in the church, I often frequented the Baptist and Independent meeting-houses, to hear their preachers. Soon after entering Oxford, I attended a dissenting chapel. But being warned of the offence I might give to the authorities, by continuing such a course, I gave it up after my matriculation; and then went to a church where a gentleman of the name of Bulteel preached in a vehement manner doctrines then almost peculiar to himself, and in the highest degree Calvinistic. On setting out for the University, I had been greatly oppressed by the fear that I should find no communion of spirit with any persons there, of my own condition. By the side of an old man's sick bed, to whose room I had been introduced by the clergyman of the parish, a friend of one of my brothers, I first met with one of the young Calvinists, who formed part of this gentleman's congregation; and he introduced me to the society of his friends, who were for the most part young men, and became my chief acquaintance. I looked upon this then as a signal instance of the Divine protection and goodness. I can now hardly forbear alluding to it with levity, as if the Almighty had said, *"if he desires it he shall have plenty."* I still feel happy, in that old Bradley, (who had put on mourning at my father's death, though he knew him not,) a few days before his own death, understood that one of my father's sons had attended upon him.

About the middle of June, news came to Oxford of the ex-

traordinary occurrences at Row and at Port Glasgow. One evening I had crossed the river from the Christ Church meadows, and
walking down the bank, through the fields on the opposite side,
with two or three companions, our conversation turned on that
subject: one said, if it were not for my books and other property
in Oxford, I should go to Scotland to make inquiry. I replied, if
I thought it true, I would sell my books and clothes if they were
all that I had, to pay for my journey. The tidings were, however,
so contradictory, that I did not credit the report.

It may be as well to remark here, that I had for many years
often fasted, and had lately added to this discipline, watching
accompanied with prayer. It was my delight to wake in the night
to pray, according to the example of David—"at midnight also will
I praise Thee." On two occasions previous to my arrival at Oxford,
during earnest prayer, I had seen visions, each of which shortly
after I saw them I found were pictures of what *came to pass in
reality,* though with certain variations; which I account for by
my disobedience to the spirit of the vision. You do not understand this, my reader, nor do I.

I cannot now enter into a detail of these visions nor of my
experiences under them. Suffice it to say, I was expecting the
fulfilment of the Divine prophecies, concerning the end of the
world, or the coming of the Lord, and as I could see no reason but
want of faith, for the absence from the church of the original gifts
of the Holy Ghost, so, such experience as I had here had confirmed
me in my expectation.

CHAPTER V

I LEFT Oxford in July, with the intention of proceeding to Ireland by Liverpool, on a long promised visit to one of my relations. Whilst preparing for my departure I met in London at my bankers, Mr. H. D., a gentleman who has since received the title of Evangelist, from the supposed inspired teachers of the late Mr. Irving's congregation. He gave me new information concerning the extraordinary manifestations at Row, and at Port Glasgow; and, at my desire, a letter of introduction to a young Scotch minister, who, having been thither, had returned convinced of the reality of the miracles. My conversations with these two gentlemen, determined me to proceed northward to make inquiry, and to take shipping afterwards from the Clyde for Belfast.

On my way, I visited my younger brother, residing at that time with his newly married wife at Sheffield. I passed a day or two with a fellow-collegian at Leeds. I passed through the principal manufacturing towns to Manchester, thence to Chester. I proceeded to Liverpool, and thence through the lake scenery of Westmoreland to Carlisle. Here I bid adieu to England, and arrived in Glasgow about September. In Glasgow I procured a few pamphlets then current, on the nature of the new miracles, and then descended the river, to Greenock, a town below Port Glasgow, from which place next morning I crossed over to Row, provided with a letter of introduction to Mr. Campbell the minister of Row, and also the chief preacher in those parts of the doctrines then denominated the "Row Heresy." This amiable, and I hope I may truly add godly, man received me kindly, and begged me to abide in his house, so long as I was inclined to make inquiry into the opinions of his followers.

By his means I became acquainted with Mr. Lusk, Mr. Erskine, the M'Donalds, Mary Campbell, and many others. From that which I heard, read, and saw, I soon became almost a convert. The effect then may be readily imagined which was produced on a highly excited and enthusiastic mind, by the awful thought that I was abiding in the presence and company of persons, in all probability moved and speaking by the Holy Ghost. One afternoon at Row, in the house of a gentleman, where I was at luncheon, I was first called out to see one of the inspired ladies, who had left the table and desired to speak to me, under the impression that she was commanded to address me. She was a plain slender young woman, pitted with the small pox. I attended her in the drawing room, and when I was alone with her, with her arm raised and moving to a kind of serious measure, she addressed me in clear and angelic notes, with sounds like these. *"Hola mi hastos, Hola mi hastos, disca capita crustos bustos,"* &c. &c. &c. She then cried out "and he led them out to Bethany and said, Tarry ye in Jerusalem until ye are indued with power from on high."

I have always felt irresistibly inclined to laugh under those circumstances which for the sake of prudence and common sense required of me the utmost outward show of gravity. So in this instance, it was with the greatest difficulty that I could command my features. At the conclusion, I asked the meaning of what I had heard. I understood that the lady thought she had been addressing me by the order of the Holy Spirit, but that she could not explain to what her words alluded. "She thought that *I* was to understand," or words to that effect. I could not help being awed; the sounds, the tone, the action, were most impressive. I felt that it was either an awful truth, or a dreadful and damnable delusion. I returned to the table where I sat down in silence. A lady on my right-hand side spoke to me a few sentences which I answered, and then again I was silent, pondering in my own heart what might be the meaning of the words I had heard, if true, and how I was to obtain a decided explanation of them. Whether the command to "tarry in Jerusalem," referred to my remaining amongst the inspired persons in that neighbourhood, or to a state of peace and confidence of mind. Whilst thus reflecting, a new and wonderful sensation came upon me: from my head downwards through my whole frame, I felt a spirit or a humour shedding its benign influence, the effect of which was that of the most *cheerful, mild and grateful peace and quiet*. The words it suggested to me were, "Like to the dew of Hermon," &c. &c. I do not remember ever having felt such, and with inward joy and pleasure I thought I recognized the marvellous work of the Almighty. I now suspect that it might have been the effect of excitement on a nervous system already undermined. Yet I look back with pleasure and satisfaction on my recollection of those hours. A mind so harassed, so tortured as mine had been for many years, may well be pardoned for being deceived, by so *sensible* a delusion; by a Pandora bringing in her box a medicine so suited apparently to my complaint, and so delightful. If a doubt suggested itself, I might naturally reply in the spirit of Camoens, "*Ainda eu imagino, em ser contento?*" Am I yet only imagining when I *am* happy?

After the party at that house had broken up and we were walking into Row, the lady who had addressed me, joined me, and begged that I would not take any thing that she had said to me, to bind me to remain there or in any one particular place. She was anxious lest I might be misled, and acknowledged that she did not understand the purport of the message. I then asked her if she was sure that she had faithfully discharged her mission, and had not withheld any part of the communication she had been inspired to make to me; for in her manner to me, there had appeared a want of freedom of action, as if the mind misgave itself concerning its illuminations, not daring to do or to say all it was prompted to. She was not aware that she had concealed any thing. I think it was this afternoon that we proceeded to the beach to wait for a steam packet, in which the ladies and Mr. Erskine were to pass over to Port Glasgow. No steam packet came, owing either to foul weather, or to a change in the regulations. It was then raining, and on finding the ladies exposed to the weather, I suggested the propriety of taking shelter, but I found a pause I could not account for, until it was explained to me, that, Mr. Erskine, one of their leaders had an impression that a steam boat would come. I was therefore obliged to leave the party, who were leaning upon this strange persuasion, to such protection as their umbrellas afforded them; I could not withstand the ridicule excited in my mind by an elderly gentleman thus misleading his flock; for I was convinced that he was mistaken in this instance at least, though I had little question of the doctrines he supported being true. I need not add that they were disappointed.

After this day, I attended the meeting of the followers of the church at Port Glasgow. Here I heard again a manifestation of tongues, and the scriptures read with an utterance preternatural, and requiring great assurance to practise, because so extraordinary. I never attended these meetings without great conflict of mind, and afterwards depression. I had an anxiety working in me, and a bond pressing down heavy on me. I knew not what I was to do; my mind was in the dark, yet I wanted to be taking *an active* part. The sounds I heard were at times beautiful in the extreme, resembling the Greek language; at times they were awfully sublime and grand, and gave me a full perception of that idea; "the Word was with GOD, and the WORD was GOD:" at times the tone of them querulous and almost ridiculous.

One evening, after having attended one of these meetings, I retired to the inn at Port Glasgow, and feeling not disposed to go so early to bed, I went into the travellers' room, and ordered a glass of whiskey. I was soon after joined by a Scotch gentleman, who also ordered some whiskey, with which, from his appearance, he was far better acquainted than myself. This kind of frolicsome squire or laird I shrank from, having a most hearty dislike to riot and extravagance. The more, however, my nature shrank from him, the more need I imagined he had of Christian charity and instruction. We fell into conversation, and I was very much afflicted, when we descanted on religious subjects, and on the reported miracles in the neighbourhood, at the broken-hearted manner in which my companion confessed and complained of his own weakness, and declared for himself he was unable to be a Christian—as for himself, he was sure that he had no kindred with Christ. During my conversation, I was dwelling intently upon the means most likely to quicken him to a sense of shame and hope; and looking, though despondingly, to be guided by the Holy Spirit in my argument. I suffered a deep internal struggle—I seemed guided to I knew not what: at last, I flung myself back, as it were, in the arms of the Lord; and opening my mouth, I sang without premeditation, in beautiful tones, that affected my mind greatly, and in measure like to an anthem, "kindred with Christ! bone of his bone, and flesh of his flesh!" The manner was that of expostulation for want of faith, of encouragement and consolation. I sang a few more sentences in the same apparently inspired manner, but without premeditation; I forget them, but I recollect after a short but animated conversation, the gentleman, greatly touched and awed into compunction, rose up and kissed me, declaring that he trusted there were still hopes for him; and he left me, promising to attend one of the meetings next day.

I could mention several instances of the same kind, when the power of the Spirit came upon me, and, opening my mouth, sang in beautiful tones words of purity, kindness, and consolation. I was subdued and humbled; it was not my doing—the words, the ideas even, were wholly unthought of by me, or at least I was unconscious of thinking of them

> Et, quoniam Deus ora movet, sequar ora moventem
> Rite Deum——

Ovid's description of the inspiration of Pythagoras tallied with my experience. This voice was given me, but I was not the master of it; I was but the instrument. I could not use it at my own command, but solely at the command of the Spirit that guided me. On another occasion, I was going to call for the first time on Mary Campbell, had crossed the ferry over the lake, and was proceeding along the shore on the opposite side, when I passed a party of ladies with one gentleman. I felt impelled in the Spirit to give a message to them. I shrank from doing so, conceiving it to be a delusion, but again fearing that I was grieving the Spirit, and proving ungrateful through my timidity before man, I summoned resolution, and addressed a few words of scripture to the lady and gentleman in front of the party when they came up. The lady, with great delicacy and command, questioned me as to what I meant, without showing offence or confusion. I replied that I did not know to what the words alluded, but that I believed I had been desired to utter them. I never could tell why. I afterwards conversed with the lady, who was acquainted with my eldest brother's wife's family. I learned that the gentleman walking with her was apparently reforming, from having been of an unthinking and wild character; and, soon after, I was told that one of the young ladies behind recognised me, having sailed across the Clyde in the same steam-boat with myself; on that day we had conversed together on the subject of the manifestations at Port Glasgow and Row. I had argued with her on the possibility and apparent probability of them, and she had expressed her desire to know the result of my inquiries. I was then able to tell her, that I not only believed in the reality of the miracles, but that I imagined I had myself been a subject of them.

At morning service in Mr. Campbell's church, one Sunday, I was led to open my mouth, and sing a part of a psalm, at a time when the rest of the congregation were at peace, and whilst Mr. Campbell was preparing to preach. *I mistrusted the guidance, I knew not what then to do;* but after inward conflict, whilst Mr. Campbell was actually preaching, I gained confidence to chant two verses of *another psalm.* I was immediately below, and behind, the pulpit. Mr. Campbell descended from it to dissuade me, and begged me not to continue. I told him quietly, "I had done." The power had left me. I knew not whether I had done right or wrong; I only knew the power was not mine, and from its nature, as evidenced to my own feelings, I concluded it divine: afterwards, in a conversation with Mary Campbell, I understood that which is written by St. Paul, that we are not to speak all together, but to command the spirits; for that God is not a God of confusion, but of order.

Afterwards I assisted Mr. Campbell to write out his apology, and attended him to Dumbarton, where he was condemned by a set of crabbed old Presbyterians calling themselves a synod, presided over by a person called "Moderator," a stout, mild, rosy-faced man, the only gentleman amongst them. Whilst waiting for their arrival, and for the opening of the church doors, I walked amongst the graves with Macdonald, one of two brothers who had originated these doctrines, and whose sister had been raised miraculously from a bed of sickness. He told me that since he had been converted, he had *lived as in a new life*—moved by a life that dwelt in him. The same young man, or his brother, whilst the mock trial was going on, rushed out of the church, crying out words with a loud voice to this effect, "Come out of her, come out of her, my people." I do not recollect the exact speech; he was red in the face. My impression at the time was that he was misled, not in faith, but in so giving utterance to it.

CHAPTER VI

I WILL not now dwell any more upon these particulars: suffice it to say, I left the manse at Row, *in my own imagination*, a living instance of the Holy Ghost operating in man,—full of courage, confidence, peace, and rapture, like a glowing flame, but still and submissive. Such, I say, was the state of my feeling in the life of that Spirit; but in the flesh I was anxious, lest I should be betrayed into error by a false zeal, or by false directions, so as to turn that power to ridicule, by attempting miracles, uncommanded, or by conduct out of order; at the same time, I was alarmed, lest, mistaking a fear of man for a love of order, I might quench the Holy Spirit working within me. I knew it was in my power to refuse to obey the Spirit's guidance, but not to command its utterance. At the same time, I knew the power of utterance was often upon me, when I considered it out of season and place to make use of it. This disturbed me, because others had told me, they could not resist the power, when it came upon them! Mr. Campbell, at my departure seemed to fear for me, that I might be misled, and expressed his anxiety; I was conscious of danger and difficulty, but I hoped what had been begun without me, would be perfected in me, despite even of myself.

I recollect one night at Mr. Campbell's, whilst reading the Scriptures, I was directed to read, or to expound to him, certain passages, which I declined doing, as out of place and presumptuous. He went out of the room, and the Spirit then guided me to several chapters and verses, containing warnings, reproof, and menaces; particularly to the first chapter of Jeremiah, verse 17.

"Be not dismayed at their faces, lest I confound thee before them;" *where the Prophet is threatened with confusion if he is disobedient.* These threats were applied to me, I was alarmed, and when Mr. Campbell re-entered, I acknowledged the inward working of the Spirit, and stated to him my opinions concerning the *"identity of the church with the Lord,"* which I had been afraid to mention before, lest I might be charged with enthusiasm. At Dublin again, after a conflict of a similiar nature, when I had left a gentleman's house to go I knew not whither, I was made to open the Old Testament, and in the books of the law, the twenty-eighth chapter of Deuteronomy was pointed out to me to read, containing the curses, that I should be cursed in my family, in going out and coming in, &c., "and the Lord shall smite thee with madness and blindness and astonishment of heart." The passages were applied to me, and I was shocked, and yet I could not see *how it could be true,* seeing *the Lord had promised to keep me,* as well as to save me and convert me.

Before I quitted Row, however, I had suspected that a new power had been conferred on me, of discerning the spirits that spoke in men around me, by their tone, and the effect of the utterance upon my nervous organs. This was a new field of observation to me when I left Scotland, and I considered it might be, if not a delusion, a beneficial guard against any spiritual enemy; but when I came to Ireland, in addition to the power of discerning evil in others, I fancied that I had the power to discern evil in myself, and to know by the sensation on my palate, throat, and hearing, whether I was speaking in accordance with the will of God, or against his will, and consequently against the laws of nature. I now attribute this sensation in a great measure to extreme nervous excitement, but at that time it led to the destruction of my new formed peace, and ultimately to my ruin. For I was conscious that I spoke often with bodily pain, in reply to trivial or religious questions, and at the same time I could not *but answer* or hold my tongue. If I held my tongue, I was embarrassed, and I caused pain and displeasure and suspicion to others, which I could not believe consistent with Christian charity. Yet I must either hold my tongue, or speak as I was guided, or speak my own thoughts; and when no guidance came, I would, at times, stumble upon broken sentences, stammer, and prove ridiculous, opening my mouth to obey a guidance which failed me before I finished a sentence, at times even before I commenced. Still less could I think it my duty to make my mission ridiculous: yet in speaking my own thoughts as I then termed them, I groaned in spirit and grieved, suffering actually bodily pain, and fearing that I was guilty of, and accusing myself of, the grossest ingratitude in rebelling even against the law of nature, and not only against the Holy Spirit, to whom I was indebted for such great mercies, and miraculous graces. This trouble of mind increased upon me towards the end of November, and the commencement of December, and was the most active inward cause of all my misfortunes.

I landed at Belfast, where I halted for the Sunday, and then proceeded to Dublin, bearing witness on my way to what I had witnessed in Scotland: on the road I recollect I lost a Hebrew Bible,—I met, as I had expected and desired, in Dublin, a gentleman who had offered me a curacy in Somersetshire. To him I related my convictions, prepared to meet with a withdrawal of his offer in consequence, which however did not follow. My kind friend appeared willing to look upon my enthusiasm with indulgence, and to leave it with the bishop, whom he invited me to meet near Bristol, to decide if it was too strong to allow of ordination into the church. I was, however, otherwise guided, and, after passing a few days in Dublin, I proceeded to fulfil an engagement in Queen's County, and from thence journeyed beyond Limerick to visit a schoolfellow, a zealous clergyman acting as curate in a small Irish town. On my way there, I spent a night or two at the house of a protestant clergyman near *Roscrea*, to whom I had a letter of introduction; he was an enthusiast of the evangelical school; he begged me to accompany him next day to a meeting at Nenagh, at which he begged me to assist. I assented with some difficulty, because I had not yet had any distinct calling or command to appear publicly. Although I often desired to have a way opened for me, yet I feared to be trespassing on paths not prepared for me by the Lord; for all the guidance I had hitherto received, after my conversation with Mary Campbell, *tended to the strictest order* and obedience to the ordinances of the church. I did however accept the invitation to speak conditionally; an express condition was, that I should confine myself to general subjects, and not be supposed to give an unqualified support to a society not acting in strict union with and subordination to the established church. I went to the meeting completely unprepared. I decided when there, what line of argument to adopt, in conformity with the will of my *singular inspiration*, and being at a loss to know how to support my argument with texts, and doubting the will or mistrusting the power of the Spirit, to speak through me uninterruptedly, I applied inwardly for guidance; and the Spirit, moving my arms and fingers, opened for me my Bible in distinct places, one after the other, supplying me in each place with a passage in regular connexion with my line of argument. According to these I spoke.

I mention these facts, to show the reasonableness, if I may so call it, of my lunacy, *if it was entirely lunacy*; to speak more clearly, to show the reality of the *existence of that power,* by the abuse or use of which, I became insane. If by the abuse of it, because the Lord confounded me for my disobedience; if by the use of it, because, though real, it was a spirit of delusion.

After paying another visit, near Limerick, I returned to Dublin about the third week in November. I there met with two individuals who had been at Row, and I was tempted to protract my stay until they returned to Scotland. My mind was no longer quiet. Incapable of speaking even on trivial subjects, without internal rebuke and misgiving, accompanied with real nervous pain, uncertain what was the origin of this, or the end pointed to, I felt inclined often to give up all care in religion, exhausted, weary, and broken hearted. One Friday evening whilst returning from a family dinner, after which I had been arguing with a friend, under my usual sense of perplexity and inward struggle, as I passed round by the college towards the bridge, I was assailed by a woman of the town, as is their custom, to whom I spoke, with a heavy heart, in the language of Scripture warning her of her danger. She left me, and five minutes after that, another coming alongside of me, led me away to my destruction. My confinement,

my sense of shame, of ingratitude, of remorse, my continual accusation of myself, that I did not feel the extent of my crime, of
my guilt in bringing disrepute on doctrines I was persuaded came
from the Holy Spirit, the abiding presence of this guiding power
influencing my actions, and awing my mind, added to the subtle
effects of mercury upon the humours of my body, during the use
of which I had the imprudence to expose my frame to draughts,
whilst washing for a long time, every morning, my whole person
in cold water, at that inclement season of the year; these causes
all combined, could hardly fail to effect the ruin of my mind; but
they were joined with others which I will mention in order in
the next chapter.

My reader, I have had great difficulty to get even thus far, but,
if after this you meet with more irregularity and abruptness of
style, and change of manner, recollect how painful a task I am
engaged in, and pass it over.

CHAPTER VII

I WAS intimately acquainted with the family of an officer residing in Dublin, of moderate and religious principles. He had constantly called on me during my illness, and when I became convalescent he invited me to pass the Sunday with him, having observed how my imagination was preying upon my mind, and fearing for me, for I had related to him the strange guidances and sensations to which I was become familiar, hoping that a cheerful evening with my old friends might be of advantage to me; and I accepted the invitation. It was about the 19th of December. Unfortunately I would have it that I was to speak in an unknown tongue, and to do other marvellous feats before this family, in order to convince them of the truth of the Row doctrines, preparatory to my departure for England, which I was wild enough to fix for the end of the week. For I conceived that my speedy restoration from the illness which had recently afflicted me, was the effect of a miraculous blessing on the means made use of, and a great mercy; and now I was well, I imagined it was a trial of my faith, and so it was, whether I should still submit to the regimen and prescriptions of my physician, or, by kicking the stool on which I had been standing from under my feet, show the power that had healed me, and at the same time my faith in that power. I say this was indeed a trial of my faith, in two senses, for it was a trial of the strength of my delusion, and of my reasonable understanding: of my real faith, which I then called human fear; and of my false faith, which I then called trust in God. It is contemptible and ridiculous, but when night came and I had to decide, I split the difference by taking half the dose that my physician had ordered me. The truth is, that I doubted my delusions, and I doubted my physician. Had my mind been clear, I might have been acting wisely, and with peace of mind; but my mind being confused, this trifling incident added to my confusion, and, my conscience being doubtful, to my imagined guilt. All this contributed to my disturbance that wretched night.

I say that I imagined I was to speak in an unknown tongue, and perform other signs before my worthy friend's household. And this, though a delusion, is but a delusion of this world, where the worthless are putting themselves forward continually as God's truest servants: the most ignorant are the most presumptuous. This delusion, however, counterbalanced all the beneficial effects of their society, for I was in a state of great excitement, both at my own feelings, that urged and led me to attempt utterances and singing, &c. &c., and at their alarm and opposition. It is said in Scripture that the disciples should *do wonders,* and amongst other wonders, more harmless, it came into my head, I am told, to put my hand *into the fire,* persuaded that I might draw it out unhurt. I was either dissuaded or prevented from doing this. During the evening I discovered I had not brought my pocket-handkerchief. My friend Captain —— sent for one of his, it was of red silk; the impression came on my mind that it was a token of ill to me, and I exclaimed —— what have you given me? you have given me blood. Conversation was going on and my words were hushed over, but I foreboded a calamity which though inevitable I could not distinctly foresee.

On retiring to sleep, I promised my host not to cry out in prayer or in hymn; that I might not disturb any of the old pensioners in the Kilmainham hospital, in a room of which my bed was prepared.

In the night I awoke under the most dreadful impressions; I heard a voice addressing me, and I was made to imagine that my disobedience to the faith, in taking the medicine overnight, had not only offended the Lord, but had rendered the work of my salvation extremely difficult, by its effect upon my spirits and humours. I heard that I could only be saved now by being changed into a spiritual body; and that a great fight would take place in my mortal body between Satan and Jesus; the result of which would either be my perfection in a spiritual body, or my awaking in hell. I am not sure whether before or after this, I was not commanded to cry out aloud, for consenting to which I was immediately rebuked, as unmindful of the promise I had made to my friend. A spirit came upon me and prepared to guide me in my actions. I was lying on my back, and the spirit seemed to light on my pillow by my right ear, and to command my body. I was placed in a fatiguing attitude, resting on my feet, my knees drawn up and on my head, and made to swing my body from side to side without ceasing. In the meantime, I heard voices without and within me, and sounds as of the clanking of iron, and the breathing of great forge bellows, and the force of flames. I understood that I was only saved by the mercy of Jesus, from seeing, as well as hearing, hell around me; and that if I were not obedient to His spirit, I should inevitably awake in hell before the morning. After some time I had a little rest, and then, actuated by the same spirit, I took a like position on the floor, where I remained, until I understood that the work of the Lord was perfected, and that now my salvation was secured; at the same time the guidance of the spirit left me, and I became in doubt what next I was to do. I understood that this provoked the Lord, as if I was affecting ignorance when I knew what I was to do, and, after some hesitation, I heard the command, to *take your position on the floor again then,* but I had no guidance or no perfect guidance to do so, and could not resume it. I was told, however, that my salvation depended upon my maintaining that position as well as I could until the morning; and oh! great was my joy when I perceived the first brightness of the dawn, which I could scarcely believe had arrived so early. I then retired to bed. I had imagined during the night that the fire of hell was consuming my mortal body—that the Spirit of Jesus came down to me to endure the pain thereof for me, that he might perfect in me a spiritual body to His honour and glory. I imagined that the end of this work was, that I was already in the state of one raised from the dead; and that any sin or disobedience in this body was doubly horrible and loathsome, inasmuch as it was in a body actually regenerated and clothed upon with the Holy Ghost. I imagined also that the Holy Ghost had in a special manner descended, and worked with Jesus to save me. I considered it a proof of the truth of my imaginations, when on rising, being perplexed by two different guidings that came upon me, I looked down upon my limbs which were white and of a natural colour; and again I looked down on my limbs, when one half of my frame appeared in a state of scarlet inflammation. When I went to dress, this had again subsided.

Before I rose from my bed, I understood that I was now to proceed through the world *as an angel,* under the immediate guidance of the Lord, to proclaim the tidings of his second coming. With that came an uncertain impression that I was to do this in an extraordinary way, and by singing—and this idea haunted me throughout my changes of insanity. I had also an *uncertain* impression of a like nature, that I was to go and show myself before the lord lieutenant or the General of the Forces, that I was to breakfast there, and to meet, either at the lord lieutenant's, a prince of the blood royal; or at the General's, a duke, to whom I was to proclaim the near coming of the Lord.

My guidance not being sure, and my folly or my faith not being firm enough, I reflected on Mary Campbell's advice, and determined to be guided by what appeared the natural path of duty. And, at the risk of offending the Holy Spirit and the Lord, to prefer showing my gratitude to Captain H. who had shown me so many kind attentions, and to attend his humble table. I now conceived again that I was to speak to them in an unknown tongue, and to make confessions, and to show signs and wonders: my words and ideas were to be supplied to me. I did not, however, dare to attempt any thing, for I felt no guidance, and I shrank from the ridicule of beginning to speak, and having nothing to say. My whole conduct became confused, my language ambiguous and doubtful. After breakfast, I prayed to be left alone, which was accorded with some difficulty. When alone in the breakfast room, I expected to be guided to prayer; but a spirit guided me and placed me on a chair, in a constrained position, with my head turned to *look at the clock,* the hand of which

I saw proceeding to the first quarter; I understood I was to leave the position when it came to the quarter; when, however, it came to the quarter, I was anxious to be on the safe side, and I waited till it was at least half a minute past. Having done this, I was not a whit the wiser; but on the contrary, I felt that I had again offended by my want of exact punctuality, proving my want of confidence. I was then directed to lie on the floor, with my face to the ground, in an attitude of supplication and humiliation. I heard a spirit *pray in me,* and *reason in me,* and *with me,* and ultimately, another spirit, desiring certain gifts of the Holy Spirit to be given me, amongst which prophecy, tongues, miracles, and discernment of spirits; soon after, I was overwhelmed with a sudden and mighty conviction of my utter worthlessness; and being asked how I could expect the Lord to take me, and on what conditions I craved his favour; another spirit cried out in me, and for me, *"Lord! take me as I am."*

CHAPTER VIII

At that moment Captain H. entered, and I arose. His family came into the room, and I again began to be troubled with the idea that I was to make confessions to them, and to speak in an unknown tongue. I had not understanding to do either, and my conduct became very unintelligible. Capt. H. sat down to write a letter, and I attempted to make a sketch partly from memory, and partly by the guidance of the power that moved my hands, of my mother's residence. Captain H. after finishing his letter, sent for a hackney coach in which I proceeded with him to Dublin. On my way, I was tormented by the commands of what I imagined was the Holy Spirit, to say other things, which as often as I attempted, I was fearfully rebuked for beginning in my own voice, and not in a voice given to me. These contradictory commands were the cause, now, as before, of the incoherency of my behaviour, and these imaginations formed the chief causes of my ultimate total derangement. For I was commanded to speak, on pain of dreadful torments, of provoking the wrath of the Holy Spirit, and of incurring the guilt of the grossest ingratitude; and at the same moment, whenever I attempted to speak, I was harshly and contumeliously rebuked for not using the utterance of a spirit sent to me; and when again I attempted, I still went wrong, and when I pleaded internally that I knew not what I was to do, I was accused of falsehood and deceit; and of being really unwilling to do what I was commanded. I then lost patience, and proceeded to say what I was desired pell-mell, determined to show that it was not fear or want of will that prevented me. But when I did this, I felt as formerly the pain in the nerves of my palate and throat on speaking, which convinced me that I was not only rebelling against God, but against nature; and I relapsed into an agonizing sense of hopelessness and of ingratitude.

We arrived at my hotel, when Captain —— left me to bring in my physician, Dr. P. [Piel]. I threw myself at the feet of my bed, endeavouring to pray. I think my physician came and again I was left alone, when, after much meditation, I prepared to go out to order a hat, and to arrange for my return to England in one of the Howth packets. But, when I opened the door, I found a stout man servant on the landing, who told me that he was placed there to forbid my going out, by the orders of Dr. P. and my friend; on my remonstrating, he followed me into my room and stood before the door. I insisted on going out; he, on preventing me. I warned him of the danger he incurred in opposing the will of the Holy Spirit, I prayed him to let me pass, or otherwise an evil would befal him, for that I was a prophet of the Lord. He was not a whit shaken by my address, so, after again and again adjuring him, by the desire of the Spirit whose word I heard, I seized one of his arms, desiring it to wither: my words were idle, no effect followed, and I was ashamed and astonished.

Then, thought I, I have been made a fool of! But I did not on that account mistrust the doctrines by which I had been exposed to this error. The doctrines, thought I, are true; but I am mocked at by the Almighty for my disobedience to them, and at the same time, I have the guilt and the grief, of bringing discredit upon the truth, by my obedience to a spirit of mockery, or, by my disobedience to the Holy Spirit; for there were not wanting voices to suggest to me, that the reason why the miracle had failed, was, that I had not waited for the Spirit to guide my action when the word was spoken, and that I had seized the man's arm with the wrong hand. I was silent and astonished. Bed time came. I requested the man to leave me for half an hour for prayer; he did so. Before that, I think Captain H. had been to me, and had explained the reason of his being there. I went to bed, but not to sleep.

In the same manner as I have already related, voices came to desire me to say and attempt many things, which, at one time, I was to utter in the spirit of holiness; at another, in my own spirit, at another time, in another spirit; which, as surely as they were enjoined, I as surely appeared to misplace, and as surely received the most cutting and insulting reproaches for failing in. At one time, I was to sing, at another, to pray; at another, to address my attendant; at another, to ask him to come to my bed, which my sense of decorum refused; at another, to desire him to make a bed for himself on the sofa, which I counselled him to do, and which I think he declined; at last, in one of these mental conflicts, hunted in every direction, my patience gave way and I mentally cursed the Holy Trinity. A cutting sense of my ingratitude, and deep grief, followed, with mute despair.

The voices informed me, that my conduct was owing to a spirit of mockery and blasphemy having possession of me. That as I was already the object of the special grace of the Holy Spirit, which had undertaken my salvation, by rendering me a spiritual body, after I had forfeited my hope in Jesus Christ, there was no longer hope for me in the ordinary means of faith and prayer; but, that I must, in the power of the Holy Spirit, *redeem myself,* and rid myself of the spirits of blasphemy and mockery that had taken possession of me.

The way in which I was tempted to do this was by throwing myself on the top of my head backwards, and so resting on the top of my head and on my feet alone, to turn from one side to the other until I had broken my neck. I suppose by this time I was already in a state of feverish delirium, but my good sense and prudence still refused to undertake this strange action. I was then accused of faithlessness and cowardice, of fearing man more than God.

And so it was, that the means taken for my care, by my friend and the doctor, became my destruction, owing to the peculiar weaknesses of my understanding. I was made to doubt my own sincerity, and to desire to prove it in spite of the presence of the domestic. Had he not been there, I might by that time have been sound asleep.

I attempted the command, the servant prevented me. I lay down contented to have proved myself willing to obey in spite of his presence, but now I was accused of not daring to wrestle with him unto blows. I again attempted what I was enjoined. The man seized me, I tore myself from him, telling him it was necessary for my salvation; he left me and went down stairs. I then tried to perform what I had begun; but now I found, either that I could not so jerk myself round on my head, or that my fear of breaking my neck was really too strong for my faith. In that case I then certainly mocked, for my efforts were not sincere.

When I undertook this action, I imagined that if I performed it in the power of the Holy Spirit, no harm would result to me, but that if I threw myself round to the right in my own strength, I might break my neck and die, but that I should be raised again immediately to fulfil my mission. I had therefore no design to destroy myself; but, I have often conjectured since, that GOD in his mercy may have meditated my self-destruction to save me from the horrors he foresaw preparing for me: they were great and intolerable, shocking in themselves, more shocking in my abandonment; I awoke from them as from the grave, to be cut off from all my tenderest ties.

Failing in my attempts, I was directed to expectorate violently, in order to get rid of my two formidable enemies; and then again I was told to drink water, and that the Almighty was satisfied; but that if I was not satisfied (neither could I be sincerely, for I knew I had not fulfilled his commands), I was to take up my position again; I did so; my attendant came up with an assistant and they forced me into a straight waistcoat. Even then I again tried to resume the position to which I was again challenged. They then tied my legs to the bed-posts, and so secured me.

Let me remark, how I became the victim of so absurd a delusion, yet having so much sense and reflection left to me. The spirits which at first spoke in my hearing, or addressed me at Row and Port Glasgow, and afterwards spoke in me and moved me; which subsequently in Ireland I heard talking to me, and communing with me invisible; had an utterance so pure, so touching, so beautiful, that I could not but believe them divine. They spake also in accordance with the word of life; they directed me in paths of peace, obedience, and humility; they flattered me even in my desire to adhere to the church establishment, and not to break the visible unity of the church; they came upon me to teach me method and order; they guided my hand to write in letters unusual to me; in so many ways they were attested, as spirits of good and of wisdom, that, now even, I dare not deny the possibility of disobedience to them, not my obedience, having caused me to be confounded, which was forewarned me in Scotland. But when I had thrown myself away, *and I was thrown away,* I was decoyed and separated from Jesus, the rock of a Christian's salvation, by my reliance on these sounds. For, as it is written, the word of the Lord came to the prophets, to Isaiah, &c. &c. When the voice came to *me,* I received that voice as the word of the Lord; and the rather, because, when I first heard it, it was like that Elijah describes, "a still small voice," and the directions of that voice were like the rest of my experiences at first, which were to my apparent good, and for my instruction. Now, afterwards that voice weaned me from my reliance upon the blood of Jesus—even through my hope in the mercies of Jesus, telling me that I could no longer be saved by the ordained means of faith, hope, and charity; but by the special interference of the Holy Ghost, and fellow-working of Jesus in me, to transform my body; this I admitted, though I could not understand it, on the authority of the spirits communing with me, the rather because it showed forth the mercies of Jesus the more extraordinarily. Thus having been once decoyed from looking up to the cross of Jesus as my only hope of salvation, it became comparatively easy for the same power, by the same means, to suggest to me a new necessity for an unusual act on my part to save me, when I had forfeited my new state of grace. For at that time I was, in all probability, already in a state of feverish delirium.

However, I did not give yet entire credit to these voices, or at least, I still exercised in certain respects my judgment and suspicion upon them, recollecting the example and warning of Mary Campbell. Particularly, finding the tones vary, I asked which is the voice of God? but my suspicions were soon lulled again, and my objections in part put down, by the suggestion that I heard the voices of the three members of the Holy Trinity, and afterwards those of the spirits of God sent to me to command me in His name.

I perished from an habitual error of mind, common to many believers, and particularly to our brethren the Roman Catholics, that *of fearing to doubt, and of taking the guilt of doubt* upon my conscience; the consequence of this is, want of candour and of real sincerity; because we force ourselves to say we believe what we do not believe, because we think doubt sinful. Whereas we cannot control our doubts, which can only be corrected by information. To reject persuasion wilfully is one crime; but to declare wilfully that we believe what we doubt, or presumptuously that our doubts are wilful, is another.

CHAPTER IX

THE next day, or the day after, Dr. P. [Piel] entered my room with another doctor. When they came to my bed-side, I was silent. I was unable to explain myself to them, because I knew that Dr. P. was reputed to be an Unitarian, and therefore I conceived it impossible to make him credit the supernatural voices and agency under which I acted. His companion seemed so stupid, and so like a man of the world of a common and vague stamp of mind, that I thought it perhaps still more hopeless to address him.

They remained about five or ten minutes on the left-hand side of my bed, and then went away. I have since learned that this wise second to Dr. P. was a lunatic doctor, celebrated in Dublin. And to that, in part, I cannot help attributing my subsequent misfortunes. I imagine that had Dr. P. acted on his own sound judgment, he would never have allowed me, however extraordinary my complaint might appear, to be subjected to the equally extraordinary treatment of confinement to my bed, in nearly one position for several days together, tied hand and foot in a straight waistcoat, in a small and close room. He would have said, whatever harm may be in him, or may arrive to him from his complaint, it cannot be greater than what will certainly happen, if he be confined so. But having submitted me to the treatment of a lunatic doctor, he submitted his own judgment along with it; through that infatuation by which so many are duped to allow these men to deal with patients contrary to nature, law, and reason, purely because they profess to undertake practically the care of men devoid of reason; affecting, at the same time, that the complaint itself is wholly

wrapped up in unfathomable mystery. I imagine, had I been
treated according to nature, if under this treatment I was restored,
through much danger, to a state fit for hazarding a journey, about
the middle of January, I might then have been recovered in less
time, with less suffering, and more perfectly, from the state of
derangement which my excitement of mind, acting on a disordered
system, had brought on only for a time. But fate ordered otherwise. I was confined in the manner above detailed; the reason of
this was the fear of violence to myself. My need of wholesome
exercise and occupation was denied. My idleness of mind and
body left me at the mercy of my delusions; my confined position
increased or caused a state of fever, which brought on delirium;
and they kept drenching my body to take away the evil which their
system was continually exciting; and which ultimately triumphed
completely over me. My want of exercise produced a deadly torpor in the moral functions of my mind, combined with the ruin
of my spirits by their diet and medicines. I foresaw a dreadful
doom which I could not define, and from which, like one in a
dream, I attempted in vain to run away. Inwardly I adjured my
Maker, and expostulated with the voices communing with me, in
me, or without me, to allow me exercise, as the only means of
saving me. I addressed no one, or scarcely addressed any outwardly, partly because I considered it hopeless, without pledging myself to attempt what my obedience to divine inspiration bade me
attempt—hopeless to persuade them of my divine inspiration,
partly because if ever I attempted to speak, I was checked and
rated by the spirits, for using my own filthy utterance, or abusing
the divine utterance. Since boyhood, I had never been confined
to my bed for more than two or three days, nor to my room, for
so much as a week together; and on an average had never had less
daily, than three hours' active exercise. Now, after a fortnight's
confinement to my room, I was fastened on my bed, with the
liberty of my arms and legs denied to me.

I do not know how long this continued, but I recollect when
my eldest brother came to my bed-side, he found me so, and many
days after his arrival in Dublin I continued to be so. It is true
my legs were occasionally loosed, but they were as quickly tied

down again on my resuming my insane attempts, or trying to get out of bed. This I used to do for two reasons; one to get water, for which I longed, and in which I think I succeeded once, either by my own efforts, or by the servant guessing at my desire, one day after my brother's arrival; otherwise, I am afraid it is too true, I had no water to drink ever offered to me, but broth, and the most filthy medicine, that tasted like steel filings in a strong acid. Neither do I recollect receiving any solid food. I usually resisted both the administering of the broth and of the medicine, being commanded to do so, with circumstances of much spiritual insult, horror, and indelicacy, which I cannot now repeat. The other reason for which I attempted to rise out of bed, was to get to the window to see if it were true, as my tormentors told me, that all my family were there waiting to receive me, and to hail me as an obedient servant of the Lord Jesus, and a willing martyr to his glory. For when I began to lose all command of my imagination, I was made to believe, that in consequence of my disobedience and blasphemies against Jesus Christ and the Holy Spirit, the Roman Catholics in Ireland, to whom I had been ordained as an angel, being miraculously informed like the shepherds, by an angel shining in the glory of the Lord, had risen up and come to Dublin, demanding my crucifixion or my burning; that in the mean time the Almighty, provoked by my great perfidy and ingratitude, had cut short the days and revoked his counsels; had determined to visit my nation with severe plagues, and me, with all the torments he had reserved for Satan, whom even he had pardoned, glad to find one, and one only, who deserved all his everlasting plagues, and to be able thereby to pardon his immense creation.

I was the one only being to be eternally damned, alone, in multiplied bodies, and in infinite solitude and darkness and torments. I was told also that the Almighty in His three persons had descended upon earth, had entered London, and had revealed all these things to the king, who was also preparing on earth the most cruel torments for me; that my father and a sister who is now no more, had been raised from the dead, and had interceded for me, and that my relations and friends had assembled round me in Dublin, and had defended me from the violence of the mob at the sacrifice of their own lives. My friend Captain H.'s coat which occasionally lay upon my sofa, for he was constantly attending upon me, was to my delirious imagination, a proof of his murder in my defence. I was agonized, and often attempted to rush to the window and to present myself to the mob and to save the lives of my friends, by my own sacrifice; at other time, to satisfy my curiosity, to see if my family and relations were really there. For, I had a species of doubts; but no one who has not been deranged, can understand how dreadfully true a lunatic's insane imagination appears to him, how slight his sane doubts. But I was not permitted to reach the window, and I was tied down again in bed; then my usual delusion came on me, that I was gifted with the power of an elephant to break my bands; and when I tried and found how futile were my efforts, I was told I did not choose to use the strength I had, from cowardice, or ingratitude, or laziness. On one occasion, I remember, after my brother had come to attend me, a spirit came to me whilst I was lying on my back, fatigued with my efforts to break the straight waistcoat, by forcing my arms and elbows out laterally, and said, *use my strength, I will show you how to do it.* The spirit then guided my arms and my hands, and with my fingers *sought and scratched the seams of the waist-coat sleeves,* soon loosened them, and I began tearing the seams asunder. The noise of the rending asunder however soon aroused my attendant, my straight waistcoat was taken off, and my arms were crossed over my stomach, in two heavy, hot, leathern arm pieces, which were not taken off from me for good, until I reached England. I feel thankful now for their removal.

CHAPTER X

THE delusions above detailed were accompanied with many other circumstances which I can hardly order aright in my memory; they were to this effect. That the angels and spirits of heaven from pity, and Satan and all his angels, being released from their torments, even by my sin, from gratitude and pity, combined to pray the Lord to suspend his judgments, to this end; that one only chance for my ultimate salvation might be given me. And this was, that by some signal act of obedience and acknowledgment of my divine mission, I might so purify my spirits and soul, before I suffered the punishments prepared for me on earth, and entered into my eternal judgments, that they, by uniting their spirits with mine, might enable me to endure them all, however cruel, in patience and obedience, so as ultimately to obtain my own pardon.

Although therefore my native genius, and the voice of one of my sister's spirits impelled me to sacrifice myself at any cost, and in any manner, rather than through my supineness or cowardice, cause the death and sufferings of so many defenders; yet another spirit, which I understood to be that of my Saviour, or of his immediate messenger, implored me not to do so, because, in so doing, *I must perish eternally,* and deprive him of the glory of making God's whole creation an universe of bliss.

It may be asked me, what course I would have had pursued towards me, seeing there was such evident danger in leaving me at liberty? I answer, that my conduct ought to have been tried in every situation compatible with my state; that I ought to have been dressed, if I would not dress myself; that I should have been invited to walk up and down my room, if not quietly, in the same confinement as in bed; that, whilst implements that might do me hurt were removed, pens, pencils, books, &c., should have been supplied to me; that I should have been placed in a hackney coach, and driven for air and exercise, towards the sea shore, and round the outskirts of Dublin. Few can imagine the sense of thirst and eager desire for freshness of air, which the recollection of that time yet excites in me. I do not recollect water having been presented to me; if it was, I systematically refused it, like every thing else; and it was not forced on me like the medicine and broth. If I recollect correctly, I got some water after my brother's arrival, and he also brought me once some grapes, a few of which I ate in spite of my false conscience, and God knows how refreshing they were.

To resume the thread of events; I felt a gradual relaxation of my muscular system, accompanied with a dreadful moral torpor and lethargy growing upon me, from my confinement and my regimen. It seemed to me at last as if humours rose up momentarily through the flesh of the face, which one by one stole from me the control of my muscles, and destroyed my moral energy. At the same time, I was accused by my spiritual tormentors of willing it, and it was *with* my will, though not *by* my will. I used to reply in inward deprecation, "I cannot help it, if I have no bracing exercise." I was then commanded to break my fetters, and told that I had strength given me to do so. I attempted it again and again; I was provoked to do it if only for exercise, but sunk as often, in hopeless indolence, and my feverishness and excitement were increased. Then, when I lay upon my pillow, a demand was made of me to suffocate myself on my pillow; that if I would do *that* in obedience to the Lord's Spirit, it would be an act of obedience, as grateful to him as any other I had been commanded. This delusion haunted me for many months. I imagined that I should be really suffocated, but saved from death, or raised from death, by miraculous interposition. I pressed my mouth and nostrils against the pillow; and I was to attend to the voices that came to me, directing my thoughts, and each tempting me to rise before I had executed the Lord's intention. I used to be deceived and to raise my head at some call, always out of time and place. I was accused of cowardice, and deceit. Night after night, and day after day, I was summoned to try it again and again, till I should succeed, under the most awful penalties. I was told, that it was necessary for the perfection of the glorified man. That all the world had done it but me; that even my sisters had done it, that they had all done it repeatedly *for my sake, to put off my damnation,* because it was necessary that the commands of the Lord should be fulfilled when once spoken, and they hoped in time that I should do it by their aid. When I felt the chill of the outward air upon my neck under the bed clothes, I was told these were spirits of my sisters, breathing on me to cool me, and encouraging me to go through with my task. I was reminded that it was my only chance of salvation; that, through my cowardice and want of fortitude, whole creations were suffering as yet the wrath of the Almighty, waiting for my obedience; and could not I, a man, do what women had done? At last, one hour, under an access of chilling horror at my imagined loss of honour, I was unable to prevent the surrender of my judgment. The act of mind I describe, was accompanied with the sound of a slight crack, and the sensation of a fibre breaking over the right temple; it reminded me of the mainstay of a mast giving away; it was succeeded by a loss of control over certain of the muscles of my body, and was immediately followed by two other cracks of the same kind, one after the other, each more towards the right ear, followed by an additional relaxation of the muscles, and accompanied by an apparently additional surrender of the judgment. In fact, until now I had retained a kind of restraining power over my thoughts and belief; I now had none; I could not resist the spiritual guilt and contamination of any thought, of any suggestion. My will to choose to think orderly, was entirely gone. I became like one awake yet dreaming, present to the world in body, in spirit at the bar of heaven's judgment seat; or in hell, enduring terrors unutterable, by the preternatural menaces of everlasting and shocking torments; inexpressible anguish and remorse, from exaggerated accusations of my ingratitude, and a degrading and self-loathing sense of moral turpitude from accusations of crimes I had never committed. I had often conceived it probable that insanity was *occasioned* by a loss of honour; I had not suspected that an imagined loss of honour could also effect such a ruin.

The state of mind mentioned in the last chapter, was accompanied by many preternatural visions and experiences. At one time, I saw the pale hand and arm of death stretched out over my bed. I felt no fear, but a sensation of confidence, that I was in God's keeping; if not for good, for evil. At another, I was desired to think orderly, and I was earnestly prayed to attempt it; but when I essayed, I was told I was doing nothing but "ruminate, ruminate all the day long." A moving light was given me, as a guide to know when I was ruminating or reflecting. It was a white light, and used to move in a circle from left to right upon the top of my bed. When I began to ruminate, it turned backwards to the left. Then my Saviour, or his angel's spirit, used to pray me to reflect, in order by any means to regain power over the muscles of my countenance. I say my Saviour or his angel, because when I imagined that I was in hell, that voice came to me, as the chief servant of Jesus in hell, directing and appointing the times and order of punishment and trial. I used also to hear a beautiful voice, that sung in the most tender, pure, and affecting notes these words, "Keep looking to Jesus, the author and finisher of thy salvation! Oh, keep looking—keep looking to Jesus!" Continually over the head of the bed, at the left-hand side, as if in the ceiling, *there was a sound as the voice of many waters,* and I was made to imagine that the jets of gas, that came from the fire-place on the left-hand side, were the utterance of my Father's spirit, which was continually within me, attempting to save me, and continually obliged to return to be purified in hell fire, in consequence of the contamination it received from my foul thoughts. I make use of the language I heard. From the ceiling in front of my bed, I used to hear the decrees of what were called the assembly of counsellors, often ushered in these terms:

> The will of Jehovah, the Lord is supreme—
> He shall be obeyed, and thou must worship him!

The word of the Lord came from the left-hand side of the ceiling of the room, and many spirits assailed me from all quarters.

When I make use of these words, *ceiling of the room*, it will appear surprising, that the visions or sounds had such effect upon me, when sensible objects were present, and recognized by me. But I understood these things in a contrary sense. Besides in part seeing the white and flowing beards, and venerable countenances, I imagined I was really present to *them*; and that my not acknowledging it was a delusion, an obstinate resistance of the divine will on my part. That, of the two, the appearance of the bed, walls, and furniture, was false, *not* my preternatural impressions.

I had at times, in the course of my life, thought within myself on the doctrine of the *communion* of saints, the ubiquity and omniscience of God, and the power I attributed to the Deity of revealing thoughts and actions. The expressions in the Scripture of the church as a body resenting the sufferings of every member, have led me to question whether, if we were in the spirit of God, we might not actually know and feel, each what the other was thinking about, or enduring, in various parts of the known world. That which had been a speculation, was now an act of faith; and I imagined that I could be in hell, on earth, and in heaven, at the same moment: nay, that I was, and that I witnessed all three states of existence; but that I did not see clearly the two extremes, because I would not acknowledge it to myself.

Indistinct ideas, also, of Bishop Berkeley's system, excepting against the reality of outward objects, from the experiences we have in dreams &c., helped this delusion. For, reflecting on that system by the light of scripture, I put this question to myself, if the creation exists in my mind, under its present appearance, by the word of God, why may not my individual character, and the character of all objects now reflected on the mirror of the mind, be changed in a minute, and reiteratedly, by the word of the same God.

I was usually addressed in verse; and I was made to know that there were three degrees of hell; with the last of which among the worms, the moles, and the bats, I was often threatened. One day, when my head was towards the right-hand corner of the bed, and I was lying on my back across it, with my feet tied to the left-hand bed-post at the bottom; I imagined I was being examined before the tribunal of the Almighty; an act of disobedience provoked the Almighty to cast me with a thunderbolt to hell, and the holy counsellors supplicated him to do so. An awful pause followed; I seemed removed to the gates of hell; and a stroke of lightning appeared to pierce the air on my right, but it did not strike me; for then the reason of my disobedience on earth, and the mystery of my sinfulness was revealed to me; and in a disconsolate and desolate state of mind, as one about to enter on a solitary and ever-lasting stage of suffering, I complained to myself that if I had but known these things before, and had I had but another trial allowed to me on earth, I hoped I might have done my duty. The voice I attributed to my Saviour recorded my thoughts aloud, as if he had staid by me to the last, and overheard me, saying, *he says so and so*. And I imagined it was agreed upon, that I should be tried again in this life upon earth.

On future occasions, I was often reminded of this engagement on my part, and I as often stipulated that the trial should not commence till I was restored to the state of health I enjoyed prev-iously; but at the time, or on another day, when lying in the same position, I heard what resembled the notes of a hurdy-gurdy, which appeared to go round me, playing a tune that affected me with extreme anguish. It seemed to remind me of all that I had experienced and forgotten of my heavenly Father's care and love towards me. My mind, amidst other scenes, was transported back to Portugal—to a day when I had passed through Alhandra on horseback on my way to visit the lines of Torres Vedras, in com-pany with three brother officers. It appeared to me, as if that day a little Portuguese beggar boy had been playing on a hurdy-gurdy in the street. But to my imagination, now, it was connected also with a time of life, when I had in person lived at Alhandra, a beggar orphan boy. When I had been taken charge of by the vicar or priest of the parish, who had loved me, clothed me, educated me, and provided for me as an assistant in the church. My pro-tector had introduced me to the abbot of a monastery, and he also, a venerable old man, had been my patron. I rewarded them, by aiding in the robbery of the monastery chapel, with certain bad companions, and carrying off a golden relique, for the loss of which the old abbot had been sentenced to the flames by the Inquisition, being accused and condemned on presumption; and I had been too grossly sensual to come forward and save him. I had returned home, and in a few days I entered the sacristie, where was the vicar, and having assassinated him, stole his money and garments; which I disposed of and had fled to Cintra. The monks of Alcobaça had there met me, and I became for a time repentant; but I was taken into their convent, and became at last, with another lad, the servant and enjoyer of their unnatural lusts.

During my residence there, I used often to visit Cintra, and in one farm house, being asked to assist in killing a pig, I had, to gratify my cruelty, plunged it alive into boiling water, after fastening up its mouth with sackcloth, to prevent its cries being heard.

This strange tale was revealed to me, accompanied with an impression of recollection, of identity with my own experience, as strongly as that by which any of the delusions of Pythagoras may have convinced him. I remember I was first desired to recollect that portion of my life; and when I could not, the sounds of the hurdy-gurdy were sent to me, as the voice said, to quicken my memory. I still had difficulty to collect any ideas, except my passing through Alhandra, my seeing the church on the right hand, and perhaps a young boy with a hurdy-gurdy in the street or market-place. But an indescribable sense of compunction, and of active interest in the place, wrung my feelings; and I was desired to recollect it as the place of my nativity.

I then heard a voice singing to the air of music

> I do not remember the hour and the day,
> But I do remember the day and the hour,
> When I was a little boy;*

My difficulty of recollecting was charged on my wilfulness; and so I understood the two first lines, that I *would* not, not that I *could* not, remember, and this partly from compunction at the crimes I

---

* I fear the death of my poor father was at the root of all my misfortunes; for I can trace the notes of this air, to the time we were living happily at Hampstead. I was then a little boy. But not now. I do not YET understand his loss.

had committed on my patrons, partly from a sense of shame and guilt at the revelation of my acts of the monks of Alcobaça, which I imagined were being exposed in the presence of my fellow-countrymen, especially in that of the Duke of Wellington, and the officers of my battalion; which also I was considered responsible for, although at the same time living in England in another body, in the discharge of my military duties.

When I inwardly expostulated and stated that when I was alive in England, I had not been aware of the union existing between me at the age of twenty-one, and a boy in Portugal of the age of seventeen; I was made to understand that an act of ingratitude in childhood had effaced from my mind the consciousness of this mystery, but that every individual besides me had experienced and delighted in this ubiquity of existence; and even that my brothers and sisters had been living in Portugal at the same time, and had then been acquainted with me, and living in England, had been conscious of that acquaintance, but could not talk to me concerning it, by reason of my moral darkness through sin.

There was a horrid idea connected with this phrenzy, that in like manner as I had boiled the pig alive, I should be plunged into a huge copper of boiling water, and should be whirled round in it on my back with my mouth covered over with sackcloth, bubbling and boiling and drowning and suffocating for ever, and ever, and ever! My eyes were also to be taken out of my head, and I yet spiritually see them *hanging over me,* looking down upon me and pursuing me round the cauldron. To add to my horrors, my dearest friends would plunge me in and stand by ridiculing and tormenting me. I actually believed that a sound I heard in the room next to mine like to boiling water, was a preparation for this awful punishment, and that my brother and one of my cousins were every moment on the eve of plunging me in and condemning me for ever. When they came into my room I saw them at times like natural men, but at times their countenances appeared horridly swollen, and their faces darkened so that they looked black. Then I was told that I was not doing my duty to the Lord Jehovah supremely omnipotent, and that they appeared as the angels of hell, already prepared to execute the purposes of his wrath, but that I was always respited, in hope of my future obedience. My feelings were dreadful.

On one of these occasions I recollect saying to my brother "—— I am desired to tell you you are a hypocrite." A voice had commanded me. This was one of the few sentences I addressed to any living being about me. I was commanded to say many things, but as the penalties were the same whether I did not say them, or used a wrong utterance, and I was constantly rebuked for the latter, and pained by a sense of ingratitude, I usually held my tongue, till urged by a new menace, or a new appeal, generally by the assurance that by the act of obedience, I should be redeeming thousands of souls who were suffering for me the agonies of hell fire, because I would not obey. Many times I called loudly after my brother and cousin, commanded to summon them and confess to them crimes of the most incredible nature. I recollect also, that I fancied myself to have been to blame for the drowning of an old woman, on the city side of the river, below Blackfriars bridge.

I saw also visions of very heavenly forms in procession; and I was invited to come up to heavenly places; my inability was my crime. I also saw on my bed *curtains,* two, if not three faces, one of my Saviour, the other of my father, and of my Almighty Father; both white with long white beards. Once, after seeing the face representing my Almighty Father, I was accused of mocking, and I heard his voice saying severely and firmly, "I have sworn by my beard I will not be mocked at," which form of words were often repeated. A young man also who attended me, was named to me at one time as my fourth brother, at one time as my youngest brother; that he was so really, but that I would not acknowledge it to be so. But the vision which made the most vivid impression upon me, amounting to reality, so strong an impression indeed, that I might almost say, the possibility of being present in two places at the same time may be capable of realization; thine it was, O Lord, to interpret it to me. When I saw the venerable countenance of my father bending over me weeping, and the crystal tears falling, which I felt trickling down my shoulders, the impression of this was so vivid, that I can hardly help now suspecting, either that water was dropped on my back through the ceiling and tester of the bed, or that I was not where I appeared to be. Still it was not altogether the countenance of my father, as on earth; and I saw a long flowing white beard. I thought, could my father's beard have been so white and so long? But I both thought it unholy to question, and besides I could not control my thoughts to unravel my ideas. So my doubts took slight hold on my reason.

CHAPTER XI

BESIDES my struggling to get loose from my manacles, and to reject the medicine and broth given me, I recollect only two active scenes. One day I was taken out at the right side of the bed, and held by men, whilst shaved on the crown. My friend Captain —— was in the room. I was desired by the Lord to be patient, till I saw his face at the window, and then to rise up and cry something. I did so. I saw the face; I rose up, and cried out, and then returned to bed. My chief grief at that time was, that I had received the tonsure of the Roman Catholic priesthood, a mark of the beast. On another occasion when I was compelled to submit by force, and without the slightest word of explanation, to certain medical treatment, I was sensible of the indelicacy: on both, the option was given me to resist, and though I partially resisted, the fear of injury to my person *seems* to have biassed me to prefer submission.

When my brother [Spencer] first appeared by my bed-side, "I have hopes now," said I, "I shall be understood and respected;" for he had written to me that he believed the reported miracles at Row. When, however, I first told him, "I am desired to say so and so," "I am desired to do this, or that"—he replied to me, in an ill-judged tone of levity, and as if speaking to a child; ridiculing the idea. My hopes of being comprehended were blighted, and my heart turned from him. I reflected; my brother knew my powers of mind, he ought to consider that it can be no light matter that can so change me. I then resumed my silence, addressing no one except on a few occasions, and by command. Afterwards, as I got worse, I imagined the Almighty had cut short the times, and redeemed all men for my sins' sake, to visit all sins on my head; then I imagined also, that men now moved in a new life, knowing my thoughts and the Lord's thoughts, and the thoughts of one another. And when I was tempted to ask and ascertain any of these facts, I was told it was of no use, for that they would read whether I did so or not in obedience to the Lord, and, if I did not, would answer falsely.

Thus my delusions, or the meshes in which my reasoning faculties were entangled, became perfected; and it was next to impossible thoroughly to remove them, perhaps, for man's word alone, impossible.

Had my brother but said to himself, "there is something strange here; I will try to understand it"—had he but pretended to give credit to what I said, and reasoned with me on the matter revealed to me, acknowledging the possibility, but denying or questioning the divine nature of my inspirations; I should, perhaps, have been soon rescued from my dreadful situation, and saved from ruin: but it was not so.

During my confinement in Dublin, I knew no malice against any individual present with me, although I often contended with them. My mind was intensely occupied with the invisible agents I fancied to haunt me. Towards them I often indulged in spiteful acts of resistance and disobedience, overcome by the cruel taunts, and malevolent and contumelious language I received from them. At times, also, an inclination to humour or drollery made me dupe them—but this, more especially, a few months afterwards. These acts of disobedience were always combined with childish and absurd delusion. At one time, I took my medicine and swallowed it, with a design to poison the spirit residing in me: at another, I refused to suffocate myself on the pillow, to try to burst my manacles, or I drank my broth; in short, that conduct which people in their (so called) sound senses expected of me, I considered sin; that which they considered folly, I considered my duty; so completely was my judgment confounded.

Gradually I got better; I can hardly recollect how; but I remember a kind of confidence of mind came in me the evening after I had been threatened, and saw the thunderbolt fall harmless by my side, and when two days passed, and still found me safe in my bed. Also another night, shortly before I was removed from Dublin, I was trying to suffocate myself on the pillow as usual, when a command was given to one of my sisters to cut my throat, and my imagination was shocked by her accepting the office. Nothing ensuing, confidence again came in me, and this night a change took place in the tone of the voices. I recollect also a dream, in which I was in a bed in another house, during which I imagined that the Holy Ghost had descended upon me, like a downy cloud of a buff or nankeen colour, and had sworn to bring me out of my troubles, and no more to foresake me. This dream left so strong an impression of reality, that it became the foundation of other delusions, but at the time it comforted me. However it was, I recollect I found myself one day left alone, and at liberty to leave my bed. I got up, and knelt down to pray. I did not pray, but I saw a vision, intended, as I understood, to convey to me the idea of the mechanism of the human mind! A morning or two after that, I was made to rise and dress, and left to breakfast; my brother breakfasted with me or after me; being desired by some spirits to leave the toast for him, a secret humour came upon me to eat it all up. I think I did so. It is to me still a mystery that I was so soon left alone for so long a time. Portmanteaus were being packed. I was made to go down stairs, get into a hackney coach, and go on board a Bristol packet. Whilst standing on the quay, I recognised a poor Irish lad, who used to hold my horse, and to do commissions for me; he had watched for me, and followed me, to see me embark. I could not express my feelings; but as he stood chill and shivering a little way off, there was an expression of distrust in his features; and I felt as if he were a truer friend than those occupied about my person.

CHAPTER XII

When I entered the packet, I descended with my brother and the stout servant who had hitherto attended me, into the cabin. I was desired to be seated; they attended to the portmanteaus. Unfortunately, either in obedience to the voices, or to my desire for action, I began walking about. In consequence, I was made to go to my bed, which God knows, I had had enough of. I soon became here again a sport of the wildest delusions. I imagined that on account of my sins, the ship and the whole ship's crew would be foundered on the voyage, unless I was thrown overboard like a second Jonah. I was desired to call out to my brother to come down; to inform him of the danger the ship was in; at one time to say one thing; at another, another; my brother came down; he put off my entreaties to let me come on deck; he joked at my fears. I then was desired to call for the captain. I called as loud as I could, but I was told it was not loud enough—that he had not heard me. That the storm was too loud—that I had, however, a voice given me, that would pierce through any confusion, but that my lethargy, my wilful, sinful lethargy,—alone prevented me using it. I was then desired to prove that I was willing to sacrifice myself, and to overcome this lethargy, by getting out of my berth, and running upon deck. My servant struggled with me, and could only get me down by lying on me. This, of course, did not contribute to my health or comfort. At last, he got a pair of steel handcuffs on me. I was told it was my duty to slay him, that I might get on deck and devote myself to save the ship and crew. I struck at him with my manacled arms, endeavouring to kill him. When all my efforts availed nothing, I was still accused of lethargy and indifference, and made to consider this indifference the more dreadful, by the report that my dearest brothers, and many of my family who had come to Dublin to suffer and to die for me, were on deck likely to perish through my slothful ingratitude and stubborn refusal to make use of miraculous power given to me. At last, my servant got the leathern cases on my arms, and I was compelled to be the passive object of the tortures of my imagination.

The next morning we were moored alongside one of the quays at Bristol. When nearly all the passengers were on shore, I was conducted into the cabin; I recollect my brother being there and our standing by the stove; I think there was another gentleman there part of the time, and the captain came in soon after. I made some observations or answers, but I do not recollect what. My mind was recovering from the shock of its horrid delusions, and I felt a happy consciousness of my safety and of that of the crew, and a desire to realize it by being on shore. At the same time I felt an indignant hate towards the voices that had so acutely terrified me. But the next minute another snare was laid for me; that all that I saw around me was but a vision, that the ship had in reality foundered, and that the crew had been drowned, but that they, knowing the secret will of my Heavenly Father, and the dreadful and eternal torments prepared for me, had prayed to suffer death for me, whilst by the assistance of their spirits I was saved from the sense of the loss of the vessel and of my drowning until I could, by obtaining a repentant mind, undergo it hereafter patiently to my glory. However, my doubts were strong, and I now no longer obeyed the commands of these voices so implicitly. On landing, I called to my mind my landing near the same spot with my battalion in 1829. I accompanied my brother to an Hotel. I was shown up stairs into a large room with two beds in it. My brother remained with me. I was seated in an arm chair. A doctor entered, and with the sagacity belonging to the tribe, a sagacity by which they are sure to lose nothing, I was condemned again to my bed. I would have given my hand to remain up; my bed was a scene of horrors to me. However, I made no reply, and to bed I went.

I was scarcely in bed when I became a prey to new delusions. It was snowing at the time. I was told that a dreadful winter was

to fall upon the country, on account of my sin. I was told that
Bristol was on fire, and made to see flames; that the house was to
fall and destroy every one in it; and this, all for my sin. My brother
was sitting in the room with me. I expected every moment to see
the walls crush him. I warned him to go away, for that the house
was going to fall. I told him I saw the town in flames, he naturally
made light of what I said. He recollected my words afterwards
when the riots were in town. I was told that the reason he did not
believe me was, that I did not address him in the tongue given to
me; I was rebuked and upbraided for it. I essayed again, but I
met with the same rebukes. I lost all patience. Again I was ordered
to suffocate myself, and to kick about in various postures in the
bed; unless I did so, that Satan would enter me, and that then my
Saviour must endure in me fresh torments, to rescue my soul from
hell. For though Satan was redeemed, yet he could only be my
most skilful tormentor and destroyer, if I were not redeemed too,
and delight also in his office, if I were at last reprobate. It seemed
to me that Satan's spirit came to the left side of my bed and entered my body, and that I allowed it, for that I was so teazed that
I delighted in the prospects of my Saviour's sufferings; immediately
afterwards I was seized with compunction and dread.

The spirits also told me that a dinner would be brought to me;
that some Irish stew had been ordered for me by my brother,
which it was intended I should eat, but that a fowl would be sent
me from heavenly places to tempt me, which I was to refuse. It
was not the first time I had heard the like from the spirits, nor was
it the last.

I did not understand what this meant, but I became very hungry. After some time the door opened, and a servant came in with
the dish, containing a boiled fowl, which appeared very large and
plump; I looked for the Irish stew, but it did not appear; the
fowl on being brought near appeared small and meagre, and again
plump, and twice its former size. The spirits then, to my inward
observations, that there was but one dish, replied, that it was resolved to tempt me by a dish of the same kind, to make my trial
more easy. That a fowl had been ordered for me on earth, as well
as the fowl in heavenly places, because it was supposed I would

at least consent to relinquish the second for the salvation of my soul, and the happiness of so many thousands interested in me; when I might eat the other. However the humour came upon me that I would dine in heavenly places as I called it, and I could not resist it; and yet it was *with* my will. For, after what I have related as having occurred in Dublin, I had no power to restrain my will, my cupidity, my avidity, from moral contamination, nay, the more I attempted to resist contamination, the more my power over my will seemed to evade me: besides this, there was a difficulty in obeying the commands given to me, because, even whilst eating the fowl, I was puzzled by the change in its appearance, and told, "now you must refuse it, because you are in heavenly places, now you may eat it because you are on earth," according as it appeared beautiful or common.

The greater part of the night I passed in great torments. Next day I was in a post chaise with my brother on my road to Bath; the snow on the ground; in my mind earnestly desiring to be at home; and the voices dictating to me the conditions on which my Heavenly Father would allow my brother to take me home, and threatening other things if I did not perform these conditions. I was to utter certain phrases, make certain confessions, and the like. I thought I recollected the road along which I had marched in 1829, but I was not sure.

We turned to the left through some gates by a porter's lodge, a few miles on the road to London, and we drove up to a door of a house on the right-hand side; we alighted, and I was ushered into a small room on the left-hand side of the passage, and shortly after a young man came in, and then an old man, a very old man. I do not recollect being introduced to either. My brother went out and came in again. A man servant came and occupied himself in taking away the portmanteaus, and in laying the cloth for my dinner, he afterwards waited on me. He had a black coat on, and my spirits told me his name was ZACHARY GIBBS. All was in a mystery to me; only I understood that on certain conditions I was to go home, which *was all I desired,* whilst on certain other conditions I was to be left here. The spirits told me this.

After the meat, a raspberry tartlet or two were brought to table;

they appeared to be very large, clean, and beautiful, and I was told they were sent to me from heavenly places; that I was to refuse them; that they were sent to try me; that if I refused them I should be doing my duty, and my brother would take me to E—— [Ealing]. The same humour came on me to eat them all the quicker, under the idea that they had given me nothing but slops and physic for a fortnight or more, and now, if they are such fools as to bring me up into heavenly places, I'll make the best of it. My brother again went out, and I did not see him enter any more; this pained me exceedingly; I thought he would at least have bid me adieu; but the spirits told me that he was so disgusted at seeing me eating the tarts, when he knew that if I could have refused one I should have been allowed by the Almighty to return to my mother and family, and that I knew it, that he had resolved to leave me without bidding adieu, and had given me up into the hands of the Almighty. I imagine now that his abrupt departure was preconcerted for fear of any opposition on my part.

Well, my brother went, and I was left amongst strangers.

If I had had any introduction to Dr. F. [Fox] at least I was unconscious of it. I was left to account for my position in that asylum, for I was in Dr. F.'s asylum, to the working of my own, and be it recollected, a lunatic imagination?

My spirits told me that I was in the house of an old friend of my father's where certain duties were expected of me, that I knew what those duties were, but I pretended ignorance because I was afraid of the malice and persecution of the world in performing them. I persisted nevertheless in inwardly maintaining my ignorance and in divining what could be the meaning of these words. What ensued the evening my brother went away I do not recollect. I went to bed in a small, narrow, disconsolate looking room with stuccoed floor, over part of which was a carpet, bare white walls, a fire-place and fire in the corner, on the right-hand side by the window: the window opposite the door, the sill about the height of a man's waist, white window blinds, a table, a wash-hand-stand and a few chairs: on the left-hand side, two beds, occupying more than one third the breadth of the room, the one nearest the window with white bed hangings on a slight iron frame, the other nearer the door, made on the floor or very low: on this my attendant slept.

I was put to bed with my arms fastened. Either that night or the next, the heavy leathern cases were taken off my arms, to my great delight, and replaced by a straight waistcoat. The night brought to me my usual torments, but I slept during part of it sounder and better than before. In the morning I recollect observing a book of manuscript prayers, and a prayer book or Bible bound in blue morocco; the impression on my feelings was very dreary, and as if I had been imprisoned for a crime or for debt; but I was occupied as usual with the agony of mind occasioned by the incomprehensible commands, injunctions, insinuations, threats, taunts, insults, sarcasms, and pathetic appeals of the voices round me. Soon after I awoke, Zachary Gibbs made his appearance with a basin of tea and some bread and butter cut in small square pieces, about the size of those prepared for the holy sacrament. He staid in my room by my bed-side, whilst I eat my breakfast.

I was not now aware that I was lunatic, nor did I admit this idea until the end of the year. I knew that I was prevented from discharging my duties to my Creator and to mankind, by some misunderstanding on my part; for which, on the authority of my spiritual accusers, I considered that I was wilfully guilty; racking my mind at the same time to divine their meaning. I imagined now that I was placed in this new position as a place of trial, that it might be seen whether I would persist in my malignant, or cowardly, or sluggish disobedience to the last. I imagined at the same time, that I was placed here *"to be taught of the spirits,"* that is, (for they all spoke in different keys, tones, and measures, imitating usually the voices of relations or friends,) to learn what was the nature of each spirit that spoke to me, whether a spirit of fun, of humour, of sincerity, of honesty, of honour, of hypocrisy, of perfect obedience, or what not, and to acquire knowledge to answer to the suggestions or arguments of each, as they in turn addressed me, or to choose which I would obey.

For instance, whilst eating my breakfast, different spirits assailed me, trying me. One said, eat a piece of bread for my sake, &c., &c.; another at the same time would say, refuse it for my sake, or, refuse *that piece* for my sake or take *that*; others, in like manner, would direct me to take or refuse my tea. I could seldom refuse one, without disobeying the other; and to add to my disturbance of mind, at these unusual phenomena, and at the grief of mind— and at times alarm, I appeared to feel at disobeying any, Zachary Gibbs stood by my bed-side observing me in a new character. I understood that he was now no longer Zachary Gibbs, but a spiritual body called HERMINET HERBERT, the personification, in fact, of that spirit which had attended me in Dublin, so intimately united with my Saviour; indeed in my mind almost identified with Jesus.

I understood that as a seal to the information I now received from my spirits, he had put on a nankeen jacket, in order by that color to remind me of the dream, in which the Holy Ghost, who was his mother, had appeared to me, promising never to desert me. That he knew all my thoughts, and all I was inspired to do, and could not be deceived. He had come to aid me; but that at the same time, to prove my faith, he would act as if he were a man in plain circumstances, if he saw I doubted.

Whilst therefore I was hesitating about each morsel I put into my mouth, he stood by, encouraging me to eat, and pressing me to finish my breakfast, or he would leave me and come back, saying, "What! haven't you done yet?" Persuaded that he knew and commanded what was going on in my mind, I did not believe his encouragements sincere; but intended also to try me. I could not stand the ridicule I met with from my spirits, or to which I exposed myself in reality: I forced my conscience, wounding my spirits; teazed, tormented, twitted, frightened, at times I was made to dupe my spirits by humour. Thus, it appeared to me that, whilst standing on the very threshold of heaven, eternal hell yawned at my feet; through my stupidity and impatience.

For about three mornings, my breakfast was brought to me in this manner; after breakfast, I was dressed, and for two or three days taken down to a small square parlour, with two windows opposite the entrance, looking over some leads into a court, thence over a garden to a flat country terminated by hills, about two or three miles off. The windows had iron Venetian blinds before them; looking through them, I saw snow on the leads; I was still under the impression that this was the effect of a dismal winter sent upon my country for my disobedience. There was a round mirror between the windows; in the left-hand side of the room, an iron fire-place with a fire in it. At the bottom of the grate, over the arch under which the cinders fall, a hideous face and mouth appeared moulded in the iron. At the end of the year, when I examined it again, I saw my eyes also had been deluded, unless the grate had been changed, for the ornament was a basket of flowers, not a face. Besides this, there was a horsehair sofa opposite the windows, against the wall; some chairs and a table; also a table against the wall in the centre of the room.

When I came into the room, there was a mild old rheumatic man there, who had on a white apron. He was of low stature, and in countenance resembling my father very strongly. My spirits informed me it was my father, who had been raised from the dead, in order, if possible, to assist in saving my soul. He was also in a spiritual body. Every thing in short, had been done to save me by quickening my affections, in order to overcome my torpor, and ingratitude, and fear of man. The chairs in the room, resembling those I had seen when a child in my father's dining-room; the very trees in the distance, resembling others in the prospect round my mother's house; almost all that I saw had been brought by the Almighty power, or infinite goodness of the Lord, and placed around me to quicken my feelings! If a man can imagine realizing these ideas, in any degree, awake, he may imagine what were my sufferings.

I asked now what I was to do. There was a newspaper lying on the table, but I could not read it, because, before I had been taken unwell in Dublin, when looking for guidance from the Holy Spirit, I had been diverted from reading the papers, except here and there, as if it were unwholesome to the mind. I thought it ungrateful now to have recourse to them for amusement, and for that reason, or "by that reply," in the language of my invisible companions, I decided my resolution, without quite satisfying them.

What was I to do? I was told it was necessary to do something "to keep my heart to my head, and my head to my heart," to prevent "my going into a wrong state of mind," phrases used to me. I was told, at length, to "waltz round the table, and see what I should see." I did that—nothing came of it. My attendant requested me to be quiet; at last, my dinner was brought. I had, if I recollect accurately, two dinners in this room—one was of a kind of forced meat; the other had bacon with it: both meals were very light, and although I did not refuse them, I recollect feeling that I could have eaten something more substantial, and also being nauseated at the forced meat and bacon, which, I considered, could not be exactly wholesome for me.

My dinner in this room was served on a tray, with a napkin, silver forks, decanters, &c. &c., and in these respects, such as was fitting for a gentleman.

Unfortunately, the second day I think after my entrance into this asylum, having no books, no occupation, nothing to do but to look out of window, or read the newspaper, I was again excited by my spirits to waltz round the room; in doing this, or at a future period, I caught the reflection of my countenance in the mirror. I was shocked and stood still; my countenance looked round and unmeaning: I cried to myself, "Ichabod! my glory has departed from me," then I said to myself, what a hypocrite I look like! So far I was in a right state of mind; but the next thought was, "how shall I set about to destroy my hypocrisy;" then I became again lunatic. Then I resumed my waltzing, and being directed to do so, I took hold of my old attendant to waltz with him; but at last, deeming that absurd, and finding him refuse, the spirits said, "then wrestle with him if you will." I asked him to wrestle; but he refused. I understood this was to try me if I was sincere; I seized him to force him to wrestle; he became alarmed; an old patient in the asylum passing by the door, hearing a struggle, entered, and assisted in putting me into a straight waistcoat: I was forced down on the sofa. He apologized to me for it many months after, saying it was in the afternoon, when all the other assistants were out walking with their respective patients.

Thus commenced my second ruin; and the history of an awful course of sufferings and cruelties, which terminated in my recovery from my delusions about the beginning of the next year, and was followed by my confinement as a madman, for nearly two years in a sound state of mind; because I entered into dispute with my family on their conduct to me, and the nature of my treatment, determined to bring them to account at law, for the warning of others, and to satisfy my excited sense of wrong. I can no longer, after arriving at this period of my trials, call Dr. F——'s [Fox's] house by any other name than that it deserves, *madhouse*, for to call that, or any like that, an *asylum*, is cruel mockery and revolting duplicity!

I have already stated, that when I came to this house, I did not know that I was insane. And my insanity appears to me to have differed in one respect from that of many other patients; that I was not actuated by *impression* or feeling, but misled by audible inspiration, or *visible*, rather than *sensible* guidance of my limbs. To the voices I heard, and to these guidances, I surrendered up my judgment, or what remained to me of judgment, fearing that I should be disobeying the word of God, if I did not do so. When I first came to Dr. F——'s madhouse, my health was somewhat restored, my mind somewhat confirmed; yet my attendant informed me at the close of the year, I looked so ill when my brother left me, that he thought I could not live. I was like a child in thought and will, so far as my feelings were directed to those around me. I knew no malice, no vice. I imagined that they loved me, and were all deeply interested in the salvation of my soul, and I imagined too that I loved them dearly. Yet I wrestled with the keepers, and offered to do so with others, and struck many hard blows; sometimes, as one informed me, making it difficult for three strong men to control me, yet whenever I did this, I was commanded to do so. I was told that they knew I was commanded, that they wished me to do so, to prove my faith and courage, but that they were commanded to prove both till they were satisfied of my sincerity. I may safely say, that for nine entire months, if not for the whole period of my confinement in Dr. F——'s charge, I never spoke, hardly acted, and hardly thought, but by inspiration or guidance, and yet I suppose that never was there any one who so completely contradicted the will of the Almighty, or the desires of those around him, and I could not help laughing now at the delusions which made me constantly choose that conduct which was most disagreeable and terrifying to my doctor and his keepers, as in the reality the most agreeable to them, if I were not overcome by a sense of the cruel state of abandonment and exposure to their malice and ignorance in which I was left.

After being fastened in the straight waistcoat, I was taken down stairs to a long saloon or parlour, to the left of the little parlour I had been as yet confined to, and on the ground floor. There was a long table in the middle of the room, allowing space to pass round it, a fire on the left-hand side, and a glass bow window and door at the further end. I was fastened in a niche on a painted wooden seat between the fire and the glass window, in the curve in the wall forming the bow at the end of the room; another niche opposite to me was occupied by a trembling grey headed old man; there were several other strange looking personages on the chairs about the room, and passing occasionally through the glass window door which looked out in the same direction as the windows of the room I had quitted, into a small court yard. I think I hear the door jarring now, as they slammed it to and fro. I marvelled at my position; my spirits told me that I was now in a madhouse, and I was told that it only remained for me to pray for the inmates, that they might be restored to their senses, and that they should be restored, but that I must then forego certain advantages. I attempted to pray, though I did not quite believe that I was in a madhouse, being unconscious of my own melancholy state, or imagining that I was placed there for convenience, not from necessity. There was an appearance of wretchedness and disorder amongst my associates, and I felt happy to be taken up to my bed-room after tea had been served in the evening.

The next morning my breakfast was brought to me as before in bed. I was dressed up stairs, and Herminet Herbert conducted me down to the seat I occupied the night before. There was an appearance of more cleanliness, order, and composure in the persons of the wretched individuals around me. Now I was told by my spirits that my prayer had been heard, that they had been restored to a sound state of mind, that they were in consequence among the redeemed of the Lord and knew that I had prayed for them, that they had in their turn desired to be allowed to remain with me one year as guides to me, and as a species of jury, to wait until I became obedient to the Almighty, and to judge me whether I was sincere in my difficulties or not; this delusion lasted for more than six months with this difference, that sometimes I conceived it my duty to recognize in their persons, relations, and friends, sometimes ministers and officers of the king.

The trembling grey headed old man was still opposite to me, and I was told that he was the Father Confessor, to whom I used to confess my sins in Portugal, and that he was there waiting to hear my confessions concerning my crimes as a poor lad at Alcobaça. Before my trials and punishments commenced, I was desired to confess to him. I tried several times, but I was checked by the noise, by his inattention, and by the rebukes of my spirits. He did not appear often after; whether he died or whether he was removed, I cannot say.

There were two or three volumes of a register in the room, and a large octavo Bible. I tried to read them but I was always puzzled and dodged by my tormentors, who could not let me rest, but made me turn from one place to another, usually guiding me after all to an anecdote about a Russian lady and a Czar of Russia, which I read over *till I was sick of it,* and which I perfectly understood. I recollect the first few days I was down in this room I was occasionally allowed to leave the niche in the evening, and sit by the fire or table, when I used to try to read these books; but one evening, Herminet Herbert on remarking my behavior, for some cause fastened me up again; after that, I did not regain my liberty of action in doors for six or more months. It was in the cricketting season after the hay was made, that I was first allowed to walk about in the room and yard amongst my fellow prisoners.

Not long after my introduction into this room, the three registers were taken away; the Bible remained. When I was allowed to use my discretion, I used to read this in the yard, until an old lunatic, whom I imagined to be the Lord Jehovah, forbade me to do so, and I obeyed. I recollect the servant bringing it in soiled and defaced in the winter from under the privet hedge, where it had been hidden by one of the lunatics.

Besides this, occasionally one or two papers were brought into the room. My delusions increased so rapidly and became so confirmed after I was placed here, that my constant train of idea and habit of thought ran upon England, and this world, as of a creation gone by; I understood at one time that, the Almighty having cut short the times and redeemed the whole world, every part of the creation was changed, but that with a view to give me every chance of saving my soul, I was allowed to walk in a vision representing objects as they were when I was in England. I did not entirely believe these communications; still they had such an effect upon my mind that my form of thought was always "when I was in England," "when I was in the world."

I recollect with what eagerness I tried to get hold of the newspapers when I first saw them in this room, to discover if events were going on as I had left them, and what courage it gave me at first to read the articles of the war in Poland accompanied with a comfortable assurance that I was still in the land of the living, like that related of one when he first saw a gibbet. But now I was told that these papers were printed to try me, that the Almighty made me read just what he would, but that if I were redeemed I should see other words printed there, *heavenly ideas* which they who were around me saw.

I thought that the lapse of time had been concealed from me, and though really in hell one moment and in heaven another, yet I was only allowed to see around me events as they had taken place in England and elsewhere in the year 1831, after my illness in and removal from Dublin. That at that time the Almighty had caused the war in Poland to break out to atone for my sins, and had visited England with a destructive winter and pestilences on account of my blasphemies, and therefore now I read in the papers what had taken place as at that time.

For I imagined that whenever I disobeyed the word of the Lord or did not fulfil it, *pretending,* as I was accused of, not to understand it, the wrath of God commanded horrible torments on me, and that His word being once passed, it was necessary that they should be endured, and that I ultimately should myself suffer them: which I must either do in His power or in a state of rebellion and despair, wherefore the spirits and persons round me and affected towards me, undertook to endure them as often as they were commanded, hoping for the time, that I should endure them to my own and to God's glory. But enough of these horrors and imbecilities for the present.

CHAPTER XIII

LET no man mock at the understanding that could so patiently or humbly submit to such seemingly absurd teachings; but rather let him fear and pray that the power of the Lord to confound the judgment and wisdom of man may not be put forth upon him.

My mind was not destroyed, without the ruin of my body. My delusions, though they often made me ridiculous, did not derange my understanding unaided by the poisonous medicines and unnatural treatment of my physicians. Then when I became insane, the knowledge of that fact appears to have given to every one who had to deal with me carte blanche to act towards me, as far as seemed good unto himself, in defiance of nature, of common sense, and of humanity. The wonder is, not that I fell, but that, having through my fall come into the net which is spread by the arts and malice of the lunatic doctors, I could endure their treatment, and, recovering from under it, exercise my own native sense of justice boldly in spite of their will, whilst still unsound in judgment, and ultimately ride triumphant over the waves of misfortune! My senses were all mocked at and deceived. In reading, my eyes saw words in the paper which when I looked again were not. The forms of those around me and their features changed, even as I looked on them. Nature appeared at times renewed, and in a beautiful medium that reminded me of the promises of the gospel and the prophecies concerning the times of refreshing and renewal; in a few minutes she again appeared trite and barren of virtue, as I had used to know her. I heard the voices of invisible agents, and notes so divine, so pure, so holy, that they alone perhaps might recompense me for my sufferings. My sense of feeling was not the same, my smell, my taste, gone or confounded.

Believing in miraculous agency, and the subject of miraculous sensations, I received these as the word and guidance of God, for their beauty and their apparent tendency to promote purity and benevolence. And if I doubted, my doubts were overwhelmed if not dissipated by compunction at attributing what was so kind, so lovely, so touching, to any but the divine nature, and by fear of committing the sin against the Holy Ghost. Whatever then appeared contradictory, or did not turn out as I expected, I attributed to my disobedience or want of understanding, not to want of truth in my mediator.

CHAPTER XIV

THE next morning after my entrance into the lunatics' common room, I observed three men, apparently *servants* or attendants of the gentlemen there. One was Herminet Herbert, whom in a black coat I was to address as Zachary Gibbs, and who I was afterwards told, on seeing him in a blue coat, was Samuel Hobbs; but under all these appearances he was one and the same Jesus. I used to call him Herminet Herbert, the simple, and Jesus Christ. He was a short, active, fair, witty, clever man. The other was a tall, spare, aquiline nosed gawky man, from Devonshire, like a groom. The voices told me to call him at times Herminet Herbert Scott, at times, Sincerity; at times, Marshall; *that was his name.* The third was a stout, jovial, powerful man, like a labourer. The voices told me he was Herminet Herbert, the simple, God Almighty, and that I was to call him SIMPLICITY; his name was Poole. Besides this, a very stout, powerful dark man, like a coach-man, with a very small voice and gentle manners, was occasionally occupied in attending on me and other patients. I called him by order Herminet Herbert the Holy Ghost, or Kill-all. I understood these were incarnations or manifestations of the Trinity. A stout benevolent old gentleman, a lunatic, who was dressed in a suit of blue, and had been handsome, was I was informed, the Lord Jehovah, supremely omnipotent, the trinity in unity, who had taken upon himself the form of an old writing master who used to teach me when a child, and whose name was Waldony, by which name, and by that of Benevolence, I was at times desired to address him. Likewise I understood Herminet Herbert Scott, or Marshall, to be a favourite servant of my Father's, who had lived in our family at Hampstead, and had been raised from the dead with my father and my eldest sister to attend on me. And Herminet Herbert the simple, or Samuel Hobbs, I was told had lived in my mother's family after my father's death, and had been very fond of me and my brothers, and familiar with us; that my brothers had known at the time that he was Jesus, but that I had not; that during an illness I had had when young, he had wrestled with me in the school-room, it being necessary for my health, and he had come now in hopes of winning me to wrestle with him again, which was continually enjoined to me for the salvation of my soul, and the keeping me in a right state of mind. Several persons about the asylum, I was told, were my father, Dr. F. [Fox], a Dr. L., and two aged keepers, one of whom I called Honesty; the other, my real father, because he most resembled him. Now, when I did not recognize any of these facts or any of these people, I was told it was on account of my ingratitude and my cowardice. That I feared to acknowledge objects as they were, because then I knew I must prepare to endure my awful torments.

Now all these persons, and each person around me, wore a triple character, according to each of which I was in turns to address them. Samuel Hobbs, for example, was at times to be worshipped in the character of Jesus, at times to be treated familiarly as Herminet Herbert, a spiritual body, at times to be dealt with as plain Samuel Hobbs. The stout old patient was at times knelt to as the Lord Jehovah; at times he was Mr. Waldony, a spiritual body; at times a gentleman. So with the rest: and these changes took place so instantaneously, that I was completely puzzled as to my deportment towards them. I saw individuals and members of the family of Dr. F—— [Fox], approach me in great beauty, and in obedience to a voice, my inclinations sprang forward to salute them, when in an instant, their appearance changed, and another command made me hesitate and draw back. In the same manner, when books, pencils, pens, or any occupation was presented to me, I turned from one page and one object, to another, and back again, usually ending in a fit of exasperation and inward indignation, against the guidance that so perplexed me.

Besides the personages I have already taken notice of, there were eleven patients in the room, to each of which my spirits gave a name, and assigned a particular office towards me. There were three I addressed as Mr. Fitzherbert; a Captain P. who was my spirit of family pride; a Captain W——, who was my spirit of joviality; a Mr. ——, a Quaker, who was my spirit of simplicity; a Mr. D——, who for a long time I imagined to be, and addressed as, Dr. F—— [Fox?] and afterwards as one of my uncles; a Mr. A——, who was my fifth brother, and my spirit of contrition; the Rev. Mr. J——, a Devonshire curate, who was one of my first cousins, my spirit of affection, and the representation of the apostle St. John; a Mr. J. who was my spirit of honesty, and my youngest brother; a Mr. ——, who thought himself the Duke of Somerset, and whom I addressed as Mr. Fazakerley, my spirit of delicacy and contrition; and Captain —— a dark man, who had lost his left leg, and the use of his left arm; and who for six months stood up in one position, and for six months sat down in one position—him my spirits called Patience; and told me he was my executioner, waiting for the decision of the jury upon me, to officiate on me, but still one of my best friends.

Besides these, the youngest Mrs. F—— [Fox] was pointed out to me as repentance; two of the housekeepers as my mother, and two servant girls, one as a sister and a cousin, and one as my deceased sister. I was told that the reason I did not recognize them was, that I could not or would not, for sin. And certainly the countenances of those about changed in a wonderful manner. And I did at one time, amongst the patients see one of my aunts, who was many miles away; and on another occasion, I saw in a patient who was introduced into the common room in the summer, an old school-fellow so like him, that I called out his name in surprise; when the vision changed, and I saw him walking in other features, and then again in new ones.

In the midst of all this confusion of triple or quadruple persons in one and the same individual, and of my understanding, that according as my spirits warned me, I was either on earth as it was when I left it, or in heaven, or in an intermediate state of felicity, I was desired to act and to do my duty, and accused of guilt in pretending not to know what was my duty, and resisting the desire of the Lord to learn of my spirits. I might well be puzzled. I might well have been puzzled, setting aside that delusion. For it might be a trial for a very wise man to act discreetly on being ushered by violence or guile, into a room full of gentlemen who spoke nothing, did nothing, or muttered a few half sentences to him without being informed of the nature of his company and of his position amongst them. I had no introduction, no explanation, no reason assigned me for my position; lunatic, imbecile, childish, deluded, I was left to divine every thing. Precisely that conduct likeliest to aid deception of the mind, to encourage and to make it perpetual, was pursued towards me, and is now being pursued towards those wretched companions I have left behind me, and to tens of thousands in a similar state.

My earnest desire, my intense inward prayer to the Deity whom I imagined conversing in me, was, "Oh! take me home, Oh! take me to E——g [Ealing]. I shall never know what I am to do here; all is so new, so strange, so perplexing. If I were one fortnight, one week, three days in the library at E——, left to myself, I should know how I was to act—what I was to do." My brothers, my sisters, and my mother were always in my thoughts; my constant longing was to be with them. Nearly all I did that was extravagant, nearly all the voluntary suffering I brought on myself was with a view to my finding myself miraculously amongst them, or them about me.

CHAPTER XV

A MORNING or two after my removal to the lunatics' common room, I was dressed and taken down there to breakfast, and this was continued until the beginning of the next year, when I had recovered my sense enough to insist on treatment more becoming my wants, character, habits, and rank in society. I came down with my attendant between half-past six and half-past seven o'clock. The breakfast was usually placed on the table about eight. The tea was poured out of two large beer cans into slop basins, and a plate of bread and butter placed by each basin. There was seldom any complaint from the patients, excepting poor Patience. He always complained, in broken and rather violent sentences, not addressed to any one particularly, of the thickness of the slices. And I observed there was always placed on his plate one slice, twice the thickness of all the rest. My spirits assured me I was brought down stairs to show contempt of me, and to punish me for my continued disobedience; or for some particular act of rebellion in the eating of my breakfast up stairs. I never made any remonstrance against this or any treatment, however bad; so fully was I persuaded that the persons around me acted from inspiration, and that my Saviour in Herminet Herbert directed every regulation, however severely, from necessity, and to my ultimate benefit.

Immediately on being brought down stairs, I was taken to my niche, seated down, and fastened into it by a strap with a small padlock, that ran through a ring in the wall, which ring could be turned round. My tea was placed before me, at breakfast time, in a slop basin, on a small deal table, with a plate of bread and butter.

And usually one hand was loosened from the straight waistcoat; at times I was fed by the hand. It was always a great delight to me to get my hand at liberty, even for a moment, and the first use I usually made of it was to strike the keeper who untied me; directed by my spirits to do so, as the return he desired above all things else; because he knew I was proving my gratitude to the Lord Jehovah, at the risk of being struck myself. My blows were usually received in good humour. The same mysterious directions came to me at breakfast here, but my confusion was greater, and my humour to delude my spirits more strong. I disobeyed and deceived every voice; although told that I polluted my spirits by so doing. The voice which kept control over me the longest was that of my deceased sister, excepting only the voices of him whom I deemed the Lord Jehovah. At last, I disobeyed and mocked at even that voice; and then I became nearly reckless about obeying any or not; only being excited to try again and again to reconcile their directions by pathetic appeals, remonstrances, threats, awakenings of compunction and of remorse.

I disobeyed these voices, although at the time threatened with terrible consequences, and aware of the dreadful terrors of mind I should go through attended with accusations of impatience and ingratitude, when my meal was over, and my humour indulged. For instance, when a few weeks later they used to take me to the bath after breakfast, the spirits called to my mind their horrid threats in Dublin, and bade me understand that this was the bath of boiling water, in which I was to be plunged for all eternity; I was threatened with finding it so, if I did not obey my spirits, or before I descended to it, reconcile them to me, by suffering something for their sakes. Two or three circumstances led to a confirmation of this delusion. In the first place, the bath was in gloomy rooms like cellars. In one room, in which I was usually dressed and undressed, there was no window at all, and the walls bare; in the other two, the light came from small windows at the top of the wall. We passed along passages to get to them, in which I saw large iron pipes, like the apparatus of steam-engines; and these I was told were to convey the hot water to the bath. I was occasionally seized hand and foot by two men, and thrown suddenly backwards into the bath: and I did not know what need there was for violence, for I never hesitated to enter it. On one occasion, Simplicity stretched out an iron bar to duck my head under the water by pressing it upon my neck; for the men seemed to think it an essential part of their extraordinary quackery, to have the head well soused. After ducking my head, he held the bar out to me in sport, and I seized hold of it, and found it quite warm, as if just taken from a fire. I attribute this now to the extreme coldness of my body in the water; for often, for half an hour after I came from the bath, I shook and shuddered, and my teeth chattered with cold; on these occasions I was usually fastened for a time alone in a large wicker chair, in the parlour I had originally been confined to. But at the time, I conceived the heat of the bar to be a proof to me accorded in mercy of what my spirits told me; that I was really in the bath of boiling water, concealed from me by their agency, but ready, on my provoking the Lord beyond redemption, to be instantaneously revealed to me. On another occasion, I entered the bath room after some other patients, when Herminet Herbert showed me a leather mask, which in sport he offered to put on me, and asked how I should like to go into the bath with it? Now my spirits had threatened me with being plunged in, after having my face covered with a pitch plaster. So these trifling incidents aided my delusions.

I may add here, that ere I had been plunged in the cold bath myself, which was not for at least a week after my arrival, I was threatened with it by my persecutors, and I used to see the patients called out one after the other, when my spirits always informed me, and indeed on any extraordinary occasion, "Mr. Fitzherbert is gone for you—" or, "Mr. Simplicity is suffering for you." I was, in short, made accountable for every event around me, and continually appealed to, "will you suffer nothing for us, when we are suffering for you, in all those around you—things you ought to suffer?" I understood then that all these gentlemen went and endured the horrors of the bath of boiling water for me, rather than that I should undergo it in a state unable to endure it to God's glory and to my own salvation. My attendant came up to me one day, and said to me—some confusion having arisen—"you seem to be at the bottom of all that's going on here; what was it? you seem to understand all these things." On another day, when Herminet Herbert was going up stairs, and I was fastened in one of the niches, an old patient said to me, "there's your Saviour going up stairs; what! will you not go after him?" All these observations corroborated my delusions. I was told I had miraculous power to burst my manacles, but that I would not use it. One afternoon, when all were gone out walking, and I was left strapped up alone, my spirits told me power was given me to open my padlock, and be at liberty. I tried, and I did open the padlock, and was at liberty some time; till on their return, Herminet Herbert found me, and expressed his surprise, "How came you loose?" and locked me up again.

I may also add, that on one occasion, when I went to the bath, Herminet Herbert asked a man who was there—whom I afterwards, if I am not wrong, found out to be a bricklayer (one of the baths there appeared to be undergoing repairs)—to help him to throw me into the water. We had come down stairs alone. Usually, the hulking fellow I called the Holy Ghost, or Kill-all, came to my bed-side, about half-past six in the morning, to help to take me down, for I almost invariably resisted going down, not from my own notion, but by the command of my spirits, as doing the thing most agreeable to the attendants. I was told that this man was another personification of the Holy Ghost, and another Kill-all. For that as Diana was worshipped in two forms, as DIANA and HECATE, so the Holy Ghost was the destroyer of those in hell. I saw this man, one day, in the passage, and his face was for a moment of a preternatural red or flame colour. He was at that time at work in a cellar opening in the front of the house, where I was made to believe that a cold bath was being prepared for me, into which I was to be plunged and immured in the dark; and to be always sinking and drowning to all eternity. I used to long to look down that cellar to see if it was true that preparations were really going on for a bath, but I never had an opportunity.

And there was, I must admit, also a singular coincidence between the state of mind, and trifling actions of those around, and the events that my spirits forewarned me of, or threatened me with, during the day. If, for instance, Mr. Fitzherbert, my spirit of family pride, who was pointed out to me as my guide came down with his shoes on, instead of looking for them in the room, or hung up his hat, my voices told me to augur such and such things during the day, which usually proved true.

CHAPTER XVI

In the morning, after the breakfast things were removed, it was a natural thought to any mind to ask "what shall I do?" How to answer this, in a situation like that of the unfortunate gentlemen in that room whose limbs were at liberty, was difficult enough. There were three books, but what were they among so many? occasionally one or two newspapers, besides this a draft-board and a pack of cards. Soon after, the books were reduced to the Bible, and then that disappeared. But that which was a natural thought to others, was to me a question addressed to invisible guides, and rendered more difficult to answer, inasmuch as I was confined to my wooden seat, and often with my arms manacled. My voices first told me to speak to each Herminet Herbert as he came into the room. What was I to say? "Herminet Herbert, will you take me to my mother's room up stairs?" "Herminet Herbert, will you take me to my mother's room down stairs?" Though I shrunk from saying these things, yet I obeyed these voices. No attention whatever was paid to me. I asked my spirits how my mother could have a room in that house? Afterwards two or three housekeepers in the madhouse were pointed out to me as my mother; I replied, I could not recognize her; I was answered, because I would not. I remarked how could she be so poor, and performing the offices of a menial? I was answered, that as part of the calamities and curses brought on my nation by the Almighty in consequence of my sins, a general bankruptcy had ruined the state and my family; that nevertheless the love of my family was such, that they had come to wait on me as servants of Dr. F. [Fox], rather than abandon

me. Poor things, they never came near me! How often did I
struggle with my attendants, and provoke their violence to get to
one or other of these rooms, imagining that my mother and sisters
were waiting there to receive me, and that all that was required
of me was to grapple with my antagonist, sincerely resolved to endure the extreme of his anger rather than shrink from doing what
was enjoined on me. After I found that my addresses were of no
avail, and I got tired of repeating the same words, I again asked
for direction. I was desired then to address the old man opposite
me, and to confess my sins in Portugal to him, as to my Father Confessor. I called to him, but received no reply; again I was directed
to address the patients around me: another time to say, Herminet
Herbert, will you take me to the w—— closet. I suffered acutely
in doing this, particularly before all the by-standers: but I yielded.
After some time, I was attended to, and taken up stairs. Here I
was usually conducted by him I called Simplicity, and God Almighty: I was assailed by new delusions. I used to rise from the
seat and throw myself forward, flat on my face, through the door,
to fall at the feet of this individual and worship him. The door
opened outwards, and I had my arms usually fastened round my
waist. I therefore ran considerable risk of hurting myself, besides
the punishment of this stout fellow. This extraordinary conduct
was suggested to me in this manner. Although I was in the house
of Dr. F. an old friend of my father's, upon earth, I was at the
same time present in heavenly places: and capable of being conscious of both states of existence, and of directing my conduct in
each, in rapidly succeeding intervals of time, according to what
was passing round me in each. But the exercise of faith was required of me, and one great trial of that faith was to see the doors,
walls, and persons round me as on earth. To cast myself prostrate
before God Almighty in heavenly places was a reasonable act: to
cast myself prostrate in a straight waistcoat, through the door of
the closet, at the feet of a servant was not a reasonable act, and a
dangerous one to boot. The apparent danger and reasonableness
were the trial of my faith: and if I flung myself forward bodily,
which through fear I seldom or ever succeeded in doing, exactly
at the word of the Spirit sent to give me the time; I should find

there was no door, no walls, no servant, no obstacle; but that I was verily in the presence of the saints, at the feet of Jehovah. I met, however, with nothing but severe falls and blows on my face and arms from the door, and rough handling from my attendant; who threw me back violently on the seat, and when there struck me in the abdomen, and then pitched into my face. My arms being tied, I used to turn my head to the right, and the blows fell on my left ear. This powerful man often struck me with great ferocity and spite: like one not contented with his situation, or perplexed by conduct unintelligible, which teazed him, whether designed or not. He was, however, generally good-humoured, and civil in his demeanour. Unfortunately, his punishment was of no use to me. I understood that I was punished for feigning, not for my act of faith, and the blows were another chance for my being at last miraculously at home, or in heavenly places. They only tended to disturb the equanimity of my mind in attempting to perform the duties required of me by my spiritual Mentors. Receiving their voices as the commands of my God, nothing could prevent me attempting to obey those commands, however absurd they might appear to myself or others, or dangerous to myself. The awful impression of dread produced by preternatural menaces; the compunction I felt for former acts of ingratitude; the appeals to my attachment, sense of honour, sense of duty, made by my spirits; the hope of redeeming millions of souls by one act of obedience, and of standing in the presence of Jesus and his Father, were too strong for me to resist. Experience alone of the falsehood of the promises could succeed in making me relinquish altogether my attempt; and that experience was long in coming, for fear or embarrassment continually made me prevent or lag behind the instant of execution; and then the failure of effect was attributed to my not acting with "precision and decision."

Returning to the common room, I always attempted to wrestle with, or asked one of the patients to wrestle with me, I was then locked into my seat. If my arms were at liberty, I would occasionally seize one or two of the patients to wrestle with me as they passed by me. I had no malicious motive; I did it in obedience to inspiration, and imagined they were inspired to know what I was commanded, how I obeyed, and how to act in consequence. My attempts at wrestling were however inculcated by the spirits on more practical grounds than ordinary. They told me that it was necessary "for the *keeping me in a right state of mind*," in other words, "to keep my head to my heart, and my heart to my head;" that I should be suffocated, or strangled, or violently exercised, or at least perform one act of obedience to the Lord Jehovah supremely Omnipotent, in a certain rhyme or measure once or twice through the day; that without that my head wandered from my heart, and my heart turned from my head all through the day, which was the cause of my being in a wrong state of mind; by which expression I did not then understand lunacy. I used to ask several individuals to wrestle with me, with a view to their giving me violent usage, a severe fall and the like, and with the secret hope that during the wrestling, one or other of them would strangle me or cause me to suffocate. I always seized the strongest men, and it is a singular fact, whilst I compelled the other keepers to struggle with me, I never did more than lay hold of the waistcoat of him I called Jesus, the weakest, unless when I was struggling with three at a time. The men usually held my arms, joked with me, begged me to be quiet, and used no more violence than was requisite to overcome me. Therefore I did not get what I wanted, until the autumn, when one day seizing Sincerity to wrestle with him, he gave me a tremendous fall that shook my whole frame. I knew then I had done my duty, and finding myself no more in heavenly places than I was at the beginning, not a whit more capable of understanding my position, I desisted from any further attempts of that kind.

But before I received this fall I was made to fancy that my insincerity prevented the man from dealing with me as God intended; that they knew I was shuffling; that I did not exert half the force I had; yet at the end of the year Samuel Poole reminded me saying, "how you used to make us sweat!" for three keepers usually came to compel me to go to the cold bath, which to me was a mystery, because I was not aware force was required to take me there, and I was told I might go to the bath with Simplicity, or Sincerity, or Herminet Herbert, according to my conduct. But in reality it was, I concluded, a display of force to intimidate; in which it failed through my delusions, for it provoked my efforts. But it answered another purpose, that my foolish opposition did not meet with such cruel violence as the spite or fears of a weaker party might have inflicted on me. Sometimes I was carried along in sport neck and crop; but usually I did not meet, on these occasions, except from single hands, with ruder treatment than might be expected from three country fellows overcoming resistance: on one occasion only I recollect a stick being brought out to beat me, but I do not recollect its being used. I am not sure.

When consigned to my seat, it became again a question how I was to employ myself. I felt in this position a sense of suffocation, which together with former delusions, suggested to me the idea of suffocating myself by pressing my nostrils against a wooden projection in the wall serving as an arm to the seat. This in fact was my chief occupation all the day long, occasionally varied by my attempting to twist my neck, standing up as well as I could and leaning on the back of my head, the face turned upwards against the wall, and then turning my body as on a pivot from side to side. Occasionally an old patient put a newspaper on my knees to read, and Herminet Herbert once or twice gave me one of the registers. Sometimes my hands were untied for a short time to read them. In the morning, and always in the afternoon, certain of the patients smoked and sat down with the servants to a game at whist. Scarcely a word was spoken except in broken sentences, or by the servants, which added to the apparent mystery of my situation. Once a day usually, one or more of Dr. F.'s [Fox's] sons came into the room and staid five or ten minutes, he addressed one or two patients, and occasionally said a few words to me; but always with a half and half manner of speech and deportment, which added to the conviction I was under, that they too came for a mysterious purpose. Occasionally they smoked a cigar in the room, and played a game at cards. I was told that one of these gentlemen was my brother D., and his name Sincerity and Contrition; the other, my brother H., and his name Joviality; he was an amiable good-looking fellow; the other, melancholy, and besotted. I occasionally asked these and other well dressed men to wrestle with me, but I did not attempt to force them, in spite of my spirits, for they were too well dressed, too decent, too childish. Generally every Sunday morning about ten o'clock, Dr. F., the father of these young men, tottered in, a grey-headed firm-charactered old man, of short stature, with a blue frock coat on, broad brimmed hat, and long cane. But to me all was delusion; I thought him a spiritual being; I called him my father.

About 11 o'clock every day, the patients were taken out walking, if the weather was fine, and I went out for an hour with Herminet Herbert, or was left tied up alone. Dinner came at one; in the afternoon the patients again went out for a walk, came home about four, went into the yard or sat down in the room till seven, when tea was brought and served as the breakfast; after which, they were taken or went alone upstairs to bed. Besides this, during the day they were occasionally taken out one by one, either to the bath or to be shaved, but I then understood when they went out singly, they went either to suffer, or to supplicate for me; when they went out together, they went as a court of justice to consult on my case.

When I was first fastened in my niche, my feet were at liberty, but afterwards they also were fastened by leathern sockets to a ring in the floor. There were two or three reasons for this, or rather causes; for had my treatment been reasonable there would I conceive have been little reason for any personal confinement at all. I imagine now that I was unwittingly the servant of a spirit employed to mock at all the conceits of a presumptuous charlatan and his careless servants, for controlling, overcoming, or managing the human mind; which spirit did at the same time work to my punishment and degradation. When I was fastened down, for example, in the niche with my hands secured round my waist and my body girt with a leathern belt to the wall, my spirits guided me to turn completely round heels over head, so that my neck came against the seat, my feet reached the arch of the niche, and, raised up on one side, came down on the other. It is astonishing I never hurt myself. They cut off this strange amusement by fastening my feet to the floor. I used also after dinner and breakfast to kick over the table with the plate at times on it, and when my feet were fastened I used to lean down and do this with my mouth; sometimes I succeeded, sometimes I did not, but my aim was to do it in *"precision and decision,"* and I did not care how many blows I received, though I feared them, if they would give me only three *in precision and decision.* I was often struck, but usually only two blows at a time; Simplicity struck me most. At last, towards the end of six months, I got three blows and three sharp raps from a spoon, from Herminet Herbert, in the time or measure I conceived was required, and finding myself still in the same situation in mind and body, I did not attempt any thing, merely to seek their blows, any longer. I used also to try and drag things to me with my feet, sometimes to fling my shoes off into the room, &c. &c., and I would actually wait in silent faith and prayer for the shoe to come back to me.

This was my position in this room for about three months; after that, I was removed to the niche in the wall opposite to the fire-place, and continued confined there till late in the cricketting season, after hay making.

About three days after I was left by my brother, I was taken out for my first walk by Herminet Herbert. The snowdrop was just piercing the ground, and from that I judged afterwards I had been brought there towards the middle of January, for I had no means of calculating time, but by the seasons, and when by chance I got a newspaper: until in the autumn, coming to my senses, I asked for a pocket-book. I walked about Dr. F.'s grounds and plantations, crying out at every carriage I saw, that it was my mother's; to every young female that she was one of my sisters, and calling aloud by inspiration, "I am the lost hope of a noble family—I am ruined! I'm ruined! I'm lost! I'm undone! but I AM the redeemed of the redeemed of the Lord; I AM the redeemed of the Lord Jehovah supremely omnipotent, and of the Lord Jehovah Gireth, and of the Lord Jehovah, &c. &c. &c. who is true to his word, and his saints love it well;" *which last words also came to me in Dublin.*

The above sentences were given to me to repeat, laying a stress on the word "am," of which sentences I now see the beauty and the connexion, though then I cried each out separately, timidly, and undecidedly. The keeper who attended me occasionally rebuked me, ridiculed me, shook me, or struck me with his walking stick. Very often we walked out in the fields, and to farm-houses in the neighbourhood, when I used to fall down on my knees before this man, and call him Jesus. I had on, generally, a great coat over a straight waistcoat; so that at any moment my arms might be fastened. I walked usually for one hour before dinner, sometimes for an hour after dinner. After some time, I accompanied the other patients, who walked out in a body, with two or three keepers, and we went through the villages: here, as before, I cried out aloud, though not so often; and I did not desist from this for a long time. I recollect on one occasion, I ran away in the grounds from the keeper, who had desired me to keep by his side. He caught me by an iron fence in the grounds, and with great violence doubled me over it. On another occasion, looking up into the sky, I saw a vision of the Lord descending with the angels and saints. Several times, the sounds of the cattle lowing, or asses braying, in the fields, conveyed to me articulate words and sentences, as to Balaam. I was often made a joke of in good humour by the keepers, on account of my delusions, and this added to their strength, for I took seriously what they said in jest. For instance, one said to me, "there's your father, go and run after him, and take him by his arm," pointing to a patient I took for my father; another, whom I called Scott, but whose name was Marshall, replied one day, *I am called Scott in good company;* another walking behind my back, with an open knife, pricked me slightly on the shoulder-blade: I then had the most horrible ideas that I was to be crucified in a number of bodies in all parts of the world, to be flayed alive, &c. &c., and imagined that my doom was put off only from day to day: each time I came home to dinner I fancied was the last. This slight action of the keeper confirmed me in my horrid suspicions. Another delusion I laboured under was, that I should keep my head and heart together, and so serve the Lord, by throwing myself head over heels over every stile or gate I came to; the condition here was as before, on its being done *in precision and decision.* I often attempted and failed, getting smart strokes from the cane of Herminet Herbert. I knew it was dangerous, but

I expected to be miraculously preserved if I did it aright. At last I did it outright, and my head struck upon a stone, on the other side. The blow stupified me: finding no advantage, I did not attempt it heartily again. On returning home, I was fastened in the niche, and remained there till bed-time.

Nobody can bear this continual turning of the mind from one subject to another; but I am not able to collect my ideas on these sufferings, so as to write orderly. I should add that I received the blows of Herminet Herbert patiently and without reply; first, being too much occupied by the agonies of my mind; secondly, conceiving that he was acting a part which he was compelled to do, to punish my insincerity and affectation; for that I was struck, not for attempting, but because I did not accomplish the object of throwing myself over the stile—through disobedience. I mention such delusions, as appear to me necessary to make my reader clearly understand the nature of my disorder, the state of my mind and disposition which I was in, and the impropriety of the conduct pursued towards me. To this end it appears I must still mention two other delusions connected one with the other. Soon after my arrival from Bristol I was told, by my invisible companions, that I was not the son of my reputed mother, but that my father had adopted me from my infancy. That my real name was Robinson. That my father and mother were Americans, from Boston. That my father had died long ago, but that my real mother, Mrs. Robinson, was still living at Bristol. I had known this until about eight or nine years of age, and my reputed father had adopted me, because he knew very well, I was ordained to be a herald of the second coming of the Lord, from my conception. And as the Almighty, in the shape of Mr. Waldony, had always walked on earth with my reputed father, in love, in gratitude, and in obedience to him, he had adopted me. I, too, had known this, until by one crime at an early age, my heart had been turned from God; after which, I had walked in darkness. At the same time, I had resolved to deny my father and mother, and would not allow any person to allude to the fact of my adoption. My reason and judgment checked me in believing this strange tale, but I bowed my reason to the authority of the inspiration!

I was told that when I passed through Bristol, I had been

specially brought there to be tried if compunction would then make me call for my mother, Dame Robinson; and that she had even entered my room, in hopes of being reconciled. That had I shown even *that* gratitude towards her and towards the Almighty, I should have been spared many torments; but that when my countrymen saw I was so ungrateful, they had prayed for and determined on an increase of my tortures. I was already to be crucified for my blasphemies in Dublin, but now I was to be crucified, and "licked, and hacked, and manacled, and brewed in a manner most distressing" all over the world, in various bodies, and kept alive during my tortures. I objected, that the king of England could only hang me, but I was replied to, "that the king and parliament had passed an act for my especial punishment, in obedience to the commands of the Almighty, when he had come upon the earth." I imagined at one time, that my eldest sister, who had been raised from the dead, had undertaken to endure these tortures for me. Sometimes I fancied she was being flayed alive in the room down stairs, to which I strove to make my way; sometimes that she was being mangled in the garden, outside our prison room; and I used to strain my neck from my seat to look through the window to ascertain the truth. About this time, also, a packet was lost off the Welsh coast, and all the passengers were drowned. Much talking there was about it, and I was made in my imagination responsible for their loss; all was done for me. At night and by day I heard their groans; and on one occasion, when I understood I had done an act of obedience, there was a burst of angel voices, in the ceiling on the left, singing out, "Victoria, Victoria! the victory's won." I knew about as much what victory was alluded to, as what sins I was accused of.

I recollect, a short time before the burning of the gaols in Bristol, in a letter I wrote to my mother, I asked her if I was really her son, and if I had ever had a master called Waldony. I was then gradually returning to my senses. My mother sent me a certificate of my baptism, in Lincoln's Inn fields, and shortly after, one of my brothers saw me, and reminded me of the real name of our writing-master when boys, and confirmed the suspicions I then had of my having been deluded. My mind, however, needed these circumstantial evidences, to be corrected entirely of its errors.

CHAPTER XVII

WHEN I was taken to bed at first, I was only confined in my straight waistcoat. The first night there was a fire in my room, which I missed the second or third night, and I was made to suppose I had been deprived of it for not performing some act of obedience. A few nights after my arrival, I threw myself off the bed, in my waistcoat on the floor, in obedience to my monitors; the command was usually given about the time the keeper came into the room either to look after me, or to sleep; fortunately I did not injure my limbs. In consequence of this trick, my arms were tied down to each side of the bed, by bands of ticking. Still I contrived to excite alarm, and subsequently my feet were fastened to the bottom of the bed, in the leathern anklets I had on in the day time. Fastened thus, lying on my back, I passed my wretched sleepless nights for nearly, if not quite, nine months! Recollect, too, that I was a *nervous* patient! I had not exercise enough during the day to procure sleep. But I lay exhausted, wearied, agonied, terrified in my spirits, hungering after rest, but unable to procure it. To add to my feverishness and misery, the servant usually tied my right arm so tight, passing the thong twice round it, that it cut my flesh, causing a red ring round the arm in the morning.

I never complained; the voices told me it was Jesus who did it, and that he did it for my good, to prevent my going to sleep, because sleep would torpify me, and as I was a spiritual body, I did not need sleep. Sometimes, however, by order of the voices, I asked the servant when he came to bed to undo my right arm; which was occasionally done. In the coldest nights I used to kick off, or throw off with my teeth the clothes, yet I never felt cold.

This restraint was kept on a great while longer than was necessary. A lunatic doctor, in one sense, is pretty sure to be on the right side; he will run no risk that will do his reputation for security, an injury. When I began to come to my senses, and to feel indignation at the treatment I had been exposed to, the voices and my wishes dictated to me to ask to have the waistcoat taken off in bed, and I fancied one day, that I was invited to make this demand by young Dr. F. who stopped me, and the keeper, Samuel Hobbs, on going out of the madhouse to walk, asking if I could not be allowed to sleep unfastened now. The keeper replied, in an offhand impertinent manner, "O! no, sir—there's no trusting him," &c. &c. &c., and I remained silent from resentment.

After I was in bed, from about eight to ten o'clock, when the keeper came up, I very often used to shout out aloud, or sing the psalm, "O be joyful," in obedience to the demon's commands. Then Simplicity would come up, and with his open hand strike me on the face most cruelly—all I could do, tied hand and foot, was to turn my face to the wall, to avoid being struck in the eye, or on the nose. His blows fell on my left ear, as below stairs, and to these blows I attribute the disfigurement of my left ear, which afterwards swelled to a great size with extravasated blood. It was cut open by the surgeon who attended the patients in the asylum, Dr. L——. It is true, Dr. F. told my mother it was occasioned by violence I did my own person, in striking my ear, but I do not recollect striking my ear, but I recollect very well I used to strike the side of my head in front of the ear, where the organ of secrecy is placed, under an idea that my blows would strike out the secrets of my conscience and memory to me; and after my ear became bad, and particularly after the operation, I tried by squeezing it against the wall, to burst the blood out, which was called "breaking my ear to my father." I imagined also, that the blood in my ear was caused by the lachrymatory duct being full of tears of blood, which I would not weep; and other absurdities.

CHAPTER XVIII

THERE were, however, other serious inconveniences attendant upon my confinement in bed, of which I fear I now feel the effects: viz: the retention of my urine. My honest doctor never thought of that, no doubt. I cannot express myself becomingly on matters of this kind. My excited feelings prompt me to use expressions of sarcasm and indignation: but again, ridicule overpowers me for I say—why? why? remonstrate upon any one isolated act, when the whole system, admitted by, and finding society fellow-workers with it, is grossly disgraceful to men of science, to men of education, to men of humanity, to men of religion, contradictory even of the principles of that tangible science, surgery; not to say medicine, of which Dr. F. and many more too like him, are professors and practitioners! *But such men, surgeons,—and yet acting inhumanly in defiance even of that sure science,* ought to know that it is no small duty of the curer of nervous patients, to have regard to the regularity of their evacuations. And there is no point for which they more require what liberty can be granted them. There is a moment, beyond which the retention of urine becomes very deleterious to the circulating fluids, and affects the nervous system with acute pains. I knew nothing of this then; I have observed it subsequently. For the agonies of my mind were too great for me to heed bodily suffering.

Connected with this subject, I have to relate conduct towards me of the most indelicate and insulting nature. I do not recollect during the first months of my confinement any attention to me in this particular, volunteered on the part of those whose duty it was to think for me. I myself first asked to be taken up stairs, in obedience to inspiration. My mind has always been extremely sensitive and delicate on this subject, and it was with much difficulty and dislike that I obeyed the command given to me, in the presence of the other patients. After my daily visit to this place, I do not recollect any opportunity being offered me of discharging my urine, during the day, so long as I was confined to my seat, except in the morning, when I went out walking, and if I went out in the afternoon; but I do not remember that I made use of these opportunities. Sometimes, indeed, I refused to follow nature, understanding that being no longer a natural but a spiritual body, these things were no longer necessary, but on the contrary, injurious to me.

It happened however towards June, or July, that I was unable to contain my urine whilst in bed two mornings successively, overcome by fear whilst waiting for my keepers, who came to take me to the cold bath in reality, but as I imagined to my eternal doom. I used to lie in agony of fear, crying out to my different spiritual companions, "Herminet Herbert come to my room and save me from my melancholy doom and destiny." "Mr. Simplicity come to my room, &c. &c.," "Kill-all, Kill-all, come to my room, &c., &c.;" and I used to augur for my fate according to who presented himself. I recollect now a sensation of fear, a sense of cruelty which I cannot yet define as the men came up stairs and entered my room to untie me. Their footsteps talked to me as they came up stairs, the breathing of their nostrils over me as they unfastened me, whispered threatenings; a machine I used to hear at work pumping, spoke horrors; besides this, there were some ducks and chickens came to be fed before the window; a breakfast bell rung, and I heard a piano down stairs: all these circumstances reminded me forcibly of my boyhood, and I think my mind was afflicted with speechless agony, at the comparison of my actual state with that of my infancy, childhood, and youth; to have been so loved, or so duped by the appearance of my family's love, and to be so abandoned in the greatest woe, under the most awful state of misfortune. But I accused myself of all, and chiefly for bringing discredit upon the new doctrines of the Rowites, on my own sincerity as a professor of religion, &c., thereby endangering the salvation of those dearest me, by alienating their affections from, and shaking to their confidence in, the truth. The dinner bell used to ring to me many changes. "This is Mr. ——'s dinner bell at E—— [Ealing], if he will be obedient to a spirit of precision and decision, or, if he *will* do his duty and not have his greed taken away from him," or "take the young hyprocrite to his mother's bed-room at E——, or to his sister's schoolroom at E——, &c."

To return, one or two mornings whilst listening to all these preternatural intimidations, and misinterpreting them, my fears or my necessity compelled me to make water in my bed. A night or two after this I was taken down to sleep in a kind of outhouse. At the back of Dr. F.'s madhouse at the bottom of all the small yards or gardens that lay on the slope of the hill behind the different wards, a range of low buildings extended along the whole of that side of the mansion excepting the laundry. These buildings contained in each ward, three or four cells with bare walls, lighted by a small skylight from the top, with a channelled and sloping wooden frame for a bed, furnished with straps, chains, &c. I imagined this to be an instrument of torture. There was a narrow dark passage between the cells and the yard, and they were built against Dr. F.'s kitchen garden wall, which was warmed by flues. The kitchen garden lay behind the madhouse; the hot-houses nearly in the centre. There was a small yard at the end of the four cells in our section with a door leading into the kitchen garden, and in the right hand corner near that door a privy.

I was taken to bed in the innermost cell, the fourth in the row. There was a mattress of straw, and a pillow of straw, both stinking of the cow-yard, on which I was laid. I was then strapped down with a broad strap over my chest, and my right arm was manacled to a chain in the wall. No explanation of any kind was made to me, and I was left alone to my own meditations.

For myself, I submitted to every thing with passive resignation, and like a child. I conceived myself in circumstances hopelessly beyond my control; the object of the direct and personal superintendence of the Almighty. I did not understand, and it was useless to remonstrate; but my attendant voices suggested to me two or three reasons for my being thus degraded; either because I had eaten my breakfast instead of refusing it; or had not struck or wrestled with my keepers, or thrown them into the bath, when ordered to do so. The real reason was never clearly assigned to me, but I conjecture it was the design to punish me for the infirmity I have just alluded to; a design as foolish as it was insolent and unjust. Foolish, because no explanation was given to me, no expostulation, and I was left a lunatic to my lunatic imagination to supply me with a reason, if I reasoned at all. Foolish, because even if an explanation had been offered, it is doubtful then if I should have believed that, instead of the wild suggestions of my inspirers; therefore foolish and cruel, because as a correction it was of no use; and had I had strength of mind just sufficient to understand it as a correction, ten to one that I should have resented it by repeating the offence fifty times, rather than not show my hatred and contempt of their malice. Insolent it was, because no man has a right in a matter of this kind to deal thus with his equal or even with a child, far less a set of ignorant empirics and their tools. Degraded it is true by a signal calamity, but yet their superior in rank and education, and entitled to respect even for the greatness of this misfortune, and to forbearance, for his infirmities. Unjust it was, for it was not marvellous that I had been twice subject to this inability of retention, but rather a marvel that I had not already *often* been so subject from their neglect.

About two or three hours after my being put to bed here, one of the keepers, Herminet Herbert the simple, or Herminet Herbert, Simplicity, came to attend to my bodily requirements in this respect, and then left me for the night.

Strange as it may appear, I felt happy in this situation. Here there was comparative peace, seclusion, freedom from intrusion. Here I had no servant sleeping in the room with me. Here I might hollo or sing as my spirits commanded, without fear of rating and beating, and although my right arm was fastened by a short chain to the wall and the strap pressed rather tightly across my chest, it was still something to have one arm free even in the straight waistcoat, and not to be galled by the fastening on the other. At first I tried as usual to suffocate myself in the pillow, the smell of which reminded me of a cow-yard; but when I was weary of attempting what I could not perform, I turned my head round and lay completely on my back, looking up to the skylight, and wildly ruminating.

The sides of the skylight were partly open, for it was a bell light. It was apparently a fine night, but whether it rained or not was the same to me. I saw a star or two pass over me, and I saw a light that moved round in the heavens, and I was told it was the light that had appeared to the wise men or shepherds in the East, and that it had been sent to comfort me. The rattling or rather grating of the chain against the wall, spoke to me in my father's voice. I was in the cell about a fortnight. The second night the straw pillow was removed, and a white plume pillow put in its place.

There are a few humane hearts that will shudder and shrink at the view of this position, recollecting my birth, my education, my talents, and that I had not been an impious or irreflecting man. But they will say it was the fault of the doctor, and though they condemn the doctor, still it was but the doctor. But no, oh! no, my elder brother came to visit me at this very time. I might almost say he seemed guided by providence to detect the cruel infamies of my situation. But he came and inspected the cell in which I was confined at night, he saw me and took leave of me in the evening sitting in my straight waistcoat in the niche, exposed to my fellow-patients, and he left me to my fate. So great, so rooted are this world's hypocrisies, so deep and wide spreading its duplicity! so weak are so called sane man's imbecilities; imbecilities, such as make me less ashamed of having been a madman, when I think of the disgrace of such conduct, of such credulity, lightness, and triviality, unaccompanied and unexcused by disease.

In about a fortnight I was removed back to sleep in my former apartment. After that the keeper came to my bed-side, regularly once each night, and without untying me, administered to my necessities, whilst I turned round on my left side as far as I could, performing for me, to my utter disgust, the most indelicate and revolting offices.

At the end of the year when I was awakened from my dream

and lethargy, I inquired of Samuel Hobbs and Marshall, the reason of my having been placed in the cells; I received a kind of half answer from Hobbs, that it was on account of my infirmity in bed, to which Marshall added an observation, that he had remarked to his fellow servants, that he thought it a pity I had not more liberty in bed, as he conceived I must suffer at times from the long retention.

I have observed I used at my own desire to be taken at first to a closet up stairs. Here I often counteracted the desire of nature. Whether I did so or not, no more attention was paid to me on that score during the day. After some time I was taken to a place in the yard, or to that I have mentioned in the small court by the cells. In this latter I was placed on a seat in which I was fastened by a wooden bar in front, and by a manacle to my right hand, and there I was left, I dare say for half an hour at a time; and there I heard many voices and saw many phantasms.

In this same place in the summer time, when the water failed in the cold bath, which was often but dirty, I was made to undergo a kind of shower-bath. I was undressed in one of the cells, and accompanied by the two servants, walked naked across the little court to the *"cloaca,"* on which I was seated and fastened in; Hobbs and the other then went and fetched two or three pails or cans of water. There were two brackets in the corner of this place over the seat on the right and left, on which Hobbs then mounted astride over me. He took one of the pails with him and with a pewter urinal ladled the contents of it over me, or poured it gradually out of the beer can. The shock used to convulse me a great deal, and besides I used to hold back my head with my mouth open and hallooing or panting, by which I was often nearly choked with the quantity of water that came down my throat. When the water was expended I was taken off the seat not without attempting to kneel or throw myself on my face before the men, who I conceived were spiritual bodies, or Jesus, or God Almighty; then I was dressed and reseated in my niche till the hour of exercise or till dinner time.

Other painful instances of neglect in the matters alluded to in this chapter, to which the other patients and I were subjected, I pass over.

CHAPTER XIX

My toilette was very much neglected, and served as an occasion for insult and gross treatment on many occasions. At first after being taken to the bath I was brought up in the morning to my room to wash my hands and my teeth. But when I began either to throw myself on the floor or to turn round and round in the room whilst the keeper was making my bed, or even when I did not set directly to work, he would take the toothbrush violently from me, and either wash my hands or fasten my straight waistcoat round me without washing me, and take me down stairs. In general the plunge in the cold bath was considered dressing enough, sometimes I had not even that, but being taken down stairs unwashed, the bowl which served to wash the tea things was brought with clean water, and I was washed in my niche before the other patients and rubbed dry with a coarse duster, an insult to them as well as to me. My feet were not washed the whole time I was imbecile. The first time I attempted to judge for myself was to ask leave not to go to the cold bath in the autumn, I felt as if soaked with water, it was granted. The second was to ask for water to wash my feet, the request surprised my servant; it was given me with some demur. They were begrimed. The toe nails had never been cut, and I had lost the nail of my little toe. My finger nails were cut by Herminet Herbert regularly, and always as low as they could be, as if to disfigure them. Two or three towels were brought to my room a week, but whether or no for my own use alone I do not know. There was for a long time no glass in my room. Once a week Herminet Herbert (Hobbs) brought my linen to my room, which lay on a chair, three or four shirts and as many pairs of stockings. I had about two pocket handkerchiefs a week, sometimes none. The clothes I walked about the country in I was quite ashamed of, or rather I thought I ought to be ashamed of when I came to myself. When my eldest brother came to see me, I recollect I was taken into a room near the sitting room and dressed like a school-boy in a new suit previous to my being ushered into the parlour. I was then taken quite by surprise, and knew not what to expect.

It is my suspicion that a great deal of this treatment was designed to insult, under the idea of quickening, arousing, nettling the patient's feelings! but there is so much of evident neglect in the management, and so much may be the natural consequence of a system calculated on the strictest economy, and whereby the case of a gentleman is left almost to the entire control of a set of ignorant, simple, at times malevolent, and perhaps not over-honest servants, that it is not possible for me to determine; and besides, my mind is astonished at the idea of reasonable beings admitting the propriety of such gross mockery, arguing in so absurd a circle, to such a cruel end. It is as if when a jaded post horse has fallen motionless from fatigue you were to seek out a raw place to spur him or lash him in, to make him show symptoms of life. Again I say to myself, if this treatment was intended to insult, why was my indignation at it when I came to my senses condemned as madness? For so it was, which ever way it is, whether the doctors are simple agents of that destroying spirit, that works in their patients rendering them their victims, or whether they act designedly, the system is a cruel mockery of the patient. He is professedly a pitiable object of scrupulous care, the innocent dupe of unintelligible delusion, but he is treated as if responsible, as if his dupery is his fault; yet if he resists the treatment he is then a madman! and if, as in my case, he is agonized and downcast by a continual and unmeasured self-accusation of his great guilt in being insane, he receives no correcting intimation that he has something to say for himself, that he is the appalling witness of the power of disease; no encouragement, no inspiration of self-confidence; but all around tends to keep down his spirits, to depress his energies, to abase and degrade him in his own estimation. A short time before I left the madhouse, a Captain W., an officer in the army, complained to me one morning, evidently deeply perplexed, saying he had asked several times for a clean pocket handkerchief, and the one in his pocket he had had three days. He attributed it to the regulations of the laundry, but then, said he, they allow us I am told three a week, and I ought to have one. I told him I imagined that it was designed to insult him, and that I thought he would admit as much if he considered other parts of the system, and I added they shall not get me to ask them for any thing. I advised him to write to his father, and I wrote to my family *commanding* them to attend to my reasonable desires; they had the folly and wickedness to deny me or to defer justice.

If the insulting and degrading treatment I have described, was indeed designed to mortify and probe the feelings, it was preposterous, without explanation, expostulation, or remonstrance; and impolitic, without a thorough knowledge of the temper and humor of the individual to whom it was applied. Why was I confined? because I was a lunatic. And what is a lunatic, but one whose reasoning cannot be depended upon; one of imperfect and deranged understanding, and of a diseased imagination? What, then, was the natural consequence of my being placed in the most extraordinary, difficult, and unreasonable circumstances, without explanation, but that I should, as I did, attribute that insult which was heaped upon me to the most absurd causes; to the non-performance of the very acts, which in a sane mind I might have condemned; or to the performance of those which I might have applauded. With me, conscience was entirely confounded—judgment perverted. That which others called sin, I deemed virtue; that which men called folly, I called wisdom. What can be said, when I struck, kicked, wrestled, endangered my own security and that of others, as the acts most pleasing to them to witness, most dutiful for me to attempt? The reader now, perhaps, wonders at treatment like this being possible; but if he does now resent it, in nine cases out of ten it is not without my having been obliged to reason with him as with a child; so rooted is the prejudice, *that lunacy cannot be subdued, except by harsh treatment.* If he asks why these things are so, I will tell him why: *because it is the interest of the lunatic doctors.* That is the end. And the cause lies in the servile folly of mankind, of which these lunatic doctors make their profit.

But such treatment is impolitic, not in the lunatic doctor, but in the conduct of such as, in good faith, desire a patient's cure; because, if discovered or suspected, it may work, as it did in me, a deadly hate towards those dealing with me, and a resolution to endure any thing, rather than bow a haughty and stubborn spirit to their cunning, address, or cruelty. In return for their insolent severity, the mind mocks at their care and vigilance, their respect and their benevolence. The question, then, lies between the power of the patient to endure, and the power of the quack to break his spirit. The latter is shamefully uncontrolled by law, in consequence of the very generous, legitimate, and simple confidence placed by chancellors, magistrates and law-officers of the crown in the humane, and tender, and scrupulous doctor. I have proved that the power of the patient is equal to that of the oppressor. But in this contest, when the patience and fortitude of the first is exhausted, look to it if the stamina of the constitution—if those foundations of sound health, are not undermined or broken through, on which, with respectful and natural treatment, cure, *perfect cure,* might have been established, and good citizens assured to the state; not those patched-up pieces of work called healed patients, now returned to the world. And again, besides the danger thus incurred, through the sullen and obstinate resentment of the patient, I have proved how, through his very disease, through his very delusions, the power of the spirit of evil mocks at such endeavours to subdue his empire over our conduct and our imaginations, without the will of the individual working malignantly with him.

Mine was not a solitary instance. Another patient in that madhouse, who, I observed, seldom or never spoke,—when one was hinting to me, that he thought the servants were directed to insult and degrade us, or, at least, did it designedly, of their own malevolence,—opened his lips, to my astonishment, and declared that when he first came to the asylum, whilst sitting one evening in the parlour wherein we were, he rang the bell, or called for a candle for another gentleman, when the servant came up, and, grossly insulting him, turned him, too, out of the room, and sent him to bed; since which, says he, I have never opened my mouth, except when absolutely necessary. Upon my pressing for further information, he resumed his silence; and though his conduct did not appear to me extremely wise, yet I can tell gentlemen who condemn it, that though it is a very comfortable doctrine for the lunatic doctors, and for a set of indolent and inefficient magistrates, to doubt and deny credit to a lunatic gentleman's word, we understand their insolence, and feel their injustice, though we cannot express our opinions, and dare not retaliate. And we beg leave to differ in our opinion. The only resource for the pride of many men is in a stubborn silence, and outward indifference. It is not surprising, then, if that is the only resource of the lunatic; of whom, it appears, all possible moral perfections are to be expected, instead of allowance being made for all possible moral weakness, whilst he is cut off from all human aid.

To return to the article of toilette. I was shaved three times a week: Saturday was one of those days. Occasionally I was taken up to my own bed-room for this operation; but usually, for one half the year, I was ushered in, in turn with the other gentlemen, to a small room belonging to another, I fancy to old Patience, on the same floor with our common room; and the rest of the year, to a small servant's bed-room up stairs. In this room, there was one patient tying his neckcloth, another sitting to be shaved, and a third pulling off his coat; besides two servants and occasionally three. After being shaved, I was washed in the dirty water the rest had been using, and rubbed dry with the servant's dirty towel; and then, with a slight shove on the back, told to go down again to the sitting-room; or else I walked down arm in arm with Herminet Herbert, as I imagined my Saviour. I used at first repeatedly to ask the barber to cut my throat in obedience to voices I heard; but I did not want it. I was always very nervous when being shaved, and found my mind more disturbed by it than at any other time, when I began to know my situation. It was also one of the circumstances that touched me with most sorrow and indignation, when I came to myself. For as a military man, I had always shaved every day; and I thought, if my friends had been disposed to show me any delicate attention during my illness, it would have been to have kept up my ancient military habits. But it is ridiculous to talk of delicacy. I recollect, also, when recovering, that one of the first shocks I felt my mind received, was in turning accidentally to the glass in the door of a dark closet, where the knives were cleaned, and seeing that my whiskers were cut short. I had never touched them from a lad, and used to take pleasure in their curls. I observed, on catching my face in the pane of glass, that my head involuntarily glanced away; and I turned back, to reflect what had struck me. I then recollected the day Marshall had cut my hair, in a chair at the end of the yard; and his manner had appeared to me very starch and sarcastic. I cannot say whether it was done for insult, or according to his idea of beauty. But it was disrespectful; for they might leave their patients, at least, as they find them, in such respects. The insult was either at the time thrown away upon me, or, as I think, my mind too much overwhelmed by my calamity and by my situation to notice it.

When I began to be more trusted, I was invited to dine in the afternoon with the young Dr. F. and his pretty little wife. I called her Repentance. Two or three patients usually dined with them at one time. Herminet Herbert waited on us, and a beautiful servant-girl, whom I called Louisa, and believed to be my sister. I contrived to get through the dinner without any very extraordinary actions or expressions, and afterwards I used to dine occasionally in the old doctor's mansion, in greater company; and though yet in a dream, my behaviour there was still more moderate. My spirits directed my attention with great rapidity to the objects of furniture, books, curtains, pillars, glasses, &c., in the room, and to little acts of civility. And I attribute my better manners to the greater occupation given to my imagination by variety of situation and ornament, and to my being in circumstances more congenial to my habits, and sensible of the impression of decent conduct and formalities around me.

I was much amused, about the middle of summer, when I was

more collected, at the style of invitation sent to me. The old housekeeper came in, and said, "You *are to send* Mr. P. and two other patients in to dine with young Dr. F." I heard this accidentally; usually, I knew nothing of the great favour intended till the hour came, or by not being fed at the common table. When I heard the message, I was at first amused; then I thought, Do they intend to insult me? or is it the servant's fault? and my spirits dictated to me to be high-minded, and not to go. But I replied, Pooh! children! they don't care for me, and I don't care for them; let them alone!

On these occasions, Herminet Herbert took me up stairs to wash my hands, or brought down a clean white cravat, and a clean pair of shoes to put on, before I entered the ladies' presence. But one day, one of these attentions was neglected, after I had asked for it; or for another reason, perhaps because I was not shaved. I determined to refuse dining with them, not thinking myself fit to appear in the ladies' society. But the opinion or will of the patient was not once thought of in this matter: to refuse was in vain. I was pushed on, partly in humour, partly in earnest, by Herminet Herbert; and just as I was going to fight him, Mrs. F. and her husband issued from the drawing-room; and out of respect to her I ceased, and went to dinner.

I was taken down to the bath generally in the morning, but occasionally in the forenoon. In the morning, a great-coat or dressing-gown was thrown over me, and I went up stairs again to dress. Often, however, I was dressed in the cells adjoining the baths, by one or two keepers. Here I used to be directed to dodge my feet about, to untie what they had fastened, to throw off what they put on, to rise up from my chair, and to wrestle with them. There was a bath repairing in one of the cells, into which I was often prompted to throw Herminet Herbert backward; but although I was told it was what he desired, I could not conquer my fear of its causing his death. On one occasion, I was alone in the cell with this man, when he was putting on my stockings; and I bent forward, as usual, to prevent him: he threw me backward with great violence against the wall, and my head came with such force against the bricks, that a light seemed to strike through it, and I was almost stupified. But such acts were not extraordinary.

I now come to an important part of the regulations of this madhouse; the mockery of sending us to church, so it was called. A large room at the end of the building, which in week days served as a laundry, was on Sunday converted into a chapel. The female patients sat in the further end, with Dr. F.'s family, separated from the male by a screen. Would any sensible people believe it possible that I was taken, in my state of mind, to assist at this service? I went there believing that I was about to attend a kind of condemned sermon each time, after which, I was to be plunged into the bath, in which I was to be drowning for ever, and ever, and ever, for not having performed one act of duty to the Lord Jehovah supremely omnipotent; for not having struck properly, or wrestled properly, with one of the keepers. But I had a chance offered me of escaping my melancholy doom, if I would get up and wrestle with one of the keepers present. Sure enough up I got, and sometimes seized Simplicity, sometimes Sincerity; who then hurried me away crying out aloud. There was attention shown to me however, in this instance, that Dr. F. F. came and sat beside me, persuading me to be quiet. This room was paved with square flag-stones, and when in my mind I objected to wrestling in it, because it was paved with stone, I looked again, and saw it was regularly boarded, but it was really in stone. It was these miracles of the imagination that made me cling to the delusion of being in two or three places at once.

After several experiments, I was left alone on Sunday evening in the sitting room, with the old gentleman I called Jehovah Gireth, who, fortunately for him, was a Roman Catholic; and so enjoyed that evening an hour's peace. But when I began to recover my intellect, I was taken to this sad exhibition, this congregation of demons as I called them, again. I found, however, that my feelings were too acutely excited by the liturgy and the recollections the service awakened, for me to command them; and that, unless I wished to expose myself more disagreeably, my only chance was to turn things to ridicule. I was laughing, therefore, the whole service through, and, fearing that that in the end would harden my heart, I applied for leave to abstain from church. This was granted; but subsequently, when I had struck one of my keepers on a Saturday, either of his own private spite, or by order of Dr. F.

as a punishment, I was desired to attend church next evening.
I refused, and was offended; but recollecting myself, I took up my
hat, and walked on in silence, seating myself in the church until Dr.
F. F. came in. I was determined then not to submit to their cursed
rule any longer, but to assert my own rights, and I rose up to meet
him, and told him it was my desire not to attend the church service. He tried to silence me, but I persisted; and he then said aloud
and contemptuously, "Take Mr. P. out; I must not let him disturb the congregation." Simplicity took me out, and as he lum-
bered after me, he tapped me with the key of the room on my
shoulder, deprecating my conduct, and saying good-humoredly,
"Come, come, Mr. P. no more of this; we shall be obliged to put
you in a straight waistcoat again." He thought that I was returning to insanity because I resisted the doctor; or else he knew that
the opposition of lunatics returning to reason, was so met; but I
was confident in my powers of mind, and resolved to dispute
usurped authority.

Now for the medical care taken of me. I was called in courtesy,
and I was in the truest sense, a nervous patient, through disease,
through medicine, through fever, and through mental anxiety.
I was brought to Dr. F. immediately. The first diet offered me I
objected to in my mind, ruined as it was, as unwholesome, namely,
a kind of forced meat, and slices of bacon. Soon after that, I, a
nervous patient, was confined in a large room with eleven or more
others, nervous patients also, and servants, and certain of them
occasionally raving, stamping, bawling, violent madmen. The
mental agony, the distress, the actions of these wretched men,
their quarrels with one another, their struggles with the servants,
the servants' rude and cruel manner, my own weaknesses and
follies, and the violence they brought on me, all were exposed to
me, and I to them. I was confined also amongst these men, hand
and foot. Often left alone for hours with two or three of them. I,
weak in body, weak in mind, not able to support fear, or to control
it as another, and, besides, overwhelmed by superstitious fears.
This was my position for six months, until after the hay-making,
and then for six months more with the difference of not being tied
up. All this was under the direction of a surgeon, a physician. A

surgeon attended the asylum, and surgeons came with the magistrates to inspect. Now talk to me of the honesty of that class of professional men, of the respectability of physicians, of the confidence to be reposed in them! Money-making hypocrites! fawning sycophants! they deserve my curse, and they have it.

I do not recollect at any time medicine being given me; neither to purify the blood; neither as tonics; except on two occasions. No! the cheap and universal nostrum was to be ducked in the cold bath; in the depth of winter or not, no matter; no matter what my previous habits. I am thankful however even for this, that I was treated usually with more modesty here than other patients, I went usually alone, the others in a body; and generally, I had the first dip before the water had been used; but not always, and it was not always overclean.

Soon after this, boils came out on my feet and knees, and I recollect Dr. F. F. putting a black plaster over them. At that time, I imagined this was the pitch plaster to be placed over my mouth and eyes in the bath of boiling water.

At one period, I fancy about May, instead of the cold bath, I was taken to a room with a stone floor, and placed in a vapour bath. Dr. F. F. or his brother attended on two or three occasions. I thought I was to be suffocated; and when I came out safe, imagined I owed it to their prayers. My mother afterwards informed me that this treatment was undertaken at her particular request, and abandoned because they imagined it excited me. This shows how ignorant and superficial were their opinions; for indeed, I preferred it to the cold bath; it felt comfortable, the other painful. They both excited in me equal alarm. But the young doctors did not accompany me to the cold bath, and the vapour bath, no doubt, gave more trouble to the servants.

About June, if I may guess, when the buttercups and daisies were blowing in the meadows, I was taken out one or two days, walking alone with Sincerity. The second day I was fastened, in the afternoon, in a wicker chair, in the small parlour upstairs alone. That day, one of the housekeepers, Marshall's wife, came up to me, and gave me a piece of bread, covered with jam, tasting strongly of garlick or onions. I thought she was my mother, though I did not understand it, and I was desired to refuse the bread and jam as usual, but I ate it. That afternoon, or next day, I was taken to a small room adjoining, and a grey-headed gentleman I had not seen before, came in with Dr. F. and Mr. H. F. My spirits told me I was to suffer something, and gave me my option to resist it or to endure it on certain terms. I submitted; and the right temporal artery was opened until I nearly fainted. I believed the gentleman was my father, and called him so. I leaned my head back on Herminet Herbert's bosom, and looking up to him, called on him by the name Jesus. After the men were gone down, he took and placed me on a close stool in the room, and held me on it. I was very weak. My spirits forbade me making use of the close stool. I was then taken back and fastened in the wicker chair; then a number of delusions about singing came upon me. I imagined my temple had been closed, as the vein of a horse, by a pin and some tow; and I tried to rub the wound open, from delusion. I remained here a week or a fortnight, during which Mr. J. whom I thought my youngest brother, was occasionally allowed to come up and stay with me. He was a wild young lad, speaking in figures and hints spiritually, not understood by those around him, though I saw the spirit had a concealed meaning. I think he had a spirit of divination.

Some time after this, when my ear became swollen from extravasated blood, another slice of bread and jam tasting of garlic was given me downstairs, after I came home from walking. Soon after, I was taken up stairs, and the same old gentleman examined my ear, and opened it with a lancet. It gave me great pain. The servants afterwards told me that great clots of blood had come out. Immediately after this, I was taken down stairs again to dinner, and treated as usual! Both times I felt very much frightened. On neither occasion had I any preparation.

I tried as soon as I was down stairs, and daily tried, to split open my ear again. What I could not do, my servant did for me. For walking out with him one forenoon, and crying out as usual, he, from his pert insolence, took upon himself to gather a switch, and to correct me with it. He struck me over the face, and the end coming round opened my wound, and the blood spirted out.

He seemed alarmed and conscious, and left me on a bench in the drying ground, near which it took place, to run to the house close by for assistance, when one came, and a plaster was put on it. After that, Dr. L. who had performed both operations, examined my ear once more, but did not open it.

When I began to come round, I think the third case I exercised my judgment in, was in asking for some opening medicine. Salts were given to me. A second time, my servant Hobbs forgot to ask for any, but being a make-shift kind of man, brought me two black pills he said he had got in Paris, and thought would do as well.

I have said that I asked permission not to use the cold bath from feeling conscious of its doing me injury: this was in autumn, but in the winter of 1831, when I saw through the cruelty of the system and its dupery, and called it by its right name, and struck one of the keepers, I was desired to use the cold bath again. That indignation naturally excited by a sane perception of my circumstances, by the refusal to attend to my protestations, and by my complete state of defencelessness amongst those whose characters I was impugning, was mistaken for insanity, to be treated with the infallible nostrum. So, at least, I suppose I am to take it, but *I acknowledge* I do suspect baser motives, I cannot give credit to these gentlemen for being quite so simple as they pretend to be. But this suspicion no doubt must be considered a remains of my *delusions.*

So one morning, Hobbs intimated to me that it was the doctor's desire that I should use the cold bath again; this was in January. I told my servant I had objections to it, and begged to wait till I had applied to Dr. F. F. I expected to see him during the day, but that morning he did not come. I then applied for pen, ink, and paper, to write to him, but like other requests, it was neglected: at last, on leaving my apartment to go to bed, I said to Hobbs "will you tell Dr. F. that it is not my intention to make use of the cold bath." I had objections to it from experience, as well as from conscience; besides the disagreeableness of it at that season of the year. Next morning I was awakened early by three or four servants coming into my room. They told me they had orders to take me to the cold bath, and that I had better come quietly. I protested and argued with them. I told them I knew it was bad for me, and that it was against my conscience. What right had Dr. F. who ought, as master of an asylum, to be my protector, to force my conscience in matters indifferent to the security and peace of others? How would they reconcile it with their duty as Christians to do so? "Come, come, it is my master's orders," said Hobbs. "Yes," said I, "but you will have to answer for it before God." "Come, come, we've no time to lose." "Then," said I, "I protest against it as an Englishman, and as an English gentleman. I am placed under Dr. F., to be taken care of, not to be insulted and tyrannized over. I am not to submit, without reason, to any stupid charlatan's conceit, because I am unfortunate enough to need his control: and I call upon you to answer me before the tribunals of my own country, as well as before God, for this conduct." They then cajoled again, and advised me to come quietly—not to make resistance. I said, "don't be afraid, I will not play your master's game for him. I will not hurt any one of you, but off this bed I will not go, unless I am taken by force. When you have laid hands on me, then I will follow." They then took me by the arms and legs off the bed, and accompanied me down stairs. I called on one of them, who used to shave me occasionally, and was more good-natured than the rest, whom also I used to call Honesty, and by the name of Wynn, to be witness to the protestations, and to the force used.

I was taken down to a new bath, in every respect more cheerful and superior to that I had used the year before. It was building when I came into the madhouse. Each room was well lighted and plastered. I looked through the windows, and saw snow lying on the tiles and leads on each side. I plunged into the cold bath, and now for the first time I allowed the water to enter my mouth and drank of it. I disobeyed the voices in doing so, but it was usually a reason for me now to do any thing, if I heard a spirit forbid it. I was sorry I had never done so before, being prevented by superstitious fear, for it seemed to bring me to my senses, and to make me calm and reasonable. Since I have been at liberty I have observed that it makes the panting and agitation caused by the shock of cold water to cease: perhaps by equalizing the temperature more rapidly. After I had well bathed Hobbs opened a small door and put me under a shower-bath, the shock of which gave me the most acute pain throughout my head, as if my whole head were *one* tooth-ache. That afternoon I was placed in a private room up stairs, and I wrote to the doctor complaining of the treatment I had undergone, protesting against it, and particularly describing the pain given me by the shower-bath; the next morning I was taken down and bathed, the weather was equally severe; on the morrow I had a cold in the head and requested the servant for that cause to pass it over; he did, saying he would speak to Dr. F. Next morning in spite of my complaints, I was again bathed, and a second time placed under the shower-bath. My head was again pierced by that acute pain, and each time during the remainder of the day my head seemed on fire. I was mad now with indignation, and terrified at my danger. Fortunately soon after this I received the letter from my mother in which she states that according to my desire, she was going to remove me. Then I again stated my wish to cease from the cold bath, to Mr. H. F., (when I began to find fault with them, I was not much troubled by the visits of the other two) and he said he would speak about it, but recommended me to use the vapour bath instead; I accepted this to secure my escape from the other, as there appeared to be affectation in the offer of it, and as though it was expected from my conduct last year that I should refuse the vapour bath, when necessity would be pretended for the other.

CHAPTER XX

THE diet allowed me was plain. In the morning and evening a basin of tea and milk poured out of a beer or water can, and four pieces of thick bread and butter. As to the manner of serving it, I was never so treated even in childhood or at school. At dinner a plain joint with potatoes and three times a week pudding, with water or small beer to drink. In my opinion a few glasses of wine would have done me no harm, and I was accustomed to drink wine. Whenever I dined with the Doctor, wine was offered, but commanded by my spirits I generally refused it. I object to the manner in which my meals were given to me, more than to the nature of them. But I do not think they were quite fit for one of my habits in my situation. The patients generally used a knife and fork. I was not always allowed a knife. The servants carved the meat, and I often had great pieces of fat given me which I devoured voraciously. I remarked that after my ear had been opened I was allowed to eat as ravenously as I had previously, and no respect was paid to my diet in particular except in the middle of the year, when the three servants who waited on the patients in our room went away on leave of absence, and their place was supplied by three others; the old man I called my Father, another I called Honesty, and handsome young man of a humane disposition. These three behaved very kindly, and much more respectfully. The old man when he put me to bed sometimes leant over me to kiss my forehead, saying, God bless you. Honesty used to cut me small portions of meat, and when I asked for more shake his head considering and saying, no I think you have had enough.

They were quiet and inoffensive and did not strike me except once, when the old man touched me with a stick when I was throwing myself over a style, saying, with hesitation, "I think Hobbs used to beat you for this."

But when I got my liberty I used to eat of potatoes and bread and butter most greedily. I did this in obedience to a spirit of humour, which made me try to deceive my spirits. They told me the spirits in the gentlemen round me refused their potatoes or their bread and butter for me, because I refused to obey the spirits that desired me to leave mine, and I was told if I made resolutions to use the same abstemiousness, they by doing so, would save me from much torments; it was my amusement to watch till their attention was distracted, or till I could reach the plates, and then I applied all their leavings to myself. Often of an evening I ate thus nine pieces of thick bread and butter; I never felt that I was oppressed by it. I fancy that I made myself as far as I could a perfect beast, but more particularly when my limbs were confined, and I was devouring the fat and skin put on my plate. I observed one young man, a Mr. J., often complained in a broken manner of the manner in which he was helped, and he was usually helped most unhandily; I have since suspected the fat was placed on my plate to try me, but it is an even chance that the servant imagined I preferred it of a sound taste. When the table cloth was being laid for dinner, the patients were ushered into the yard where there was an alcove. Then Patience who had been standing on his legs all the forenoon, went out also into the yard; but first all the lunatics cleared the room. When I began to recover, one rainy day I refused to go into the yard preferring my seat by the fire, but after some demur I yielded, rather than cause confusion. I used to wonder also at so many madmen using their knives so harmlessly, only one day young Mr. J. cut at my legs under the table in sport with a knife. I do not think he intended to harm me, but I got up and desired to have another chair given me rather than run the risk. One evening also still later in the year, an old patient, jabbering a great deal, struck me a blow at tea, to which I replied by a smart box on the ear, which made the whole company laugh. It was seldom they did laugh. My hand struck that blow, but it was involuntary on my part, as if my hand had been moved by a violent wind. A spirit seized my arm with great rapidity, and I struck as if I was a girl. I recollect feeling grieved that the gentlemen should laugh to see a young man strike an old man. But old Benevolence told me, you have done perfectly right; I was obliged to strike that old gentleman myself when he first came into the asylum, without that there is no keeping him in order.

When I say I ate my meals voraciously, I allude to the manner rather than the quantity, for I was not helped more than twice to meat and once to pudding, and once to cheese. I began eating quietly and attending to the directions of my spirits but gradually I lost all self-possession. The day after I was bled from the temporal artery, I had a dinner of fish given me, and I was fed for many days with a wooden spoon, fastened up in my wicker chair.

CHAPTER XXI

DURING the whole period of my confinement I was never tempted to commit suicide; under my delusions I was often commanded to commit acts endangering my life and safety, but always with a view to my salvation, or that of others, and so far from any intention of self-destruction, that I expected to be raised again immediately if any evil happened to me. At Dublin I was to twist my neck, afterwards I was to suffocate myself, at Dr. F.'s I used to provoke the keepers to strike me or to throttle me. One morning after the bath, Hobbs did at my request strangle me with the strings of the straight waistcoat after he had fastened me in the niche. He did it perhaps in sport, perhaps saying to himself, we'll see what will come of it. It did me good so far, that finding I was disappointed in the miraculous results promised to me, I desisted from requiring it. I used to throw myself over the styles, I used to throw myself forward flat on the face on the ground; and besides this the voices told me to throw myself to the right, or to the left, which I did repeatedly, and once or twice down a steep green bank round a mound in the yard to our apartment. In this I was prevented sometimes by an old patient continually reciting incoherent sentences mingled with Latin, who mixed up his recitation with calls to the servants indicating my danger. In all these acts I sought a miraculous benefit. If there was any thing miraculous in the result, it was that I escaped with whole bones. I was not conscious of pain from the blows I received at the time, but I knew afterwards I must have suffered pain, from the bruises on my body. So I recollect when I sat in the niche opposite the fire-place, I observed in the morning my feet covered with red chilblains. But my spirits said it should be a sign to me, and that I should not feel them if I was doing my duty to the Lord Jehovah supremely omnipotent. They then occupied my attention by their injunctions during the day, which I endeavoured to understand and act up to. I felt the chilblains after breakfast, and once again after that, but my mind was immediately occupied again, and I was rendered unconscious to the irritation.

I used repeatedly to refuse my meals in order to be choked by their being crammed down my throat, to endure something to the honour of the Lord Jehovah supremely omnipotent. I was accused however of only affecting and so to provoke choking, I tried again and again. At last one afternoon Sincerity came to force down my meat, which I had refused with this object. I resisted with all my power till he literally crammed it down my gullet, bringing back the end of the spoon with blood on it, and chipping one of my teeth. He then came and with a coarse duster brutally wiped my face, bringing blood from my lips or gums, and saying, pretty boy! with a strong nasal twang. This took place whilst all the patients were at their dinner. The Rev. Mr. J. whom I used to call Affection, got up in great agitation, and stamped with his foot, and stretched out his trembling hands crying, "Good God, Marshall! you'll strangle him! Marshall I say!" but I made him a sign with my left hand which was fastened against the wall, meaning, be quiet, it's all for my good. I was not violent, but puerilely patient, but determined not to swallow the food but by force, and I was puzzled when my spirits told me I had done my duty so well to Sincerity that he should wipe my face so brutally afterwards.

Dr. F.'s madhouse stood in a very fine and picturesque country, and near a steep and wooded bank that bordered the river. At one elevated spot that commanded a view down the valley, a natural or artificial precipice yawned in the red soil, crowned with a small parapet, in rear of which was a small terrace and a summer house. When I went out with the patients we were often conducted here. They called it the battery. The view was enchanting, but I looked down on the people working and the boats moving in the valley, with feelings that they were dead to me, and I dead to them, and yet with that painful apprehension of a dream, that I was cut off from them by a charm, by a riddle I was every minute on the point of guessing. I sat on the parapet looking down over the precipice, and Hobbs stood by me. My voices commanded me to throw myself over, that I should be immediately in heavenly places, that I was brought here to prove my faith in the Lord, that I should not be hurt if I threw myself over in his time, that if I was hurt I should be raised again immediately. But either the danger was too apparent, or the servant stood too near, or I had received enough rude treatment to no effect, to have less confidence in the assurances of my being a spiritual body; I did not venture. And after the second visit I did not approach the parapet, but sat in the summer house to avoid the temptation. The other patients sat on the battery. I consider it a most imprudent place to take them to.

My family chose the situation for me, partly on account of the beautiful scenery. Their kindness was ill-judged; for I have no doubt the noble views excited my spirits, awakened by imagination, and redoubled every blow of affliction, reminding me of my former health, and force of mind, and liberty. About the middle of the year, I was taken out walking with the patients, though I had not entirely given up my shouting and hallooing. We walked one after the other, I thought like a string of wild geese, nine or ten of us in a row. The hills are pretty stiff, and were, in fact, too much for me, causing my pulses to beat too rapidly. From the top of a high hill, at some distance from our abode, there was a commanding prospect to the sea, over Somersetshire into Wales: on this hill, before we descended, Samuel Hobbs cut out his initials on the soil. Now when at first I had doubted the words of my spirits, that Hobbs was my Saviour, I was desired to look on his waistcoat, and there I saw the initials S.H. marked in red silk. I was made then to understand that these initials meant Salvator Hominum; and when I came to know that he was also S. Hobbs, my spirits assured me that Jesus had chosen those two names, to preserve the initials he was entitled to, and at the same time to strengthen my faith. I was directed now on the hill, and I did carve with his stick J. upon the soil before S.H., to show my faith that he was indeed *Jesus Salvator Hominum*.

But to resume: when I had more liberty, and was aware of my

situation, I stood one day in my bed-room, before the little square glass, reflecting upon self-destruction, upon which I had always looked as a cowardly, mean, and ungenerous action; perhaps it was after having heard a patient make some painful remarks on it before the other gentlemen; perhaps it was after hearing a servant describe how one of the patients had put his head under a cart-wheel; but at the time I was considering, also, how a man could summon boldness to endure the bodily pain, as well as obliterate moral feeling; when my right arm was suddenly raised, and my hand drawn rapidly across my throat, as if by galvanism. I then justified our law, which acquits an insane man from the verdict of *felo de se;* and I determined not to advert to the subject again, seeing that I had not control over my spirits, until I was free from provocation: in which resolution I persevered.

CHAPTER XXII

Now with regard to my treatment, I have to make at first two general observations, which apply, I am afraid, too extensively to every system of management yet employed towards persons in my condition. First, the suspicion and the fact of my being incapable of reasoning correctly, or deranged in understanding, justified apparently every person who came near me, in dealing with me also in a manner contrary to reason and contrary to nature. These are strong words; but in the minutest instances I can, alas! prove them true. Secondly, my being likely to attack the rights of others gave these individuals license, in every respect, to trample upon mine. My being incapable of feeling, and of defending myself, was construed into a reason for giving full play to this license. Instead of my understanding being addressed and enlightened, and of my path being made as clear and plain as possible, in consideration of my confusion, I was committed, in really difficult and mysterious circumstances, calculated of themselves to confound my mind, even if in a sane state, to unknown and untried hands; and I was placed amongst strangers, without introduction, explanation, or exhortation. Instead of great scrupulousness being observed in depriving me of any liberty or privilege, and of the exercise of so much choice and judgment as might be conceded to me with safety;—on the just ground, that for the safety of society my most valuable rights were already taken away, on every occasion, in every dispute, in every argument, the assumed premise immediately acted upon was, that I was to yield, my desires were to be set aside, my few remaining privileges to be infringed upon, for the convenience of others. Yet I was in a state of mind not likely to acknowledge even the justice of my confinement, and in a state of defencelessness calculated to make me suspicious, and jealous of any further invasion of my natural and social rights: but this was a matter that never entered into their consideration.

Against this system of downright oppression, enforced with sycophantish adulation and affected pity by the doctor, adopted blindly by the credulity of relations, and submitted to by the patients with meek stupidity, or vainly resisted by natural but hopeless violence, I had to fight my way for two years, wringing from my friends a gradual but tardy assent to the most urgent expostulations: not from the physicians; their law is the same for all qualities and dispositions, and their maxim to clutch and hold fast.

The first step adopted towards me by my friend, Captain ——, in Dublin, was injudicious and indelicate. If I had been incoherent, I had hitherto only rendered myself ridiculous; and if, by one act, I had run the risk of injuring my person, it was also evident that I had relinquished my purpose at the request of his family. I trace my ruin to the particular trials, to the surprise, the confusion, the puzzle, which the sudden intrusion of a keeper brought upon me. But at that time, unfortunately, I did not consider my dignity so much as my relationship to the Almighty, as his redeemed servant, bound in gratitude, and from self-abasement, to exercise forbearance and humility. If it be replied, My ruin might have been brought about another way; I answer, I do not know what might have been, but I know what did take place.

The first symptoms of my derangement were, that I gazed silently on the medical men who came to me, and resolutely persisted in acts apparently dangerous. No doubt there were also sypmtoms of bodily fever. But from that moment to the end of my confinement, men acted as though my body, soul, and spirit were fairly given up to their control, to work their mischief and folly upon. My silence, I suppose, gave consent. I mean, that I was never told, such and such things we are going to do; we think it advisable to administer such and such medicine, in this or that manner; I was never asked, Do you want any thing? do you wish for, prefer any thing? have you any objection to this or to that?

I was fastened down in bed; a meagre diet was ordered for me; this and medicine forced down my throat, or in the contrary direction; my will, my wishes, my repugnances, my habits, my delicacy, my inclinations, my necessities, were not once consulted, I may say, thought of. I did not find the respect paid usually even to a child. Yet my mind was at first sound, except as far as it was deceived by preternatural injunctions; in a certain respect, it remained sound throughout my illness, so that it faithfully recorded the objects and the events that took place around me; but I looked to the inspirations I received for the interpretation of them. If at any time my ear could have been closed to my delusions, I was then fit to be at liberty; but the credit I gave to my delusions, rather than to my judgment, was my disease. I was not, however, once addressed by argument, expostulation, or persuasion. The persons round me consulted, directed, chose, ordered, and force was the unica and ultima ratio applied to me. If I were insane, in my resolution to be silent, because I was sure that neither of the doctors, or of my friends, would understand my motives, or give credit to facts they had not themselves experienced; they were surely no less insane, who because of my silence, forgot the use of their own tongues,— who, because of my neglect of the duties I owed to them, expunged from their consciences all deference to me; giving up so speedily and entirely all attempt at explanation; all hope of sifting the cause of my delusions; all hope of addressing my reason with success; all hope of winning me to speak. If I needed medicine and light diet, still, I say to myself, surely that was not all; surely air and exercise, and water, and occupation or amusement, and a little solid food, would have done me no harm. Certainly, if they wanted to ensure a case for medicine, and broths, and ultimately for a lunatic asylum, the neglect of my nature, as an animal and intellectual being, was consistent. These two poor gentlemen in Dublin were, however, comparatively innocent. *They went like a donkey blindfolded,* round and round in the mill, the same to them whether the cord that draws up the water was broken or not. They, with whom I had to do in England, were perverse as well as infatuated. There, when I began to understand my wants, to know my rights, to claim them, to upbraid, remonstrate, threaten, in order to procure respect for them, the reply was still the same. "The doctors advise, and your family are bound to follow blindly their advice; and you must submit, whether or no."

My position was in every respect more depressing when I came to Dr. F——'s. I was no longer in rooms that I had chosen, but in a new place, to which I had been removed without my will having been consulted, and left there without explanation. This gave inlet to, and confirmed the delusion, that I was no longer a free agent, but under the control of beings superiorly enlightened. I may say, that I met with no persuasion, explanation, or exhortation throughout the time of my residence here; but to speak more strictly, no remonstrance was addressed to me in a manner befitting my age, character, or situation. I have already mentioned how I was disappointed in my brother's conduct; he made light of my delusions, and I said to myself, he must be a perfect fool, to know what power of mind I had, and to think I am acting without a very strong cause. After being treated with so little reflection by him, I was not surprised at strangers behaving in the same manner; but, in truth, whilst they were pitying my folly, I was shocked at, and pitying theirs. My delusions had rendered me imbecile, but I was not aware of it; and they addressed me as a child, and I did not understand them, because I knew I was a man.

Dr. F——'s system was to class all the errors of his patients under the head of imagination. A safe and plausible term, used to catch others, and to disguise their own ignorance; at the same time, that it augured little of respect or hope to the patient, the effects of whose imagination on him were often as real, as the impression of sensible objects on the supercilious doctor. It was not likely, therefore, that I should confide the difficulties of my mind to men who, by slighting the origin of them, betrayed their presumption, whilst affecting excellent acuteness.

The doctor's manner of address to me, and that of others, always puzzled me, and made it difficult for me to act or to reply: it was coupled, too, with a kind of half-and-half manner, as if my sincerity were mistrusted, which corroborated the communications my spirits made to me, that they came to try me; and when I regained better health, became very offensive. Sometimes, if I called out aloud, the young doctor would assume a winning smile, and put his finger playfully to his mouth: once he asked, "What do you mean by saying you are the redeemed of the Lord Jehovah, supremely omnipotent? don't you think that I am? I hope I am, and these gentlemen too." The tone and manner rendered these questions perplexing, and would have excited my ridicule, if my mind had not been too much occupied to give way to it. The reply perhaps most on my tongue was, Do you take me for a child? do you think I do and suffer all I have gone through without reason? They suited their behaviour to that which I appeared to be, taking advantage of my weakness, instead of correcting it. Because I did not respect myself, they disrespected me; whereas they should have brought me to my senses by greater reserve and respect. They forgot that, amidst all my lunatic childishness and simplicity, I was a grown-up man, and probably knew not myself. And if it is true of any creature, that he knoweth not of what spirit he is, it is strikingly true of a lunatic.

The first and most blameable error of the doctor was to place me in a noisy and crowded parlour, the common sitting-room of the madmen. He a physician; I, a nervous patient, and a gentleman. The conduct of my relations was as blameable, to leave me so far from home, under the guidance of men, complete strangers to me and to them, and my inferiors in rank and profession, careless or wittingly exposing me to so much rude contact and observation. Had I been lunatic on any ordinary subject, it would have been their duty to have reflected, that in all probability my conscience was affected, and that I might require a friend and a clergyman, to whom to confide my troubles. But they knew that my mind was deranged by overstudy on religion. And they left me exposed to strangers, and what is still more humbling to human nature, and to the pride and religion of my country, they who stand in no mean situation for wealth, talents, rank, or morality—they who are not merely fashionable professors of religion, and many of whom are even zealous in evangelical opinions,—took so little thought, as to consign my soul and spirit, in the hour of my utmost need, to the absolute control of a physician who was a sectarian, whilst my body was committed to his menials. Dr. F. had been a member of the Society of Friends; and, naturally enough, the spirit of the burlesque doctrines of that sect crept into his system, where they only warred with the interests of the patient; so that when, in the next year, I complained of the degrading footing of familiarity on which I had been placed with the domestics, and of the conduct in which they had been allowed towards me, he replied to me, in a letter to this effect, "Had not Jesus made us all equal?"

Placed amongst strangers, the idea of opening my thoughts and unburdening my spirit to them scarcely entered my mind. Confession and confidence were acts from which, however salutary, I was precluded. Deranged and imbecile as I was, I was not yet so brutal as those who left me, and exposed me to the temptation of unveiling the secrets of my conscience; of betraying the dealings of God with me to individuals unknown to me; of laying myself open to their secret and prying curiosity; and my weaknesses, first, to their inward ridicule, then to their outward mocking;—to be forced to run this hazard, or to have my mind preyed upon by its agonies, was cruel. At that time I shrunk even from crying out the sentences the spirits dictated to me, acknowledging my ruin. Since then, my sufferings, my despair of being attended to, have hardened me, and made me reckless.

When I began first to write to my mother and my brother, complaining of my situation, and aware of my state, my feelings were acute in this respect, and my instances earnest and repeated that my correspondence should be private. Delicacy towards my family, if only that, dictated this. I received no attention. The same bigotted credulity that abandoned my person and soul to the doctor's management, abandoned also the secrets of my heart to his impertinent examination. I cannot describe the hatred with which the recollection of this conduct still inspires me: then I hated, I despised, I was enraged, I became hardened. I loathed myself for keeping any terms with my relations and those around me. In the end, I scoffed at religion; I blasphemed the name and nature of God. The doctor alone benefited; for his benefit it was designed. Liable to his subtle misrepresentation, I concealed and disguised my feelings, or wrote for his inspection, braving his malice and duplicity. My real distresses I left to time or chance to take away, or to unravel. I was brutalized.

Thus, in a state of derangement, I was abandoned to my fate, and so condemned, that I could not seek health by sane conduct. I could not recover sanity, but by ways which can alone be justified by insanity; from which I shrunk, even insane: ways, which the very nature of a sound understanding, the very nature of humane feeling, make impossible. But this is one example only. When I grew older in my afflictions, I found that no patient could escape from his confinement in a truly sound state of mind, without lying against his conscience, or admitting the doctrine, that deception and duplicity are consistent with a sound conscience. Those who do otherwise are not sane, they are living in a lie. But what does that signify? they are good subjects, and the doctor's best friends.

CHAPTER XXIII

I RECOLLECT, when I first began to be aware of the insults and affronts put upon me with my daily food, and felt the impropriety of my situation, I still did not accuse or lay the charge to the doctor indiscriminately; but I determined to seek information before I judged. Mankind will, I think, consider it an affecting sight, when they behold a young gentleman, at the dawn of returning light, awakened to the consciousness of the cruelties around him; of the advantage that had been taken of his darkness; of the degrading treatment he was exposed to, yet examining and hesitating before he condemned. I reasoned with myself, for I was without a friend,—first as a citizen, then as a private individual: as an Englishman, I laid charge to the government, to the magistrates; more especially to the prelates, who supinely abandoned the trust committed to them, over the souls of the diseased members of the church, to the doctors, who serve as eyes to the magistrates. But these were evils I could not remedy. As a private individual, I knew not which most to blame, the doctor or my family. I recollected the two or three first days of treatment; my private parlour, my meals neatly served, the silver forks, &c., and I doubted whether, for my misconduct, I had not been degraded; and had my family been made acquainted with the change, or was the doctor imposing upon them. Therefore, in great distress of mind and anxiety, I wrote to my mother, stating my complaints, asking if they were aware of my position, and insisting upon a private apartment, and a servant to attend on me alone. Part of the answer I received was to the effect, that my elder brother *thought* that I was to have a room to myself, or that I was to be allowed to go to my bed-room. I was shocked at the indifference which this uncertainty betrayed. When I wrote that letter, I still considered more the evil effect my misfortunes might have had on the inclinations of my mother and sisters to believe the doctrines of the Row heresy, to which I yet adhered, than my own necessities. I put several questions connected with my peace of mind. I received no answer to them. What I wrote, I saw on the paper, or heard dictated before I put it down; often printing it in capital or other letters, as I saw it printed. But I wrote in trouble and agony,—abruptly and without much connexion; which was not surprising, for I was not alone.*

I was then in the small parlour with three other gentlemen with whom for a few days past I had been allowed to dine and pass the evening there: probably selected on account of our better behaviour, and because the room below was too crowded. I wrote the letter under the promise three times given me before I sent it, by Dr. F. F., that it should not be opened. I knew that I was ex-

* The above was written in Paris last year from memory. Since my return to London, I find, on referring to papers I have preserved, that my first letter was written on or about the 29th of November; for I have a copy of a letter I commenced on that day, which I afterwards altered: it was to my elder brother. This letter was detained until about the 22nd of December; for I find the copy of an envelope, dated the 19th of December, and directed to my brother, in which I complain of the detention of that letter, and enclose one to my mother, written about the 11th of December. These letters, and others, I have thrown into an appendix to this volume, not to break the thread of the text, and to prevent any further delay in this publication.

I acknowledge I am confounded at the bare-faced impudence of the doctor in detaining my first letter so long. I do not know whether to attribute it to cowardice,—from a consciousness that I was not entirely wrong in my accusations, and to his knowledge of the security and impunity with which he could treat me so unjustly,—or to his habitual indifference to complaints of the patients against his system, from the infatuated prepossession that his asylum was a second paradise. The excuse that he made to me was, that he hoped I should see fit to change my sentiments before I wrote to my mother, that he was loath to send a letter that might wound their feelings.

I know what I know. But in this world I must talk of a supreme and benevolent Providence, and of certain individuals being honourable and sincere, or be ejected from society. I *know too little*, or too much; too much, without more courage to act according to my understanding; too little, without more understanding to put my knowledge in practice.

pressing myself without control over my feelings, and my delicacy and modesty shrunk from what I wrote being disclosed to strangers, or pried into by self-interested, empirical, or idle curiosity. I had also other reasons that I did not like Dr. F. to be aware that I was suspecting him of dishonesty, or to charge him with it without grounds, and I might betray family matters. My letter however was opened by old Dr. F.; this was communicated to me the day after I had delivered it into the hands of Dr. F. F., when dining with the latter and his wife. My first expression after that of astonishment was, "Well, I am glad of it," for I only felt, then the Dr. knows the state of my feelings not by my fault. But I afterwards felt exposed, insulted, indignant, betrayed, when I recollected other parts of the letter, and foresaw that I could have no peace in communicating with my family, unless I was secure of the privacy of my correspondence. If they had not been deceived, they were perhaps unworthy of my concern. I insisted on that privacy as much for their sakes as mine: but although repeatedly mentioned by me, my request was not even once alluded to; yet even although it might have been an excessively extravagant request, if it gave me peace of mind, it was right to have attended to it. This silent, and as I felt it, contumelious contempt of my most earnest request, and expostulations, repeated on several occasions nearly drove me mad. If the show of an argument for not acceding to so simple and usual a wish had been given me, that would have proved attention at least, and some sort of respect: but to be passed over in silence, and apparently for the very reason, that a reason ought to have been given, because I was myself bereft of reason. I could not make it out, and I could not endure it. Now after these things, when I upbraided my family for their contempt, they argued from my accusation that I was a madman; because how could I imagine that such kind, excellent, affectionate relatives, wished to show me contempt. Not reflecting—and I wrote back to them—that contempt is contempt, but that the wish to show contempt is flattering to the pride and vanity of the object of it, because he knows that the contempt is affected. Henceforward, however, this was the hopeful tribunal to which I had to appeal for three years, they judging themselves and their conduct by their own excellent opinion of themselves, and me as a madman, for accusing such excellence, and refusing me my appeal to a jury, my appeal to law, my rights and privileges, on the plea that I should at length confess my errors, and be sorry to have so dealt with such excellent people, who left me in the mean time to pine and rot in a lunatic asylum.

To return to my letter, I obtained also, three times, a promise from Dr. F. F. that it should be forwarded immediately. Consider my wretched circumstances, consider my state of mind, my state of health, the resentment I felt at the treatment I had already endured, the acute suffering that treatment still occasioned me, my suspense, believing my letter to be sent, and no answer; and then you may conceive my danger, my exasperation, my despair, when on inquiry, many weeks after the letter was written, I found it had not been sent. Dr. F., with empirical sagacity, wanted me to write something more connected, to alter the expressions concerning his asylum more favourably. Yet on his son's deprecating my sending such a letter to my family, whilst I was yet writing it, and when I asked him for his last promise to send it without reading it, I showed him the words which I had written, explaining the reason why I preferred sending my scrawl as it was, to correcting it; whilst I covered with my hands the rest of the letter. My reasons were, that my brother's considering my hand-writing and my style, might try to find out for me the cause of, or the mystery of my malady. Poor fool! I might as well have written to the stones, or to the winds. They showed me no real desire to inquire, no delicacy, no beauty of feeling.

They who have not been confined in a lunatic asylum, cannot conceive the dreadful and cruel suspense that delay, and not only the neglect, but the refusal of every day civilities, together with inattention to just and obvious complaints, occasion. They do not know our wants and fears, because they do not know the danger we are in. They may judge our danger, however, from what these men do; and from what they have done, they may judge what they dare to do: being encompassed, even more than a king, with a hollow impunity, and clothed in the deepest hypocrisy. They who have not endured this confinement do not know how the very suspicion of being a lunatic, coupled with being cut off from all pecuniary resources, shuts the minds of others against sympathy, impedes the proffer of assistance and the exercise of protection, and aught but the show of pity. Neither how it embarrasses the suppliant in his applications for redress, awakens anxiety, excites mistrust, and closes the door of his hopes; whilst he finds himself left defenceless to the sarcasm and persecutions of those he is accusing. This is an awful peril for a man in a sound mind to be exposed to, lest he become deranged; lest he be tempted to violence, *the object* of his tormentors, which would then be construed into an open act of insanity; and if not immediately accepted as damning proof, by imbecile magistrates, at least cruelly try the mind, by tantalizing the expectations. How much more fearful is such a trial for one who knows that he cannot plead innocence of lunacy; one who, in mind and bodily health, is weak, and thereby more exposed than another to follow a wrong course; exposed to suffer even from treatment which men in sound health might almost laugh at, still more from that which he dreads from having experienced it, and against which he is exasperated; and also, still more liable than the other to lose that gift, lately lost, so dear now, being newly restored to him,—the gift of a sound mind, and convalescent health; perishing again from want of wholesome communion, shattered by assault, or insidiously undermined.

By this time I had broken off all friendly intercourse with the Drs. F. He had explained to me that he acted with the sanction of my family, and they, by his guidance: and my eldest brother in a letter stated, only (so loosely had he acted) that he thought some agreement had been made with regard to my having a private apartment; but on further reflection, as my mind grew stronger, considering my rights and my state more accurately, I concluded that the doctor was responsible to me, that he had forfeited claim to my respect, and deserved great blame, both as a physician and as a man of honour and gentlemanly feeling, in exposing me in a state of nervous excitement and great weakness, to the violence, confusion, and open observation of the society and servants in his common room: particularly when he knew my name, and the kind of society in which I had lived, to which I had been brought up; and the circumstances of my illness. As my fall was great, so was my trial severe, and his conduct the more highly to be censured. But the year before, an officer in the army, now to be put under the sticks, the fists, the knees of his menials, at their discretion: deranged through enthusiastically religious principles, and left amongst a motley group of blaspheming, infidel, and irreligious lunatics. Yesterday a gentleman, moving in the most refined and honourable circles, to-day in a room full of fanatics coarse even by habits, and of vulgar education; to select such a time to heap all these painful trials and cruel contrasts upon me! But no matter; the ruin of the soul has been accomplished; the work of villany has been done; what is now the use of complaint, what the use of remonstrating against such bare-faced and impudent mockery: moreover, I did not feel it then; I could not resent their cruelties; I was overwhelmed by other afflictions: the waves that wash over the body of a drowned man shock and lift the limbs, it is true; but they fall again on the sands, listless and impassible. Be it supposed, I did not feel it then.

The want of feeling with which we were treated, however, is difficult to be credited, and the degree of folly to which it proceeded, scarcely to be imagined. Communications, when they came from our families, were made to us in the presence of the rest, vivâ voce. Letters were given to us to read, and materials to write, in public. I received no tidings from my family, as near as I can guess, for three months: I understood afterwards, from my mother, when released, that in this, as in other parts of her conduct, equally contrary to nature and reason, she obeyed the advice of the doctor. They had got a stranger into their nets, and they were determined to keep him all to themselves. I am surprised at their self-sufficiency and impertinence. The natural result of this neglect was to produce in my mind surprise, wonder, a sense of strangeness in my situation, and alarm, to find a satisfactory clue to which, I had nothing but a disordered imagination to draw upon, which supplied me, as I have indicated, with ludicrous and horrible ideas enow. I was led also to entertain a mean opinion of myself, and to condemn myself by too severe a judgment. So that when I began to address my friends, I was at a loss to know how to approach them. What was I to augur from their silence; had they cast me off? did they look on me as a reprobate? did they scout me?

At last, a message in a letter, or a letter to me, was delivered to me in the common room one forenoon. It was from my mother. Either on that, or on a subsequent occasion later in the year, I was asked if I would write an answer. I applied to my spirits, as usual, for guidance as to the feelings I was to express, the acts I was to perform. I hallooed aloud, and behaved boisterously by their direction. I got pen, ink, and paper brought to me, and a table; kicked them over; had them replaced; and at length wrote to my mother to this effect: "that I was so happy where I was; that I loved the people so about me; that I longed to come to E——, and to bring Herminet Herbert with me," and I alluded to my spiritual friend, Mr. Waldony. I wrote with great perplexity, and opposition from many of the spirits. Unfortunately, my family were too willing to believe this silly rhapsody, although there were a few words that might have afforded them a clue to the truth; and I was informed, when released, that the contents of that letter greatly influenced them in rejecting the complaints I made, when I began really to appreciate my situation. I did not call to mind what I had written, until they recalled it to my recollection; and I was then very angry that my family had never frankly alluded to my previous statements, in order that I might have come to an explanation. I wrote two or three short letters in the same style: in the last, I begged my mother to excuse me from replying to her, as it gave me great pain. I then did not hear from her for a long time, and I was afraid she understood that receiving the letters she wrote gave me pain. My meaning was, that I could not answer her for the contest of my spirits; for many came to write for me, or to dictate to me, and I became agitated, and vexed which to put faith in, which to choose. In other words, I imagine it was a contest of mind, between the spirit of a right understanding and the spirits of delusion. Had I been alone, I might by chance have written soundly, my senses being calmer and more collected. But besides the delusions and the simplicity which obscured my intellect, I doubt not that my sorrows and sufferings, called for actions and expressions I unconsciously shrunk from before strangers; and if I behaved in an unusual manner, if my agitation made me leave the table, or lay down my pen; if I wandered in my attention, one of the servants would come and incite me to go on, or take away pen, ink, and paper together, saying, "what's the use of giving it to you if you make no use of it;" or "come, come I think you have written enough for to-day;" then another entering the room, and staring at me, cried out, "has he finished the letter yet," and if not, then "take it away, take it away from him; he'll be all the day about it."

CHAPTER XXIV

In June, about the time of hay-making, my eldest brother, on his way from T—— after his election, called to see me. I was unfastened, led into another patient's room, and dressed in a new suit of clothes, like a boy at a private school, and taken into the entrance room to see him. After speaking to him, some gooseberry pie was offered to me; and then I walked out with my brother and the keeper; tried to throw myself over the stiles as usual, and came home. Next day, I again walked out with him; he took me to a seat, where he asked me to explain him a proposition in Euclid, which I comprehended perfectly, but was prevented by my spirits from following consecutively; it seemed to me as if I had other business; and I thought he was come to try me, and was inspired to know all my thoughts. From the seat I drew a sketch, with some difficulty, partly guided by the spirits, partly of my own handy-work; and I desired him to give it to my elder sister. My brother took leave of me in the evening, in the common room, at tea time. I was then fastened up in the niche. I was told by the voices that he would have taken me to E—— [Ealing], which my heart was set upon, if I had performed one extravagant act or another, which I had failed in, or refused to do.

Before my brother's arrival, or soon after, my mother had desired the doctor to supply me with books, and had written to know what books I should like to have sent to me. She had also desired them to propose to me to draw and to learn the flute; Mr. H. F. asked me to read Virgil with him, and Dr. F. F. suggested the occupation of turning. I sent for a Euclid and my Hebrew Bible; I agreed to try my hand at drawing, and a schoolboy's copy-book and one pencil were given to me. Was it intended to turn me to ridicule? to provoke me to exercise my judgment? or, was it from simplicity and hypocrisy; pretending to do what they cared nothing about? As to the music-master, I did not believe that the offer was sincere. I thought that they came to try me, and at any rate that it was of no use, for though I could understand what I read, and might blow on the flute, I knew I could not apply to study, until I understood the calls of the spirits, and how to follow or reconcile their directions. In the same season, I was astonished at Dr. F. F. proposing to me the use of a turning machine: and I could not believe his sincerity, for I knew the first day I should put my finger where it would be crushed, in obedience to a voice of one kind or of another. I asked for Gibbon's Roman History, but it was never brought to me, and as they fought off from this request, my suspicions were increased. Long after, when books were again offered to me, I again asked for the History of the Decline and Fall of the Roman Empire, instead of which I was presented to my amusement with the history of the Lew-chew Islands. But, Herminet Herbert (Hobbs) exercised a summary control over all these petty occupations, and on one pretence or another often took my pencil and books away from me, or prevented me bringing them down stairs. Small as these means were, they doubtless aided my recovery; occupying me on realities, and for a time rescuing me from sloth, apathy, and idleness. It was one of my first complaints by letter, that they were taken away; and, I think, the only one that was immediately attended to. These attentions, such as they were, I owed chiefly to my mother's persevering instances, together with other particular alterations. Unfortunately, I did not know until I was released, how much I had been even thus far indebted to her.

My brother was evidently agonized at my appearance. His visit gave me self-confidence, and insured me some respect. More advantage might have resulted from it, had my situation been more becoming. But a visit of this kind, and the style of delivery in which communications were made from our families, and the patients requested to reply to them, are instances of the mockery and treachery of such a system in a madhouse. By placing you in an unnatural and cruel situation, and at the same time counselling your friends to keep aloof from you, in presence and in letter, they create the feelings which render it impossible for a man in a sound mind to receive intelligence from them at last, without extreme agitation: then they abruptly communicate that intelligence, or hand the letter to the patient, and neither consulting his modesty or his distress, deny him a little retirement to read these lines in private. His feelings, at a time that he is declared incapable of controlling them, are thus called upon, in the very circumstances, from the cruelty of which he ought to have been preserved, by those from whom he hears, for which they ought at least to express their sympathy, and regret, if not atone and apologize. But no, the letter contains a mere meagre account of every day occurrences; cold, unmeaning, paltry trivialities, trifling with the time and tone of a mind whose imagination is strung up to the highest pitch of delicate and romantic enthusiasm. The violence, or agitation, or ridiculous conduct that ensues, is then attributed to the receipt of the letter, instead of to the brutal heedlessness with which it is delivered. But this is in favour of the doctor. Another apparent cause is given for withholding at least, if not denying altogether, one rational mean of a patient's recovery; and however specious may be their conduct, and their excuses to mankind and to themselves, their end is to make money, not to make whole; and their system is adapted in one way or another to this end: whilst the essential interests, the mental wants of the inmates of their prisons are neglected. It stands to reason. Tie an active limbed, active minded, actively imagining young man in bed, hand and foot, for a fortnight, drench him with medicines, slops, clysters; when reduced to the extreme of nervous debility, and his derangement is successfully confirmed, manacle him down for twenty-four hours in the cabin of a ship; then for a whole year shut him up from six A.M. to eight P.M. regardless of his former habits, in a room full of strangers, ranting, noisy, quarrelsome, revolting, madmen; give him no tonic medicines, no peculiar treatment or attention, leave him to a nondescript domestic, now brushing his clothes, sweeping the floors, serving at table, now his companion out of doors, now his bed-room companion; now throwing him on the floor, kneeling on him, striking him under all these distressing and perplexing circumstances; debar him from all conversation with his superiors, all communication with his friends, all insight into their motives, every impression of sane and well-behaved society! surprise him on all occasions, never leave harassing him night or day, or at meals; whether you bleed him to death, or cut his hair, show the same utter contempt for his will or inclination; do all in your power to crush every germ of self-respect that may yet remain, or rise up in his bosom; manacle him as you would a felon; expose him to ridicule, and give him no opportunity of retirement or self-reflection; and what are you to expect. And whose agents are you; those of God or of Satan? And what good can you reasonably dare to expect? and whose profit is really intended?

Gentlemen of England, the system I have described is not only the system of English men, it is the disgrace of English surgeons, of English physicians. It is practised or connived at by the innocent simplicity of that race of presuming upstarts, who in various guises admitted by your condescension to terms of familiarity, sit at your tables, hiding their conceit in a false humility and in silky smiles; whilst they ape your manners and dupe your generosity. Be assured, whoever ye are, who have to deal with children or lunatics, if you are not looking after them yourselves, you are not respecting them. The doctors know that, and take advantage of it, to construe your disrespect into worse even than it is. Their servants take advantage of it. Bystanders draw false conclusions from it, much rather the poor object of it. His nature resents it; though he is not always aware of anything but his delusions: and his delusions contending with his feelings for the mastery over him, make him a madman. His self-respect, also, for so he respected himself partly for your sakes, is destroyed; and he delivers himself up to every grovelling thought and lewd idea, reckless on account of *your* ingratitude; even if his weakness and total want of wholesome exercise, wholesome occupation, and wholesome repose, does not render such a surrender inevitable. If, however, he has sense to resent consciously your desertion, he has also ten to one the high-mindedness to do it by scorn, contempt, and silence on his part; perhaps he does so by expressions of hatred and attempts at violence in your presence, devoid of discretion, and impotent over his revenge. These the doctor, consciously or not, easily gets you to interpret into signs of the complaint, when they are in truth the signs of his devilish treatment, and of the patient's unguarded honesty: which, also, a few respectful words of repentance from you might make vanish like the morning mists. Not however, if you repent only to offend again; if you mock at one who, whatever may be the source, is preternaturally enlightened. I am sure that no lunatic who has undergone the trials I describe, can meet his family on terms of cordiality, but through practising dissimulation, or through being a simpleton. At this distance of time, I cannot forgive my family the guilt they incurred by their abandonment of me. I am at a loss to find any argument which will justify me in doing so: I dare not expect to be able to do so. But if haply perfection requires this moral excellence, by what happy fortune are you entitled to look for it in the inmates of a lunatic asylum?

I have complained that the behaviour adopted towards me, was calculated to humour the state of mind I was then in, not to correct. The servant, for instance, whom I used to call Jesus, and Herminet Herbert, ran with me, jumped, joked, walked arm in arm with me, rattled the spoons in my face as he put them into the cupboard, pulled me by the nose, &c. &c. If I was not insensible to the impropriety of this familiarity, at least, I could not express my sense of it. But it will be evident, this was not the way to correct a gentleman's diseased mind. This conduct may be partly accounted for by having been placed under a quondam Quaker, to whom in theory and in practice, as far as it only interfered with others, and suited his interests, perfect equality of rich and poor was a matter of faith. There was, however, this unfairness in it, that I observed the joke ceased whenever the domestic had had enough of it. The lunatic's presence of mind and tranquillity might be broken in upon, but not so the keeper's. There was but one step from joking with them to violence and ob-jurgation. Later in the year, a young handsome lad used to invite me to box with him every evening in my bed-room, striking me in sport a few blows: at length, I expressed a kind of awkward resentment at it. I have perhaps written enough on this subject.

CHAPTER XXV

ONE Sunday morning, old Dr. F. entered the common room as usual; and on his entrance I, who was tied hand and foot, sang the psalm, "O be joyful," &c. to the edification of those present. The doctor tottered up to me on his cane, and argued against the impropriety of my conduct in singing, in such a place, such a psalm on a Sunday morning. This was the kindest and most reasonable address made to me during my imbecility in that madhouse. But it was lost upon me, because I did not believe it sincere. My spirits had told me to sing the psalm in his honor, and purposely to please him. That I was not to mind what he said, because he spoke so to see if I preferred serving God or him; and that he was really delighted to hear me sing it, as a proof that I was returning to a sense of my duty to the Lord Jehovah; and trying to fulfil my mission as an angel who was to sing his praises. Sunday morning appeared to me an additional reason. His using that argument aided the spirits in deluding me. Therefore as soon as he re-entered the room from the yard, I pealed forth again, "O be joyful in the Lord, all ye lands," though not so decidedly. His word helped to make me doubt the word of the spirits.

One forenoon, after I was allowed to walk out in the common room and yard, Mr. F. F. whilst standing near me and three other patients, asked me suddenly before them, "Pray, Mr. —— was it your father who was shot in the house of Commons?" I do not know whether I replied; but I recollect being greatly troubled by my spirits to make a reply, though inwardly at peace. I then looked silently in the faces of the bystanders, and then turned

my back on him, and walked away to meditate on what had occurred, alone. I will not say what I feel now. The next part of
the treatment I will allude to, is my having been walked about the
grounds and the country in a state of insanity. The chief thing
to be desired in the treatment of an insane person (as any but
charlatans would have inferred from the name they give them,
"*nervous patient*") is quiet, peace, security; security from intrusion, observation, exposure. A lunatic appears insensible, but
his is, perhaps, the most alive of any mind to ridicule, and to
the contemptibleness of his state. But he is, as I may say, unconsciously alive to it. He does not acknowledge his own feelings,
because his mind is deeply engrossed in painful and excruciating
conflicts; he is already troubled by a thousand horrible and fanciful ideas of danger; the victim of inward and preternatural sarcasm, contumely, and derision. But he acts strangely, from what
he suffers unacknowledged and not understood by himself. If
indeed, he were in quiet, peaceful circumstances, if he were secure he might find his mind reflect to his conscience perfectly,
what the trouble occasioned by internal and external alarm prevents him noting; but the opposite is his position.

Though all men in the world are daily acting more or less
from these unacknowledged sensations, I shall not be understood
without mentioning an example. Whenever I went out to walk,
on leaving the common room and turning round to the left
into the passage, I had to pass by the door of the housekeeper's
room, before I reached the hall door. Into this room I often ran
from my keeper at the command of one or other of the spirits, and
began to admire the maid's work-baskets, and similar objects which,
though trifling, appeared to me so simple, neat, and beautiful. I
used often to wonder at myself, and to be surprised, that what
formerly I passed over with neglect, now so greatly attracted me.
When I was in a great measure recovered from my delusions, and
in better health, keeping also a constant and minute watch and
control over my actions, and observing the causes of them, I
went out, one day, walking as usual, when on passing the door of
that room, I observed the shadows and voices of persons entering
the hall door on the right. I ran immediately, as formerly, into

the housekeeper's room, unable to check the impulse. I recollected myself, however, and then recognised that it was acute sensitiveness or shyness; the consciousness of my being unfit for the eye of man to look upon, that caused me to rush into the servants' apartments, with whom I was in some degree familiarized, rather than meet the gaze of a stranger. I said instantly to myself "then the physician is unconscious that we have any feeling; and is mistaken in his system." I felt the hopelessness of my situation, at the same time that I saw how necessary seclusion was for my happiness and peace of mind, to preserve me from acts of folly.

From what I state, it will be obvious how improper for many patients any exposure, or any conduct likely to draw attention on them in particular must be. Nature tells a man, who has any great grief, to be for a time secluded. Nature makes a man, sensible of any great infirmity, seek retirement, still more under such an awful infliction as insanity, when from the proud station of a reasonable being, he is degraded below the beasts of the field: fallen from his throne; bereft of his dominion. Nature, however, comes not into any part of the doctor's plans, but self-interest. He does not consider what is the sanest treatment for the sufferers, but what will attract most customers. They see the patients apparently unconscious to the shame of their situation; and that conduct, which really proceeds from an unacknowledged sense of it, they look upon as a sign of the specific disease they labour under. They act then according to that they find, instead of reflecting that want of sense is probably part of the disease, and that it is their duty *to restore a sense* of propriety by more regard on their part, not to harden the feelings by constant exposure. I may apply the same remarks to the custom of walking me about the grounds, where I met the carriages of the visitors, and others about the farm-houses, and subsequently, with a string of patients through the villages: what could be more painful to a man of any feeling? what could be more dangerous if you wished to restore good-feeling? what more cruel if it was the design to probe the feelings, through a heart already broken down, and benumbed by disease and affliction?

I may be wrong, but I cannot help suspecting that it was the key to Dr. F.'s system to probe the feelings; if not, why put such brutal questions? why take the patients by surprise at the visit of relations? why expose them in public to receive private communications? why insult them and degrade them in every circumstance of domestic life, toilette, meals, couch, &c. &c.; besides on one occasion, when I remarked to Marshall that the boots were not very well cleaned, he replied with his strong nasal twang, "they'll be better when you get out, d'ye see."

When I began to make remonstrances with my family, I complained of the absurdity of their having allowed me to be exposed in this manner, at the same time that the professed object of my being detained so far from home, was the desire pretended for *my* retirement, to save *my* feelings in not meeting my friends. I alluded, amongst other facts, to my having been allowed and encouraged to go out to play at cricket, with strange gentlemen of the neighbourhood, whilst yet hallooing out, and acting under the wildest delusions. And when the propriety of my being in retirement was again recurred to as an argument, to prevent my confinement in London, or in a neighbourhood where I hoped to meet those who would truly befriend me, since my relations on pretence of duty, delicacy, or decency, abandoned me to the malice and economy of the doctor, I replied, that such an argument was sheer mockery; that not my pride, not my delicacy, not my modesty were being consulted, not my care for privacy, but my family's desire to hide me; for otherwise they would make my privacy effectual by placing me in a private family as I required; and whether was it better to have my griefs and infirmities exposed to friends who would enter into my feelings, respect, pity, and protect me, or to the strange tenantry, strange household, strange patients, and strange visitors of a doctor perfectly unknown to me, except through his stupid inhumanity.

O sirs! the conduct I have had to endure, the gauntlet I have had to run through was dreadful; but it cannot be remedied now; when my mind recurs to it, it is too great to be resented articulately.

I desired my family to order Dr. F. to let me walk nowhere

but in his kitchen garden, the place least liable to the intrusion of strangers, and that I might be alone. This was attended to; and I am thankful it was, otherwise I might never have been restored to LIBERTY.*

* One afternoon, a thunderstorm came on whilst we were in the field at cricket; my spirits were then as usual puzzling me, when suddenly a rattling peal of thunder shook the vault of the heavens, to my ears it articulated the most terrible imprecations, and I stood mute with astonishment, expecting almost to be struck to the earth by the lightning, and doubting whether to attribute my being spared to the mercy and long suffering of God, or to the infinite counsels of his wrath reserving me for greater damnation. A passage of Scripture has since been brought to my mind, when a voice came from heaven, but some said it thundered.

CHAPTER XXVI

My recovery was very gradual, but its periods remarkable. Three times my spirits prophesied to me, that a great change would take place in my situation. I expected a marvel, but the change took place in me, by natural causes, altering my apparent relationship to the persons around me. I had been continually haunted by the idea, that the sufferings I saw or fancied others enduring, were endured for me, and that it was my duty to try to partake in them or to alleviate them, or to perform some act of duty, for my neglect of which they were punished in my stead. For instance, when one day I saw the young clergyman, Mr. J. fastened opposite to me in a niche, by an iron manacle to the wall; *in great agitation I prayed the servant* not to do so, but to put it on me instead. For he had been kind to me, and I heard the spirits say or sing to me, "Mr. J. is manacled for you." But after one of the prophecies mentioned above, I began to hear these words added to the message of the spirits, Mr. J. is manacled, or suffocating, or whatever it might be, for you; to meditate on and reflect on too, or to think on with grief and contrition too, and the like. Then I knew that I had been deceived; and my mind received quiet. I was relieved from the oppression that I was continually causing the misery of others by my misdemeanours, and from the harass of being always called upon to perform some hazardous duty in order to relieve them. I began to hesitate before I acted, waiting on any appeal from a spirit, to hear if no interpretation or additional sentence explained the first. I joked inwardly at the absurdity of my delusions. By this a great alteration took place in my mind. Objects began to stand around me in a new light. I began to be less ready to give up the dictates of common sense, to the injunctions of invisible agents. At another time, my spirits began singing to me in this strain. "You are in a lunatic asylum, if you will"—"if not, you are in," &c. &c. "That is Samuel Hobbs if you will—if not, it is Herminet Herbert," &c. &c. &c. But I had been so long deceived by my spirits that now I did not believe them when they spoke truth. However, by listening and finding that the patients called him Samuel Hobbs, and by other accidents, I discovered at last that I was yet on earth, in natural, although very painful, circumstances in a madhouse. My delusions being thus very much abolished, I soon after got liberty of limb during the day-time.

Then new delusions succeeded those that were dissipated. I was on earth, it was true, in England and in a lunatic asylum; but I understood that it was the law of the land, that those lunatics who after a certain trial did not recover should be made away with, in order to spare the country the expense of maintaining them. I was still a disobedient angel whom the Lord had made pass for a lunatic in order to preserve me. But I was watched with jealousy. Several times my spirits indicated to me a gentleman who was, I afterwards discovered, a patient in another ward, as the Chancellor of the Exchequer. He had come down purposely to examine and report upon my case. He was not the only person I dignified with title and office. Before that, when the magistrates paid their first visit, I imagined that one was the Lord Eldon, the other Mr. Goulburn, and a third my mother's attorney. They had come to look after me, both out of respect to my father, and from the peculiar interest that my case excited. But, when I came to see my delusions, I received these grave old useless gentlemen with bursts of laughter, both at their demeanour, and at the absurdity of my deception. I shook off the greatest part of my delusions a short time before the riots at Bristol.

About this time, one of my brothers came to see me. I did not receive him very kindly. I was beginning to suspect that my family had behaved ill to me, though unable to express myself, or to arrange my ideas. There was an inquisitiveness also in my brother's manner which I did not think becoming, accompanied with the same tone of suspicion I had observed in the Mr. F——s', which wounded my feelings and aroused my pride. During our conversation, my brother asked me why I spoke with my mouth shut, and whether I had been used to do so. I did not understand the question, but on his repeating it, I put my hand up to my mouth when speaking, and to my surprise found that whilst I spoke I kept my teeth close together. Soon after, he noticed my hair was cut very close and cropped in front, but long and full behind. I was not aware of that either until he drew my attention to it. He asked me if I liked it being cut so. I said to myself, if he is such a fool as to ask such a question, I am a fool to talk with him seriously; but I suspected that this was a part of the insulting system I had been submitted to, and that my brother asked me merely to try if I resented it. The absurdity of such a system, whoever imagined it, cannot be better evidenced than by my never having noticed the affront; and the result of it, when I noticed it, was, that I resolved to show no resentment, whatever I might feel. I then proposed taking a walk with my brother, to show him a view over to Bristol, which I admired very much. The attendant followed us.

On returning, my brother went up with me to see my bedroom. He asked me also if I should like to see an aunt and a cousin, who were interested about me. I replied unfortunately, that I thought it would be of no use. I felt that I should only be grieving them, and that they could not find out for me the clue to those puzzling inspirations which troubled my mind. But their coming would no doubt have cheered and enlivened me, and as they both loved me, they might either have felt and remedied the impropriety of my situation, or have taken me home with them upon trial, for I was then perfectly inoffensive. In that case, ease, quiet, and security would have rapidly effectuated my cure.

The same evening I dined with my brother at Dr. F's. The conversation turned on Mr. Irving, and other topics: I did not feel satisfied with the style of those who took part in it. I heard all that was said; but I was conversing chiefly with my spirits.

At one time they were teazing me about the manner in which I was to eat or leave my potatoes, and at last, not being able to please myself or them, I threw down my knife and fork on the plate: this attracted a moment's observation. Mr. F. F. said a few silly words in joke, and I resumed my tranquillity and gentleness. Next morning, being Sunday, I saw my brother again in Mr. F. F.'s company after church for about half an hour, on the lawn by the old doctor's house. I behaved very coolly, and I suppose he felt no encouragement to see me again. On Monday morning, he took leave of me at the hall door of the madhouse, and mounted one of the doctor's horses to ride into Bristol. He is no great horseman, and I re-entered the prison I was confined to with Samuel Hobbs, holding my arm, and laughing and quizzing at his want of jockeyship.

I was sensible to the impertinence of this familiarity, but my feelings of resentment against my family made it in some sense not unpleasing, particularly as I thought there was an expression of sympathy in the man's countenance, and of disappointment' at the result of my brother's visit. They have not touched the right string, he seemed to say, they have been too dull to guess the secret. To resent familiarity, however, on the part of the domestics, was to break through at once the whole system of polite education I had been submitted to. This man had walked arm in arm with me, recited Shakespeare to me, sang songs, trifled, fooled with me. His language was neither restrained by reverence or decency, and often he swore. He always talked in an insolent radical manner of the gentry. My spirits often desired me to rebuke him, when I was shocked at his oaths and language. But I refused; for, I replied, if these offences are really rebuke-worthy, I will keep my rebukes for those who really need them; not for those who sin designedly, to tempt me from curiosity, or from some other motive. Besides, I used to reply, if this is the Lord Jesus Christ, he cannot really sin, and I will not expose my want of faith and stupidity to ridicule and mockery by rebuking that, which since the universal redemption I have been informed of, is no more rebuke-worthy. But when I had recovered a sounder understanding, I knew that this man was substantially and indeed

Samuel Hobbs, the servant of a doctor of lunatics, whatever might be his spiritual character. It fell out one afternoon, about the time of the Bristol riots, when the speech of our servants became very licentious, and the threats of what was to be done to the gentry very wondrous, and yet alarming, that he was sitting with his back towards the table, his feet upon the fender, and his pipe in his mouth, and slandering many great men, and the gentry generally. I then felt for my companion, Captain P. whom my spirits had called my spirit of family pride; and when at last he fell foul of the Duke of Wellington, I told him to hold his tongue, and to mind his own business; that the Duke of Wellington was a greater man than he or I were ever likely to be; and that till we could imitate his great actions, we might make allowance for his slight faults. After this, I never heard Samuel Hobbs speak disrespectfully of the nobility again. Whether or no he was ashamed of being rebuked by a madman, he acknowledged the justice of this reproof.

No doubt Dr. F. and others will express their surprise on hearing these facts, and say they disown them to be, and ask why they were not complained of. I reply, would it not have been a sensible and a reasonable course to pursue, to complain of these things? Were not we confined because we were deranged in our reason, and bereft of our senses? Am not I right then in saying that the world, in their treatment of lunatics, are as insane as the lunatic himself, inasmuch as they expect from one expressly devoid of reason, the conduct of a reasonable being. Again, supposing that by chance one or two of the lunatics acknowledge the impropriety of the conduct that passes round them, yet, *if their moral sense is not blunted to the enormity of it,* by their habitual degradation as well as by disease, why should they complain either to the magistrates or the doctor, when they do not know that such conduct is not connived at, when they know that whatever they say is looked upon with mistrust and suspicion, and that in either case they are left exposed to the malice and brutality of those whom they complain against; to whose evidence they may have to look also shortly for the recovery of their liberty.

Soon after liberty of limb had been restored to me, my mother, to whose exertions I owe, after all, whatever was likely to restore me to sound reason whilst under the care of Dr. F., begged that I might be allowed to work in his garden; this was indeed beneficial, as it gave me occupation and more privacy. Later in the year I was employed with two gentlemen and a keeper, to cut out a small path in the shrubbery. I was entrusted with the mattock and the spade. My spirits however teazed me so much, by contrary directions, that after repeated trials I threw them down, contenting myself to wheel the barrow, to pick up sticks, and to handle the bill-hook. It was about the time of the Bristol riots. The seditious conversation and tone of the servants, and their accounts of the state of mind of the peasantry, gave me great anxiety. The heavy dragoons were quartered in the neighborhood, and one day I saw a troop of them exercising their horses down the road. They talked loudly and swore. I augured ill of their trustworthiness and discipline from their conduct, and throwing down the sticks I had been collecting, I rushed into the thicket in tears, exclaiming, "oh! my country, oh! my country." Then my spirits checked me; I began to sing a psalm, and was beguiled by my delusions. At that time, I longed to see a train of artillery coming down the road, and looked for it daily; for I knew that they would keep order; but the government then acted the part of madmen if not worse. The night the city was on fire Hobbs and Poole came into my bed-room to see the flames; I was tied in bed; Poole proposed to untie me, that I might see it; but Hobbs replied, "Oh! no, no, he will only be playing his tricks."

One day whilst working in this plantation, the string of patients passed us on their way home. Hobbs took me by the arm and laughed saying, "come let us see what you have been doing, they say you do nothing but pick up the sticks like an old woman." He came at last to the bundles I had collected to light his fire; he seemed to reflect, and was silent.

Another day, old Benevolence presented me with a fine nettle, in white bloom which he had gathered in a hedge, and told me it was a green house plant. The size made me hesitate for a moment, but I saw immediately it was a joke. Then my behaviour in the asylum struck me in its true light; the scales fell from my eyes. I knew that I was looked upon as a child; what, thought I, you take me for a child, for a fool! but you do not know what has made me so! On another occasion whilst amusing myself with the bill-hook, an old clergyman came to me to request me to yield it up to him: I said, quietly, "No! I like to use it myself;" he went up to the keeper, and I saw them laughing heartily. I reflected then on what I had spoken, and could not help laughing myself, whilst I walked up to him and gave him the bill-hook.

We were not the only gulls; Dr. F. had in his premises, on the lawn before the house, four or five fed, which had been brought from the sea. They strayed across the field into the plantation in which I was employed, and I drove them back with my pocket handkerchief. It was the first time I was trusted alone. A female came out and thanked me; then the sight of a female at all beautiful, was enchanting to me.

I now began to recover my reflection rapidly, and to make observations upon characters and persons around me. I met the doctor who had bled me in the temporal artery, when going out one day at the hall door. Some of my spirits desired me to resent the manner in which this operation had been performed, without my permission, and in a brutal way; and I do to this day; but, others desired me to forgive him. These on the whole prevailed. I shook hands with him to show him that I bore him no ill-will; and on his alluding to my state, I said, "Oh! sir, I have been in a dream, a fearful dream, but it is gone now.'

I had asked Mr. F. F. for a pocket-book in order to know the date, and to keep memoranda. He gave it me one day out of a gig, whilst I was employed in the shrubbery: I vaulted over a gate to receive it. I had told him before this, that I should make my escape if I could, that I might not be accused of being guilty of breach of trust if I ran away. He remarked, I see you are active enough to attempt your threatened escape, but I suppose you do not really mean it. I replied, I really did. So simple was I, and so resolved. I should say that by this time my mind had arrived from a state of imbecility and infancy, through a state of childishness, to the simplicity of boyhood; open and undisguised, and designing adventures, without calculating its strength.

Later in the year my imagination began to reflect the most divine and beautiful figures, in all kind of lascivious and wanton combination; until then my mind had been as chaste as it was free from malice. Now I saw these angelic forms, more beautiful than pictures, because they changed their attitudes, and sported in action. My spirits however told me that I had been looking on these scenes all the time that I was in the madhouse, that that was what they meant by heavenly places, and when I reminded them that I never had been able to get to heavenly places, they said that was my fault; that my spirit had been there, and that they had often desired me to come up there in one spirit or another; but that they could not help it if my spirit only came, and I chose to remain behind. With these visions I heard voices, reconciling me to the sight of, and desiring me to become a partaker in the lewd acts I saw committing; obliterating my disgust, and all sense of guilty shame, and substituting a purer feeling of delicate submission and modest consent. The holiness of the images purified the imagery of all that was revolting; and if my spirit refused to acknowledge the pleasure I took in contemplating these scenes and actions, and the desire I had to partake in them, then I was made to imagine as if in spirit I was forced to submit to the same, with every accompaniment of violence, insult, degradation, and sarcasm, as a puritanical and ungrateful hypocrite; undeserving of my Heavenly Father's love, in thus revealing his goodness to me, and unveiling his true nature, of which the world were ignorant, and kept in ignorance by him, through their hypocrisies, and malice, and envy one towards the other.

CHAPTER XXVII

I will now turn to the conduct and treatment of my wretched companions in confinement, and in affliction. I will begin with the oldest and most noisy of them all. A grey-haired, bald-headed, thin old gentleman, whom I first called Dr. F., and then my uncle, Mr. D., whose name also he bore. He was a solicitor or an attorney, he wore an old-fashioned, long skirted, square-cut black coat, and a broad brimmed hat, and when in good health, he was very respectable in appearance. He was usually very red in the face, idiotic, noisy, jabbering sentences of Virgil, Horace, English, &c., &c., occasionally applying them with a hidden meaning. He would halloo, strike the others in sport, and was altogether mischievous and troublesome. He often scratched his head till it was quite sore in many places; once he baptized me on my seat, whilst fastened up, with a mug of beer: once he threw brickbats at me. This was the gentleman my arm slapped in the face after he had struck me a blow at tea. He was usually to be seen in a room up stairs, with his red wild face staring through the blinds; here he was confined alone. When I began to walk about the yard, he would put his arm round my shoulder, ask me to walk with him, seize me by the right ear, and pulling it ask me, "Is that the ear Dr. L. opened for you?" Occasionally he pinched the wounded ear, but more gently. He did it to arouse me. He would ask me questions on Latin poetry;—I suspect it was he that hid the Bible. When he walked out with us, I observed that at stated distances he picked up a large stone, and carrying it a little way, threw it into one place, till at last there was a pretty large heap of stones collected at one of these stations. When I was recovering, he confided to me part of his story by snatches, under a chaos of confused sentences, allusions, and quotations. He told me he had been a lawyer, practising on the western circuit; that he had written a letter with a benevolent intention, at the time of my father's death, relating to my family. He inquired into circumstances connected with his views in that letter, his ideas were rational and distinct on the subject; though he could hardly speak three sentences coherently; like the under current of a stream, which remains clear and steady in its course, though broken at the surface and at the banks into a thousand eddies, and by a thousand waves. There was another subject preyed upon his mind, connected with his conduct at the Taunton assizes, where it appeared there was danger of the rescue of certain prisoners, and he had taken an active part; he appeared to be scrupulous about his conduct having been correct, and he mingled also allusions to his daughter; but there his mind failed him; he could not explain himself directly. Another day he spoke of my treatment by the servants. He told me he thought I had been ill treated, and that the behaviour of the servants was very bad. I replied, that I did not think it was intentional: he said, "I do," and then ran off on other subjects, as if afraid to say too much. He was more than seventy years of age, and I thought it a sad thing to see an old man in so great affliction, who had been so respectable, confined in such circumstances, and I wondered at the want of feeling of Dr. F., who was himself an old man.

I will mention next, Captain ——, the most prominent character in the room. My spirits desired me to call him Executioner, and Patience. He was of a brown complexion, with dark glossy hair; he had lost one leg, and besides had a withered arm, the sleeve of which was fastened to the breast of a blue surtout coat: he had a cork leg. He stood for one half the year at the end of the room facing the window, sitting down only at meals, and never leaving the room except to be shaved, or to go to bed, and once in the forenoon. He was usually silent, but occasionally cried aloud strange words; "Bruim!" &c.; or spoke a few disjointed sentences, in which he anathematized the Duke of York, and Sir Herbert Taylor, or abused the servants. He had dark penetrating expressive eyes. A newspaper was often brought to him, which sometimes he tore up, sometimes he allowed to be read in the room. He often complained aloud of the thickness of the bread and butter at breakfast and at tea. I remarked that there was usually one slice of bread and butter twice the thickness of all the rest, put on his plate. This is one of the reasons which make me suspect that the patient's feelings were often provoked designedly, either through the impertinent jocularity of the keepers, or through the mistaken quackery of the doctor. One forenoon about the middle of the year, a chair was brought in, and fastened below by an iron chain to the wall, and two servants seized this gentleman and forced him violently to sit down upon it. After that he remained seated in one position the rest of the year. He reminded me very much of the Brahmins I have read of, who imagine that they devote themselves to God in keeping one attitude all their lives. When the chair and the iron chain were brought in, I was very much frightened; I was then fastened up, and I thought he was going to be tortured for me. I was to have had my stomach squeezed between the chain and the floor, because I was such a glutton, and refused nothing for the sake of any spirit, but in pity for me, Patience had undertaken to endure it for me. I hallooed out to spare him, and was greatly excited. I saw him forced on the seat, and not under the chain. Then the spirits told me that he had endured it, but that they would not let me see it, they had hidden it from my eyes. Perhaps nothing can prove more strongly the power of my delusions, than that I gave credit to this absurd explanation. The reasons were that I believed in the tale of the destruction of Sodom and Gomorrah, when the eyes of a whole mob were blinded so that they could not find Lot's door! I conjectured that Jesus had escaped through the midst of the people by being rendered invisible to them: and I had myself been often perplexed by seeing persons who were not around me, instead of persons who were: by seeing words in books that were not printed there, and by other illusions. There was nothing else striking in the demeanour of Captain ——, but that he occasionally in manner and in speech, exhibited his resentment of the disrespectful conduct of the servants.

Mr. N——, my spirits called Mr. Fazakerley, and my spirit of delicacy and contrition. He was a short, thin, sharp featured man, with light grey eyes, a mouth always pursed with sardonic smiles, a head partly bald and partly grey. He carried his hands usually in his waistcoat or trouser pockets; walked with a nonchalant obstinate air, and with an awkward gait, halting on one leg. He was a man of pride. He sat usually in one chair by the fire-place, his elbow leaning on a table, and never spoke to any around him; once or twice only I heard him ask a question, and give directions to the servants, who treated him with decorum. Two or three times a day he rose from his chair and went into the yard, where he stood with his head raised up, his hands on his hips, his face wearing the appearance of choking, and cried aloud, "I take my oath before God, &c. &c. &c., that I *am* the Duke of Somerset, and that I give and bequeath all my jewels, large possessions, &c. &c., to his majesty and his heirs for ever. So help me God. Amen!" When I went into the yard at liberty, the spirits desired me also to take his position, and to cry out in like manner; "I am the lost hope of a noble family;" but after attempting it three or four times, I shrunk from so exposing my feelings, and my situation. Then my spirits said, cry out, "God save the king," or any thing you like, but you must suffocate. Mr. Fazakerley suffocates himself in this position, you must do the same. I took this direction literally, and I tried to sing the words, and at the same time choke myself. And I conceived myself a hypocrite because I could not perform an impossibility; which however perhaps, I had no intention of performing sincerely. Not succeeding in my attempt to suffocate, or in understanding the directions of the spirits who offered to teach me, and feeling the exposure of my situation, I used to stand in that place the greater part of the morning and of the afternoon. In the autumn when I had left this off, Hobbs showed me that part of the privet hedge, behind which I stood, saying, "look here, what you have done;" it was literally stripped of its leaves, yet I was not aware of having plucked them; this will show the nervous state in which I had been, and how great was my mental agony. I do not know what Mr. Fazakerley thought, but I rather think my conduct cured him of his folly, or diminished the exhibition of it. Once always in the afternoon Mr. Fazakerley rose and marching towards the cupboard near which I was confined, took out of it a cup which he filled from a can of water, left in the room after dinner. My spirits desired me repeatedly to ask him for a cup of cold water also, but he never gave me one; but he whom I called Affection, did.

This was a Rev. Mr. J., a clergyman from Devonshire, a tall sallow complexioned man, with light hair, a firm, but kind and gentle, though vacant countenance, somewhat slovenly. The agony of his features was often very great. He made observations aloud, often of a spiritual nature, not very delicate in language, sometimes reasoning on the anomalous character of the servants, as if arguing with himself what was his proper line of conduct towards them, occasionally replying in a very loud tone to the remarks of another patient. He stamped also with one foot, with a remarkably earnest expression of countenance at the same time. He was often treated violently, and manacled to the seat opposite to me. I never could tell why, for I never saw him offer violence to any one, except late in the year, when he had a quarrel with an impertinent young man, and they scuffled. He bore the ill treatment of the servants with a most provokingly calm superiority of humour. It was this gentleman who was so agitated, when they were forcing the meat down my throat. He was repeatedly pushed out of the room for his noise. I heard him once reasoning aloud on the sacrament, and made a few observations to him. He addressed me several times by name, always in an earnest and friendly manner, and now and then turned away again laughing, as much as to say, this young man does not want preaching or wisdom, he wants to be at fun and mockery all the day through. My spirits called him my cousin ——'s, spirit of family affection, also that he was my cousin, the most affectionate of my relations and friends, also when I desired them to show me St. John the Apostle, they directed me to look on him, whilst they told me that I was like to St. Paul or to St. Peter.

One afternoon in the summer time, I staid in doors with other patients, whilst the rest went out walking; when they came in, after Hobbs had locked the door, I was standing by the fire-place,

and Mr. J. was passing along the other side of the table towards
the yard; he took off his hat and put it on the table, making some
observations aloud. Hobbs who had come near me on my side of
the table, spoke sharply to him and lifted a cane he had in his
hand. Mr. J. replied, pray who are you; then offering his arm
said, you may strike me if you will. Hobbs struck him three or
four sharp cuts over the arm across the table. Mr. J. smiled contemptuously at him, stamped with his foot, put his hat on his
head, and passed out of the room. Had I been a little more in my
senses, I should probably have thrashed the servant.

The gross want of respect to situation, rank, character, or profession, manifested by these men on all occasions, is shocking to
the imagination, and revolting to reflection; and also, that whilst
a lunatic is exposed to immediate and unsparing chastisement
from them, for any ebullition of frenzy; he may be tempted to
acts of violence repeatedly, both in self-defence, and in common
justice to others; which nevertheless, by the ignorant and shuffling
magistrates who visit him, would be infallibly perverted into a
proof of his continued insanity, upon the report of those who are
most interested to distort facts to detain him, and to revenge themselves upon him for his noble and spirited resistance, and uncom-
promising representations. The very acts of impatience and im-
petuosity which gave me self-confidence and hope, and assured
me I was returning to my sound senses, too sound to be liked by
those feeding on my supineness and imbecility; the very acts which
I hailed in my fellow-prisoners as symptoms of restored life, and of
gallant, though God knows, imprudent resentment of galling
mockery, insult, and oppression, were looked upon, and held up
by my doctor to the keepers as the signs of mania; the very disorder
for which I was to be detained. But that which my mind found
more terrible, was that whilst temptations to violence should have
been removed from me, on account of my express state, we were
continually provoked to use violence, with justice and honour to
human nature; the result of which however, might have been fatal
to those who excited our acts, and then have consigned the unfortunate perpetrator of them to be entombed for life in a madhouse; as far at least probably as any inquiry before a jury would

have availed him, and certainly if he had property to pay the
doctor well for keeping him.

One morning when Mr. J. had asserted that he had done
nothing to deserve confinement, Samuel Hobbs replied, "how
can you say so sir, didn't I come to fetch you, and when I came
hadn't you kicked through your brother's door, and weren't they
afraid to keep you in the house, and you would not go out of it."
I do not know if these are sufficient grounds for shutting a man
up in a madhouse, but Samuel Hobbs thought so, and he got his
bread by it.

Mr. W—— was an old gentleman, about sixty years of age,
bald-headed, of short stature, rather stout, an aquiline nose, and
silly smiling countenance. He was the first of the patients who
tried to enter into conversation with me, and with whom I endeavoured to exchange any reasonable remarks. I called him Mr.
Simplicity. He used to stand by me when fastened upon my
wooden seat in the niche, leaning slightly against the wall with his
hands in his pockets, jabbering with an appearance of great self-
complacency a great many unconnected sentences, mentioning
my name, alluding to my father in a tone of surprise and encouragement, sometimes addressing to me appeals against the conduct
of the servants. He was an Irishman, and a Quaker; he had been
partner and coheir in a bank at —— in Ireland, and had run
away from the bank at the death of his father or of one of the
proprietors, on account of his fears of being made liable for the
overdrawing or speculations of a relation and copartner. He had
been secured, and since that time for many long years confined in
this madhouse. I collected these facts from his own lips, after
painful and repeated attention to his wanderings; sometimes in-
terrupting him, sometimes leading him back. I can give but a
faint idea of the want of connexion of subjects betrayed by his
conversation. He would speak thus: "yes, sir, yes, sir, Lord K.
was a very good man, a very good man! Do you know Lord ——
sir, he was Lord Lieutenant in my time. Yes, sir, and Mr. ——,
and Mr. ——, the same as brought in the bill for emancipating
the Roman Catholics, you know sir; my father was at that time
head of the firm. Sallust, you know Sallust, sir, one of the Roman

authors, he kept a bank at ——, county of Limerick. S—— and Co. My father knew the Duke of Richmond very well. Yes, sir, it was a very respectable firm. Mr. ——'s, son in a madhouse! they say he's not mad but only pretends to be so. Yes, sir, he was an old man. We are Quakers. That rascal Hobbs threatens to put the manacles on me (here he used to seize his wrist, tremble, and speak very loud and fluently), he threatens to strike me, sir; I wonder if Dr. F. knows of it. Dublin, yes, Dublin is a very fine town. So when my father died I suspected it was not all right, you see, sir, I ran away. There was a great disturbance in Cork, and Mr. —— was member for the county; they wanted to make me liable; so I thought it better to run away. There's a great sum owing to me now. I spoke to Dr. F. about it; I asked for some writing paper, but Hobbs takes it all away, he takes every thing away from me, sir. The doctors say that my case is that of pavor lymphaticus, pavor lymphaticus, sir."

And so it was, poor old gentleman, for at the slightest appearance of menace from any of the patients or servants, he called out lustily, took his hands out of his pockets and stretched them out trembling from head to foot, though a stout man. At the latter end of the year I was disgusted by seeing Marshall seize him on two or three occasions by the collar of the coat and throw him on the back upon the floor; it was in sport, but improper and rude sport from one old man to another, and from the servant and keeper of lunatic patients; to a patient under lymphaticus pavor. This old man was quiet and timid like a child. I soon found out that there was some foundation for his complaints against Samuel Hobbs. He was generally allowed after breakfast to go up to his bed-room to read, and it was amusing even there to see him eagerly steal away delighted to get out of reach of danger, but Hobbs often stopped him in his flight, saying, "halloo, Mr. —— where are you going to, sir, you shall not go up." Or after *hearing him* rating him on the stairs in a loud voice, he brought him down again; whether from caprice or not I cannot tell. I found when I was allowed to be up stairs myself, that the old man studied Sallust, and wanted me to construe to him some passages; this accounted for the mention of that author. Having been at Dublin,

I often tried to talk with him of that city, for there was no one else cared to know what he was gabbling about.

In the autumn, Captain W. a young Irish gentleman, an officer in the line, having been brought to the house, made jest of poor Mr. Simplicity, threatening to throw things at him, to strike him, &c. &c. Captain W. read a great deal in the Prayer book. This gave me hopes of reasoning with him on the impropriety of his conduct: besides that, he was really a gentleman. But to my astonishment and amusement he argued quietly and in sober seriousness. I am sure he was sent to me by God Almighty to keep me from melancholy, I should die in such a stupid place if I had not him to make fun of. My spirits called this old gentleman like many others, Mr. Fitzherbert: he was but a slovenly old fellow standing always with his hands in his breeches pockets, a posture for the hands however not unusual or surprising in a house where we were all devoted to idleness and sloth.

Beyond him, on my left-hand side, sat a little, thin, withered, yellow faced man, sprucely dressed, with a well brushed blue coat and brass buttons, neat frill, waistcoat, and drab trousers, white stockings, and shoes, his grey head neatly combed, his legs uncrossed before him, his white handkerchief spread on his knees, and his hands on his thighs. My spirits called him Decency; he occupied this seat morning and afternoon invariably, except when out walking or at meals, when he took a turn or two up and down one side of the yard. He was a Dr. S——. I heard that he had been confined for twenty years, and had fought a duel. He was a quiet, silent, inoffensive man. I seldom heard him speak at all. Once only he spoke to me in the autumn, in a very squeaking voice when he showed me a withering leaf, and told me the mottled colours on it reminded him of an apple. One day I saw him go up stairs with a clean pair of blinds, I presume to fasten before his window; unfortunately Hobbs was in the way, caught him, made him come back, and snatched the blinds out of his hands, and rated him, saying, "I told you you should not go up, I'll take the blinds and throw them to the devil."

By the side of Mr. Decency, sat Captain P., another of the numerous family of Fitzherbert, that the spirits pointed out to me. When at last I asked what was the meaning of that name, and how so many came to bear it who had no relationship to each other, they replied, that Fitzherbert meant son of Herbert, and that these being spiritual bodies, were all sons of the almighty Herminet Herbert, whom I had seen in the three persons of the Trinity; Herminet Herbert, God Almighty; Herminet Herbert, Jesus Christ; and Herminet Herbert, the Holy Ghost; and also in Herminet Herbert, the Trinity in Unity; and that the name of Herbert, signified from the German, Lord of Hell. The Mr. Fitzherbert in question, was my spirit of family pride, and gentlemanly decorum. He was the most gentlemanly and courteous individual in the room; tall, well made, with dark hair and eye brows, good features, and a countenance inclined to ruddiness, always clean and neat, without affectation. For a long time his actions served as signs to me. He usually occupied the same seat in the room, occasionally leaving it to play at cards: he seemed to feel his situation very acutely; often appeared to labour with great internal struggles, when he muttered deep in his throat something that seemed to be a quotation from a tragedy of a very bloody import, leaning forward at the same time, and wringing and turning his hands clasped within each other. It was he who stated to me the reason of his silence, for he scarcely ever spoke. I saw Hobbs once asking him to read a letter for him. The young doctor told me he laboured under certain delusions similar to mine.

At dinner, a Captain W. usually sat at the bottom of the table. He was also a Mr. Fitzherbert, my spirit of joviality, and of joviality in contrition. He was a short, stout, red faced, in happier circumstances I might have said, jolly looking man; quiet, mild, inoffensive in his manners, silent like the rest. That which particularly characterized him, was his being constantly in the yard, where he walked up and down, generally not under cover, and in all weather, unless it literally poured with rain. I thought this a symptom of derangement, but when I came to myself and spoke to him, he told me that he did it to be alone, he did not like the noise or the exposure of the common room. Besides this I may add, it was some occupation even to use the legs. This poor man had served in the Peninsula. He answered any question I put to him and with perfect good sense, great deliberation, and much agitation. I ceased to speak with him as he never offered to begin conversation with me, and seeing him apparently in the possession of all his faculties, I judged that he might have reason for finding discourse painful, particularly with a stranger.

Here let me observe, if you want any proof of the madness as well as cruelty of applying a system such as this to insane patients, where can you find one more perfect than in the fact, that you drive them in self-defence to conduct which in ordinary circumstances a man cannot fail to look upon as a sign of unsettled mind? You look upon the unfortunate object of your pretended concern, and of your occasional malevolence, with pity for irregularities and extravagances, which however singular, however extravagant, are alas in him but too reasonable, through your own unreasonableness; or putting him in circumstances of extraordinary trial; do you expect from him, from him whom you confine expressly for his weakness and deficiency, an example of fortitude, a pattern of self-denial, perhaps not to be found in the annals of human nature? By reason of your own conduct, your judgment if honest and scrupulous must be in ambiguity; for you can never tell if the patient's eccentricities, are the symptoms of his disorder, or the result of antipathy to the new circumstances in which you have placed him; and he, who is struggling against the guilty tyranny and oppression of the doctor; he who is dying daily to hope,—to life,—to the desire to exercise those qualities of the mind, which for the sake of woman endear a man to society, and society to man; he in whose breast the seeds even of a divine nature, in spite of your cruelty and contempt, rise to new life hourly, hourly to be crushed and murdered, acknowledges amongst the cruelest of his wrongs, and the hardest of his chains, that he must either tempt his nature to bear more than he can endure, or be condemned as insane, for actions and conduct arising from the faultiness of the conduct pursued towards him, the childishness of those who deal with him, and judge of him, forgetting his actual situation. To prefer walking in a cold drizzling rain, to sitting by a warm fire side, were folly, if your kindness were not coupled with that mockery, which makes the inclemency of the season and weather comparatively less cruel. To be silent and incommunicative is a singularity; but that singularity becomes reasonable, when a man is denied liberty of expression and action, and confined with perfect strangers, amidst those whose interest it is to suspect and pervert his ways; aware of that which you, enthroned in the conceit of a more sound understanding, are daily forgetting, that the weakness of his mind renders it peculiarly improper for him to open the secrets of his heart to men with whom he has even no acquaintance. To halloo, to bawl, to romp, to play the fool, are in ordinary life, signs of irregularity, but they become necessary to men placed in our position, to disguise or drown feelings for which we have no relief; too great for expression, too sacred for the prying eye of impertinent, impudent, and malevolent curiosity. I will be bound to say that the greatest part of the violence that occurs in lunatic asylums is to be attributed to the conduct of those who are dealing with the disease, not to the disease itself; and that that behaviour which is usually pointed out by the doctor to the visitors as the symptoms of the complaint for which the patient is confined, is generally more or less a reasonable, and certainly a natural result, of that confinement, and its particular refinements in cruelty; for all have their select and exquisite moral and mental, if not bodily, tortures.

Captain W. was a man of a humble and humbled mind, susceptible, tender; the agitation of his feelings was often visible, in the trembling of his hands and arms. I used at first to kneel to him at night, to be saved from the tortures I thought prepared for me.

Mr. A. was a young man—fair, slight, quiet-mannered, stupid, good-tempered. He used to have novels lent to him, which he read usually whilst standing under the alcove in the yard—he put them by in the cupboard. I understood, on his remonstrating with me or another for taking the volume, that if he did not take care of them they would be taken away: so childish was our treatment, and so absurd. Was it in the first place more essential, that the only recreation and occupation by which a young gentleman could be called awhile from himself, and from contemplating his unfortunate position, should be secured to him; or that a novel in boards should be defaced—the price of which, after all, might be set down in the yearly accounts, in more perfect imitation of the private school system. Hobbs took away my books; but they were restored to me, when I complained of it, with an injunction to take care of them. I felt astonished and disgusted to be treated so like a child. But when I consider the propriety of the injunction, I ask, how were we to guard our effects, who had not so much as a drawer with a key to it, not even what boys have at school, a private locker. Oh! it is revolting to conceive this degrading treatment possible, and this in the midst of grown up Christian people, under a grown up old Quaker doctor, under the noses and eyes of big, bullying, grown up national church *justices*. It is revolting. It makes even this language, discreditable as it might be on other subjects—creditable, through the immensity of their folly, heedlessness, or *"supercherie."* Yes, I say "supercherie," for the magistrates know well whether they are doing their duty, or affecting to do it. And if they reply, we act according to the statute; I answer, very well, gentlemen, then we'll look out for the making of some statute that will aid humanity, at the expense of your lauded indifference.

But again, to defend our property or trusts in a room full of madmen, where we were often left alone without the servants, and where we were confined ourselves with them, as too dangerous for society with all its understanding and force to cope with; too likely to invade the rights of others! He whose predisposition to violence was feared, exposed to collision in defence of his honour, and that amongst those shut up for their likelihood to invade honour!

Mr. A. conversed rationally, and joked with other patients. The spirits told me he was my brother D——, and my brother D.'s spirit of contrition. His countenance often wore the appearance of great lasciviousness. One day I recollect his standing by me with Mr. J., and quizzing me whilst manacled in the niche, when the other patients were out. He was an amiable young man, he went away in the autumn to Dublin, with Honesty, a kind and respectful servant. Long time before he went, the young doctor used to come and speak to him of his intended departure, and letters received. At last, to a question of Mr. J. as to whether he was going, he replied with a forced laugh, "that he did not believe he was going at all;" expressing himself contemptuously of the doctor —that he only came to sift him, and to pry into his feelings. Young Mr. J. replied quietly, "do you think so, I think you are going." "I don't," replied Mr. A., and resumed the novel he was reading.

Captain ——, the gentleman whom my spirits called "the Lord Jehovah supremely omnipotent, the Trinity in unity," incorporate under the form of Mr. Waldony, Benevolence, &c. was a stout, good-humoured, elderly man, at times even handsome. He wore a suit of blue clothes, the skirts wide and old fashioned. He was the most trusted of all. I never saw any irreguarity in his conduct, and once or twice I heard the servants say they looked to him to put down any disturbance in their absence. At times, however, he became agonized, and inflamed in the face, his features distorted, and he would lean forwards and thrust a handkerchief in his mouth, as if to stifle his feelings. It was then my spirits told me he was suffocating for me. He used to sit smoking, with his hands in his pockets, or play at cards, or read the papers. It was he that asked my pardon for assisting in the beginning to put me into the strait waistcoat: and when I was leaving the madhouse, he told me twice or thrice he should be ready to give evidence, if I called upon him as to my peculiar ill treatment; which he said had been very bad. He often used to joke good-humouredly with me, to show me kindness, and when under delusion I seized him to wrestle with him, he used to take it in sport, seize me by the collar, and shake me. He was a Roman Catholic; but they called him an infidel: as a Roman Catholic, he did not attend the chapel. I imagine he was a Deist. He used to take away the Bible from me, saying, "you have read enough of it; it is that which brought you here." I thought it strange that the Lord Jehovah took away his own word from me: but my spirits said, that since the redemption, all was changed, and that word was no longer necessary. I obeyed; but I did not understand. When I knelt to him as the Lord Jehovah, and to Herminet Herbert as Jesus Christ, in the evening, they would kneel before me in fun, which puzzled me extremely. Was this the goodness and condescension of the Lord? But my spirits told me the Lord took off my manner, and not the matter of my address. One day, on my calling him Jehovah, he replied with great promptitude, "Well! I *am* the Jehovah." I was constantly deluded to think that he, as my heavenly Father, would take me back to E——, where my family resided. Many absurdities did I attempt to perform in this hope. By ill luck he had resided in that neighbourhood when a boy, and knew all the lanes and houses about. He talked to me of lanes in which he had seen little groups of angels in the trees: this I was simple enough to believe; and all his remarks tended to confirm my deceptions.

One afternoon, I was left alone with him when yet fastened up; he brought three chairs, and lay down upon them, near me; holding in his hands a book or a paper from which he read. My spirits told me it was a delusion; that it was my fault if I did not mount to heavenly places, and see other things around me. They desired me to listen, and I heard two voices, one of Captain ——, reading the paper in a low voice to himself, another of a spirit from the same mouth, whispering things spiritual.

Mr. J. was the youngest patient in the room, and in my opinion the most cruelly treated. A young, gentlemanly, active, little man. I saw him occasionally naked in the bath, he was lightly and gracefully made. His hair was light, his face pale, his features plain; but at times his countenance was divine; at times, he looked dirty, sallow, mean, and loathsome. He used to talk a great deal and ask the other patients questions, or make remarks likely to offend, and impertinent, but, in my opinion, the utterance of a spirit of discernment or of divination. He used language figuratively, but I was not always able to understand his drift. He would ask, "have you brushed your coat this morning?" "will you let me brush your hat for you? are those shoes you have got on?" often he said to me, "do you fence?" I was so stupid as to take his questions simply at first; and I replied to him, that I had had lessons from Angelo; he then rejoined, "Angelo! aye, Angelo, they say Angelo fences well; for my part, I think he never had a foil in his hand in his life." Looking up into the sky once, he said to me, "do you see that beautiful woman?" He occasionally alluded to the doctrines of faith and good works; and I understood from him or others that he had belonged to a society of young men in Cambridge, who used language in a figurative manner, and held wild notions. I felt that he had meddled with matters too high for him. I need not say that no one appeared to comprehend him. Though all showed a dislike to his remarks, as if they knew they were being spoken *at*, as well as spoken *to*. Hobbs used to act and look as if he suspected that there was a method in his madness; and I think Mr. Waldony knew as much, though he would not acknowledge it.

He often stood by me, when I was fastened up, and made allusions to my situation, asking me, have you been at your father's house this morning? do you make no efforts to get out from there, Mr. ———. Now the only thing I did besides singing aloud, hallooing (for which I got rated and trounced or flanked by the servant's duster) was to try and twist my neck, or to suffocate myself by pressing my nostrils against a small handle of wood fixed in the wall, which served as an arm to the seat in the niche. I imagined that he rebuked me, for not having yet executed my purpose, through cowardice and insincerity.

My spirits told me this was my youngest brother. I understood them literally at first, and I was perplexed because I could see but an imperfect resemblance in the features. But I was told that I did not like to see him; and therefore could not. Afterwards he was pointed out to me as my younger brother's Honesty; and I acknowledged a resemblance in character. He was allowed to remain with me alone up stairs, when I sat in the wicker chair after the opening of my temporal artery. One day, when I was at liberty, and the servants were gone out walking with most of the other patients, I sat at the table, after having attempted to play a game of drafts with him, in which we did not succeed. I then began reading, and he sat down opposite to me, making observations on me aloud, which appeared to be condemnatory of me, and reflecting on my conduct. My spirits desired me to reply to them, or to leave the room. But I would not, and I contended against the spirits that called me out, if I remember, to defend my honour, obstinately resolved to do nothing till I was reduced to a state of the meanest and most debasing feelings. I sat, through his remarks, in a spirit of malignity towards him for his impudence, and towards my Maker, resolved not to give up my position, for after being wearied and deluded by contradictory and unintelligible commands, I at times avenged myself by a complete revolt. A few days afterwards, whilst standing on the bank in the yard reading, I saw him coming out of the saloon, and walk down the alcove, his countenance was like that of Hyperion. He observed me, took displeasure at my demeanour, and halted, making a remark. My spirits told me if I did not change my place or attitude, I should ruin his state of mind, and drive him to hell: for the love of God to change my place. I recollected the afternoon before mentioned, when he drove me to hell; and maintained my position, replying, that God who had insulted me through him, and had not protected me, might now protect him; in a few minutes he went down the yard—in appearance to me a devil.

He was often severely handled. He and Mr. J. the clergyman, were made to use the same indecent shower bath I was myself exposed to. I am afraid to say how long he was confined to the backyard, without the privilege of exercise or of change of scene in accompanying us out walking: but I fear during the whole summer, he did not walk out so much as twenty-one days. A spirited, active, intelligent young man! I saw him once ask the servant to allow him to go out with tears in his eyes: but his hat was taken away from him, and the door locked in his face. Once he was not allowed to go out for ill conduct to myself, which Hobbs observed, for Hobbs often defended me from his impertinent intrusions. I would willingly have staid at home for him to go out, but I could not explain or express myself; and though his keen observations insulted me, I know he spoke to me the condemnation of a spirit in him, to which he was sincere, although I did not altogether understand him, for I had no time or place for reflection, or for self-examination; and my thoughts were too much confused. I was told his disorderly conduct prevented the keeper taking him out, and at the latter end of the year, when a powerful young lad whom I named Simplicity and Honesty, came to wait on us, there being then thirteen or fourteen patients in the room, I saw he was fastened to the lad's arm out walking, and struggling to get away from him. When left alone in the yard, he amused himself with picking up stones, climbing up into a small tree and sitting there looking over the country, and one day he picked nearly all the leaves off this tree.

I remember one day his shying small stones with great force in front of the lunatics' faces who were walking under the alcove; but I observed the stones never hit any one, and we were too near to be missed if he had meant us any harm. He cut at my legs with a knife under the table, but still to intimidate, not to do mischief, for he had opportunity to hurt me if he had designed it, before I changed my seat. I loved the young man, and one day by command of the spirits, I laid my head in his bosom, on the bench in the yard, but I could not understand the mind of the spirit in him. Towards the end of the year, I was provoked to strike him twice. One winter evening I was seated by the fire, reading a speech of my eldest brother, when my manner offended him who was sitting at the corner of the fire, on my right-hand side. He asked me with a sneer, "is that your speech or your brother's, sir," and on my making no reply, he alluded as the doctor had done once before, to my father's death. I was provoked to smite him over the lips with the pamphlet; he rose up sparring, and I rose and knocked him down. The servant coming in, and hearing the origin of the quarrel took my side; he went out of the room. I was applauded. The scene reminded me of passages in Roderick Random; and I was full of grief.

Another evening in January, after I had been removed up stairs, and had been disputing with the doctor, and with my family, and had also received that treatment of my letters, and the replies, which exasperated me so much, and having had no exercise during the day, I went down to walk in the yard. Mr. J. took offence at me and shouldered me in passing two or three times. I took an attitude of preparation when he next came to me, he halted, and began sparring again; I was in no humour for sport, and fearing him, I struck him in the face, and gave him a bloody nose. His blood was very black. I am truly sorry for these blows, for I do not think now the young man designed to hurt me, but he was obeying a spirit of frolic and gaiety; on neither occasion did he offer to strike me again; but I could not command myself, being then desperate.

I have seen this young lad occasionally cleaning the shoes and knives in the knife hole, under the alcove; he always acted in a fitful manner, as if guided like myself by spiritual direction. When I began planning my escape, I observed him narrowly inspecting and considering the same points that I examined. When my spirits desired me to sing in the room, he stood by me and took up the air I began, or the song I was trying after, so as to help my memory. One day when I came home from walking, in the midst of the other gentlemen, I observed Mr. J. standing on the opposite side of the table at the further end. Hobbs passed behind me and along that side of the table, advancing towards him. I saw no violence or impropriety of conduct on his part, but in a minute a scuffle ensued between him and his keeper. During the whole of the struggle Mr. J. only exercised a passive resistance; determined, with great coolness to oppose and resist force, but not to exercise violence in return. He was dragged with extreme rudeness, resisting mightily, into the yard, and then down the alcove to a wooden seat, to which he was often manacled by the right wrist. I followed, desired by my spirits to take Mr. Fazakerley's position in the alcove as usual. The servant wanted to fasten Mr. J. on the seat by the manacle. Mr. J. resisted. The rascal got the young gentleman down on the bench, and whilst he vigorously, but still calmly, and only defensively struggled against him, seized him round the throat and strangled him. I was extremely excited, frightened, and grieved; for not having seen any cause for the attack upon the young man, indeed there had not been time for any, I more readily believed the voices that told me he was suffering for me, &c. And when I saw his bloated and inflamed cheeks, and the eyes starting out of the sockets, I offered to do any thing to rescue him. My spirits desired me to whirl myself round and round as fast as I could, which I did till I staggered against the wall, and nearly fell on the stone pavement. I attempted it a second time, being accused by my spirits of cowardice and insincerity; but either I really was afraid of a fall, or other sensations made me cease. The habitual submission of my spirit was such that I did not once think of attacking the servant. Now had I been in my sound senses I might have rushed on the man, seized him unawares, and dashed his head against the pavement. I speak as a man; for who can control his passion under every excitement, and what is nobler than to resent and punish cruel and brutal oppression? Then that which to a free man would have been counted an act of justifiable homicide in defence of a fellow creature, or at least but as an act of manslaughter, would have doomed me to perpetual banishment from society, as a madman, though an act noble in proportion to the danger that threatened me, whether I failed or succeeded. There are those in the world, I know, who will cruelly and coldly reply, that there was a difference, inasmuch as *the keeper was doing his duty;* and that at any rate to interfere in my case, would have proved my madness. These are the doctor's true friends. Vipers! I only hope I may catch them in the discharge of this *duty,* as I now am; and I will try to enlighten their consciences. When again I reflected on the brutal treatment which was attempted also on myself; I exclaimed, good God! but what must a man expect, even though not a surgeon, at the blood being thus forced up and coagulated in a lunatic's head. But with this shocking scene I must close my day's labour; painful, too painful at all times, but in this case, too much for me to reflect on patiently. God grant that I may not have undertaken this too late to do good to those I have left behind me!

Captain W. came into the common room in the summer time: when he first entered and peeped into the yard, he appeared to me as a son of Mr. Stuart Wortley's, a schoolfellow and a friend of my fourth brother; again he re-entered from the yard, and I saw another of my schoolfellows, an Irishman and one of my friends. The likeness was so strong that I called out the names each time involuntarily. Mr. F. F. then introduced him to me as Captain W.; but having seen him before under the countenances of my friends, I did not believe him, but rather my spirits. He was a talkative young man of a religious mind, but slovenly. He told me that he had been obliged to leave his regiment on account of the state of his mind, and that his was a case of love madness. I said to him, if so, why not show more respect for his person, for the sake of his lady; he replied, oh! it did not signify here, in the world it signified, but what did it matter now? what were we sent here for? I thought it mattered here more than elsewhere, for he was not likely to get out unless he showed attention to his person. He was fully aware of his position. He had come with his father, and had heard the arrangements made for him, which he detailed to me one day when complaining about pocket handkerchiefs not being supplied to him. I was entirely ignorant on what footing I was placed there. It was he that quizzed and terrified the simple old Quaker. He told me one day that he had attempted to make away with himself from the bars of a window upstairs; he used to talk of suicide openly, which was painful to hear. As I came gradually to my right mind, I used to burst into fits of laughter, at the discovery of the absurdity of my delusions, and of the still grosser absurdity of the conduct pursued towards me and the other patients; for at one time I could not control my humour, at another my anger; for I said, if it were only ridiculous, but now it is grossly cruel, selfish, and disgusting. Captain W. observing this, told me I should never get out of confinement, it was invariably observed that lunatics who laughed excessively, were incurable. I thought to myself, I'll not only get out, but laugh at you too into the bargain, good gentleman.

In the autumn, a respectable, silver haired, old clergyman, was added to our number. He was a tight, neat, busy, little man, and behaved, during the whole of his sojourn amongst us, with great decorum. He tried even to introduce the custom of saying grace at dinner, but it did not succeed. I saw no marks of insanity in him except at meals. The first time he sat down to dine with us, he refused his food, and in the presence of us all, for he was then sitting at the right side of the table, I was at the head of it; Hobbs seized him, and forced the victuals down his throat. It was a disgusting and frightful sight, to see the old man trembling, resisting, and to hear his suffocated sobs and cries. This scene was repeated several times at breakfast and dinner. At last the old gentleman was considered to be in his senses, and went to church to give thanks for what was called his recovery, before he went away. This patient talked to me sensibly and rationally, he also worked with me in the shrubbery. One afternoon in the yard, he began praising Dr. F.'s asylum, the kindness, the humanity of the treatment. I replied, that I begged leave to differ with him in toto.

He asked me for an example of conduct contrary to his opinions. I begged his pardon if I wounded his feelings by mentioning his own case; I asked if it was respectful to his age or to his profession, that he should have been so exposed before us, even if it were necessary to force his food down his gullet; and if it were considerate or humane to the spectators in any sense, but more especially considering their state as lunatic and nervous patients. He never spoke to me afterwards of the humanity of the asylum.

In truth, the humanity of the asylum consisted in the conduct of the patients, not in that of the system and of its agents, for, had the patients felt or manifested half the indignation that nature or honour required of them, they would probably have been half murdered if not wholly so.

After the entrance of the Rev. Mr. ——, another Captain came in. He was a slovenly, imbecile, man, stooped very much, and laughed a great deal to himself. I understood that he had been removed from another asylum. I recollect nothing particularly of him, but that he flew out into very high words at tea one evening when I was left behind the other gentlemen gobbling my bread and butter, and mixing with it salt, pepper, and mustard, from a cupboard, in obedience to my spirits; he left the table saying, that he would not sit at it if I did not behave as a gentleman; I made no reply, but I was astonished at his interference; I felt, so long as the servants do not entertain the same opinion it matters very little to me here what you may think. I shall obey my spirits, do what you will with yours.

In the autumn, another elderly man was ushered one evening into the common room by one of the young doctors; it was immediately after the riots at Bristol. After a few words he was left alone. He was a decent, grey headed, short, hard featured, stubborn man, and appeared in every respect to be of sound mind. I imagined he was a gentleman who had come to visit one of the patients. My ideas were soon set right. It was towards tea time, and when he sat down at the table, he asked in a decided tone for some coffee; his request was at first met with silence; he repeated it, then Marshall, whom I called Sincerity, replied, "Oh! there is no coffee here, the tea is good enough for you." I thought, you have a severe lesson to learn, sir. The old man was of a very active body and mind. He had no employment, no one to converse with. At first he talked a great deal, with some wit; then he began to play tricks and was scouted; then his mind completely gave way: he used to go into the yard and daub himself with red soil calling it paint, and in a few weeks he was confined as I had been, in a straight waistcoat, upon the self-same seat, in the niche. His fall was rapid and shocking. One day before he was fastened up, whilst walking in the alcove, begrimed with dirt, and playing his pranks, Marshall ran behind him, and in joke, hit him a violent blow in the small of the back; the old man was put to great pain, for he said he had long had a complaint in the kidneys.

He was stiff in his joints from old age; when confined in the niche, he did not lose his spirits, but was still the noisiest and most talkative of us all; so that Captain W. asking us once which was the happiest man of us all, replied when all were silent, "old Mr. ——;" but I knew he was mistaken, and mistook spirits for happiness: the noise which men resort to, to hide themselves from themselves, and from one another, for real gaiety. He found out my name, and addressed me with a kind of forced and vulgar familiarity: he told me he was a merchant of the city of Bristol, and that one of his ancestors or relations had married a relation of my uncle, Sir John ——, whose family were of Somersetshire. He was a fine old man and I wondered at so much fun and enterprise in age, when youth seemed so supine.

He had originally been supercargo in an East Indian ship, and had visited China. One day he showed me a privet leaf, saying it was a tea leaf, by which I understood his spirit meant it resembled though he may have intended that it was, a tea leaf. He pretended to know a great deal, and to be able by skimming over a book, to acquire its contents. He asked me to show him a pamphlet I was reading, in order to give a specimen of his talent; but he was not quiet; he did it to hide from others his own feelings, and to escape from his own ennui.

The treatment I had endured was shameful, but yet I was a young man. The treatment of this old man was horrible. All day long he was confined as I had been, on a wooden seat, amidst noise, insult, flippancy, and confusion. The common wants of nature were neglected in him. Oh! it was shocking. Of an evening, at his request, a request unheeded by Marshall the servant present, I held the box into which patients that smoke spate, for him as an urinal, emptying it afterwards in the yard. Often he was without even this decent aid. After sitting a whole day, in the evening I heard him begging for one of the hair cushions of the chairs, to put under him; no one attended to him; I did: the servant desired me not to do it, but I gave it to him. One Sunday young Mr. J. commenced flanking at his legs with a duster; I was so grieved that I put myself before him, to cover him, receiving the blows. I did not offer to strike Mr. J. for then I would not have lifted my hand voluntarily against any man, considering his body as the Lord's temple; but watching my opportunity, I snatched the duster away, gave it to Captain W. to keep, and went out of the room. The old man was grateful.

When I received and answered my letters, he used to ask me for pen and ink, pretending to write or direct a letter himself, but scrawling nonsense. He often inquired if there was no letter for him, and was disappointed and grieved in silence that there was none. He expected one from his child. I knew he would have to wait long. At last one came, and he received it eagerly.

One night I went up stairs to bed alone, and heard him call to me, for he slept in a room opening into the same passage: the servant not being yet with me, I went into his room. He was lying almost naked on the bed strapped down as I had been, but with a belt over his belly. He asked me I think for some water, which I gave him, and for other assistance which I was unable to render him; then I got to my own room not to be observed. He used to defile his bed night after night, for which the servants rated him, but I do not know that they struck him. Probably in behaving so he acted under a delusion, or nature gave way to necessity, having been controlled in the day-time from delusion; perhaps also he was neglected.

On a Sunday evening, about three weeks after his entrance, when all were gone to church but Mr. Waldony and myself, he being very restless, I was surprised to see him get up, and collecting hastily chairs together, attempt to scale the alcove at the only feasible point for effecting an escape. Having formed as he thought his ladder he began changing his coat, to put on that of another. I said nothing but watched him, for he was putting in practice the scheme I had thought upon, and I thought if he succeeded I would be after him, if not, I was not suspected. One of the servants came in just as he was mounting.

Before I left the asylum, I was one day ordered to go down into the common room whilst Hobbs prepared to walk out with me, for then I used to walk out alone in a retired walk behind the kitchen garden. The room stank abominably; the rest of the gentlemen were in it, I inquired the cause, and I found it was owing to this old patient, who was seated at the end of the room tied up in his niche, not having had his bodily necessities attended to; yet he was left there an offence to himself and an insult to the other gentlemen. Once the same accident happened to myself, when the three humaner servants waited on us; but I was relieved from my situation as soon as they discovered it. I have suspected since that my dinner had been drugged.

I have already mentioned that I began writing to my family in November, to complain of the treatment which had been pursued towards me, and to find out to whom the blame was to be imputed. At the same time I demanded a private apartment, with a servant of my own choosing: that letter was opened and detained, in opposition to my wishes. I then wrote concisely to my eldest brother, that he might desire my letter to be given up to him, and insist upon my correspondence with my family being respected. The two letters were forwarded together. I was not sanguine in the expectation of obtaining my demand. I replied thus, if my family have been guilty of so great folly, as to submit me to such mismanagement, contrary to nature, reason, and religion, there is no folly they may not be guilty of in respect of me: I was not surprised then as at a thing unexpected and impossible when my mother wrote to me word that she must be guided by the doctor as to my having a private apartment. I was still less surprised at a distinct refusal from *him*. Interest, prejudice, and pique, might influence his judgment; but I was astonished at the hardness of heart and

want of understanding that could make an affectionate and indul-
gent parent doubt the reasonableness of my request; particularly
when I knew that I was termed a nervous patient, and reflected
that for years my mother had suffered from extreme nervousness,
during which she could scarcely endure, and even forbade a newspaper being unfolded in her room; so greatly did she feel the need
of quiet. Now I am sure that next to myself, no one will more
acutely resent my ill treatment when she understands it, than my
mother, and it is fearful to think how an habitual hardening the
heart to misgivings of the mind respecting the trustworthiness of
other men, and a supine surrender of the judgment, and of the
dictates of honest feeling, to the impudent pretences of shallow
hearted swindlers, may betray individuals, and whole classes, to
the most shameful and inhuman acts of madness. Alas! it is too
true, the treatment I have described can only be that of madmen
or of villains. So opposite in nature to the end proposed!—I was
not however able to brook my disappointment, it drove me almost
mad through passion. Then it was that I struck the servant over
the eye, and wrestled with others; then it was also I struck Mr. J.;
then too, I foresaw and tried to prepare myself for all the difficulties and disappointments in the way of my obtaining my liberty
with honour, resting my only hope on the enlightened character
of the Lord High Chancellor, if by any means I might be able to
gain his ear: I thank God he left me this hope, it buoyed me up
though it proved partly false, my mind being blinded to the
estimate I had long before made of men of public character, viz.,
that they are men great in one line, but devoid of real understanding; because, deciding wilfully, they reject light that restrains
their activity, and contradicts their imperfect convictions.

In consequence of my striking the servant a blow, I was desired
to descend again, schoolboy fashion, into the common room, where
I wrote with a sprained thumb as well as I could, my second appeal
to my mother; in it I swore that I would have the life of one of the
servants if I were not removed from that madhouse before three
months were out. I could not patiently endure my situation, and
it was indifferent to me if I was confined for life, so as I could
avenge by blood the indignities I had been subjected to, and put

an end to an agonizing state of suspense. If I were myself slain or hanged, death brought a joyful release, and no disgrace can I care for, having drunk the bitterest draughts of ill deserved ignominy, and despising as I do the accursed folly of the world. Fortunately I detailed in that letter a part of those indignities: my pride was wounded in so doing, for I could not brook that advantage was to be taken of my misfortunes to doubt my honour, but under the English lunatic doctors and the English country magistrates, I was obliged at last to have every feeling brutalized. My family had not, or pretended not to have been aware of my ill treatment. My mother desired by return of post that I might have a private room, and in a short time I had one. Then the ideas of all around me seemed to have changed towards me: my meals were private and served to me as to a gentleman, the familiarity of the servants seemed to cease, and to my broken spirit the exertions made to comply with my demands seemed excessive.

Fortunately there was a worthy and elderly physician residing in my mother's parish, who had formerly had the care of insane patients; she applied to him. He was a sensible, honest, humane man, but too mistrustful of his own sound judgment. He advised my mother to attend to my desires immediately, but on account of my violent language he could not look with calmness on my having a private lodging, or being with a private family. I learnt this from his own lips a year afterwards. I then demonstrated to him the extreme folly as well as cruelty of the conduct which had been pursued towards me even in this instance, and against which I had protested and remonstrated again and again without effect, viz., that resolutions were taken as to the disposal of my person and property, and communicated to me with about as much ceremony as if I were a piece of furniture, an image of wood, incapable of desire or will as well as of judgment. Steps were taken, but the reasons never shown to me, God knows it, never. My mother wrote to me to say that I was to be removed from the madhouse I was in, and to be confined in another; where, or under whom, was not mentioned, or why. Had she mentioned her reasons for choosing another madhouse instead of a private lodging, I could have removed them immediately, and a long and painful

altercation might have been prevented. I was not a madman acting with indiscriminate violence, but I was exasperated by the
recollection of, and by actual suffering from insulting, degrading,
cruel treatment. I had no ill-will to any individual, but to those
concerned in the murder, the repeated murder of my spiritual and
moral nature. On the contrary, I was in disposition like a child,
in conduct, as I proved under these trying circumstances, calm and
deliberative until rendered desperate. My resolution even to take
the life of the keeper, though violent in expression, was determined
in resolution and feeling, it was the cry of outraged human nature,
not the victory of passion over right understanding. I still almost
feel over again what I then felt.

So little care was taken by my relations to be precise or ex-
planatory in their conduct towards me, that the previous letter I
received from my mother, desiring me a private apartment, merely
contained a refusal to remove me from the madhouse of Dr. F.: the
next told me that a private apartment was being prepared for me
in a madhouse elsewhere. By that time I had been again insulted
and injured by the forced use of the shower-bath and cold bath. I
considered my life in danger under insolent and violent servants,
malignant, prejudiced, and nettled physicians. The magistrates
called, and I claimed their interference: I stated that I was much
grieved to be compelled to appeal to them against my mother, but
that her conduct was so unjust that I was afraid I must look to
them for legal assistance if she did not answer my letter according
to my reasonable desires. They in a loose way promised me the
assistance of a lawyer, but had I needed one they left me the name
of no party to whom I could apply, and I must have waited three
months to make my next appeal. So the convalescent madman
who needs most help, is left most of all to his own resources; and
the doctors have ample time to drive him insane again, or to provoke him to acts of indiscretion, that may be construed into proofs
of derangement.

I now took up this attitude against my family. I argued that
although I was unsettled in my judgment and still partially lunatic, it did not give mankind or them any legal right to exercise a
brutal and tyrannical control over my will, without respect to the

nature of my calamity, and to the degree of restoration I had attained to. Instead of being treated as I was, *de haut en bas,* with complete contumely, no argument or address being made to my understanding, I conceived that my being a lunatic required on the contrary the more scrupulousness on their part, the more caution, openness, and explanation. That it was their duty to make my way more straight and clear before me because I was by my disease already sufficiently prone to delusion, and even to unprovoked suspicion. So at least the doctors desire you to believe, but I question if the suspicions of lunatics are not often most sane, and engendered necessarily by the underhand dealings of others towards them. There is a distinction to be made between the suspicions of lunatics and that of lunacy. I considered that though surrendered by law to the charge of a physician, it was to be protected, and to be prevented from injuring others, not to lay me open helpless and defenceless to his villanies, and his treachery; to the violence of his servants, or to experiments of his quackery upon my constitution and feelings under the pretence of cure, and that even if it were so, the law could not justify him in a system brutally perverse and contrary to all science, surgical or moral; a system unnatural and impudent; that the silence of the law could not be an excuse for it, if no patient had hitherto had understanding or courage to plead against it. I determined therefore for safety, for example's sake, and for revenge to appeal to the law against my physician. I avowed the three motives.

In order to succeed I desired first legal assistance to set forth my case and to save my rights; secondly to be taken to London to be for a short time under the care of a surgeon who had known me from a child, that he witnessing my state of mind and body, and hearing my complaints, might be able to argue and to give evidence concerning the necessity of requiring me to use the cold bath, at that inclement season, the propriety of using force considering the degree of understanding I was restored to, and the danger to my health of body from the shock and cold, and to my mind from the needless excitement. These requests were denied. I then wrote to my mother, stating to her, that if she really was not aware of the cruelty of my situation, she had been deceived by Dr. F., and then might justly join me in demanding legal satisfaction, but that if she did not do so, I could not be reconciled to her, and must hold her also responsible to me at law, for she was certainly the most culpable. Moreover, that though I knew I was still lunatic, yet I knew too, from sad experience, that I was capable of taking care of myself in a more reasonable manner than the wretched physicians she confided in; that I was not a lunatic incapable of controlling myself, although I felt so sensible of my need of observation that I would not accept my liberty if it were given to me, but should place myself immediately under the eye of some one I could rely upon; but that if she insisted on placing me, where under pretence of observation, I should be defenceless, open to violence, impertinent intrusion, indelicate treatment, and deprived of tranquillity, peace, rest, and security, I should claim my freedom, though lunatic, as one not mischievous, and hold her responsible for my future detention.

In taking this resolution I was actuated also by the desire of convincing the consciences of my mother and of my family, to see the sin they had been guilty of. Knowing the terrors of the Lord, knowing what it was of horror to feel that repentance comes too late, I stood in awe of God if I did not rebuke them, and shocked at their doom if they should die unconvinced and hardened against my rebuke: for I call God to witness, although accused by my family at the instigation of the doctors of lunacy as if devoid of affection, I endured continual and deep agony of mind, affection and attachment, contending within me with feelings of duty and just wrath. The conduct I endured was not to be endured in life with patience: the stupidity of spiritual death alone submits to it quietly. The judgment that I came to, that it was my duty to sacrifice affection and attachment to the maintenance of my rights, and to rescue myself and others from treatment revolting to humanity, to enlighten the minds of others by bringing down condemnation on the guilty, even though that guilty one was my ———. I cannot write the word; and this, under the charge of being cruel and unnatural, to save the soul: this judgment may have been mistaken, but it was not that of a madman, and no man can rebuke me for it who has not passed through like extremities.

I might as well have appealed to the winds. I received letters from my elder brother and his wife, canting about submission, patience, and the Holy Spirit; to which I replied in mockery and disdain. I knew that my patience had been proved in a fire they could not have stood under for a moment; that it had not given way until they had neglected my representations, and made me desperate; and they talked to me of patience, ignorant of facts and circumstances, whose business it was to have humbled themselves and to have applied patiently for information to me. *They* wrote to me of the Holy Ghost by *whose* conduct I was driven well nigh, and at last altogether to blaspheme the holy name of God, and to doubt his Providence. *They* talked to me of my Heavenly Father's will, *who* if they had allowed their stubborn stupidity, and hypo-critical reliance on the doctor to have been pierced by one cry of agony, ought to have known that they were already guilty before my Heavenly Father of that perverse will by which I was aban-doned, through which I was destroyed, and wander about, the ruin of what I was, and to which I was still compelled to address threats, argument, and representation. Another wrote to me actually de-fending the doctor in opening my letters, taking the part of my enemy, and reasoning against me. I was so disgusted at his indeli-cacy and presumption, for he always wrote to me as if *he* knew what lunacy was, not I who had endured it, therein proving the stubborn and innate lunacy of human nature, rushing to give an opinion where nothing is known to found a right opinion upon; that I wrote on the note a few laconic lines to say, that I returned him his note, and that until he changed his mind and expressed his sorrow to me for having written it, I could not have any com-munion of spirit with him, and therefore desired not to speak with him.

When indeed I desired my correspondence to be respected, it was from feelings of delicacy towards my family, as much as to myself. But I met with no delicacy in return. I wonder at their insensibility, how that intelligent and sensitive souls can become so besotted. But I am wrong, human nature has yielded to the absurd and immodest assumptions of the papal church in regard of confession; there are other vipers as subtle. But others behaved in like manner. When I made my first appeal to the magistrates, in doing which, confined in a madhouse, recovering from lunacy, weakened by long sickness, I had to conciliate resentment and exasperation, with respect and filial duty, vindictive feelings, with affection; I had to speak in presence of nine or ten magistrates, servants, and doctors. None had the delicacy to withdraw, no one had the gentlemanly feeling to desire me to see them in private. They stared with impudent and unmeaning curiosity. Nay, I have one exception to make. Captain W., confined like me as a lunatic, left the room; he afterwards apologized to me for being in it, saying, he was unaware of what I was going to speak about, but that the moment he heard me he retired. I thanked him, and told him, that I should have been glad, amongst so many unfeeling, stupid, and suspicious judges, to have had one honest, clever, and gentlemanly witness to my complaints and demeanour.

At last the letter came to announce my mother's determination to remove me from that madhouse to another. I wrote immediately objecting to my person being bandied about across the country at the discretion of others, I knew not whither, without the slightest respect to my inclination or judgment. I demanded again a private lodging and a servant of my own choosing,* by which I meant, that I should have a voice in his appointment, and continuing with me, the only true safeguard against disrespectful conduct. I refused to accede to her desires; I held her responsible for my detention; and I desired that I might be placed in a neighbourhood where my name was known, and my personal character might be respected by the magistrates. I repeated my request to be brought to town if only for three weeks to see the surgeon alluded to above, and to take the advice of a lawyer; also to have my teeth attended to, which were in a state of decay, not having been washed for a whole year. I also prayed that whithersoever my journey, I might not be compelled to travel more than six hours a day: for I feared that fatigue and excitement might overcome me, my nerves being

---

* This expression was unfortunately mistaken, as if I wanted to have a servant of my own instead of selecting one of the doctor's; for this reason it was refused; but the reason was not communicated to me, or I might have explained it, instead of being condemned without knowing it, as absurd.

so shattered, my frame so weak. Learning afterwards that my elder brother was to remove me, I wrote a letter to him, rebuking him for his conduct to me, for his neglect of my letters, and inattention to my requests; I refused also my hand to him, and to speak to him unless he acknowledged his fault, and asked my pardon: I consider it my duty to deal truly by them, and I was obliged to act concisely, because I was often deprived of the power of speech, and could not trust to myself to moderate my expressions, or to them to respect me if I spoke in a broken, irregular manner. My spirits often counselled me to disguise all my resentment until I was clear of Dr. F.'s establishment. It might have been better for me: but then I replied, "I must play the hypocrite, which I cannot do long," and my mind shrunk at the idea of deceiving my own relations with a design to punish them, besides, I was not able to endure the treatment I received any longer, therefore I chose the straightforward path.

When they arrived, I returned to my other brother, as I had intended, the note he had written. I was amused, perplexed, and provoked at the same time by the familiarity of their demeanour towards me, in spite of my reserve. I understood my position immediately, and saw my little hope, and the great difficulties before me: that I had no chance of success so long as I argued with my relations alone. For why? they looked on me as a misguided child; but I despised them as dupes of their own conceit, and guilty of grosser lunacy and insanity in their dealings towards me without the excuse of derangement, than I had been the victim of in my trouble. A wise man can hardly accept or admit the rebuke of a wise man; how much less could my infatuated brothers admit the justice of the rebuke of one whom they condemned as lunatic without discrimination.

To check the misplaced familiarity of my elder brother, I asked him if he had received no letter from me, he said, yes, and I resumed my silence; but I think when we halted for the night, I found he alluded to a letter of a previous date. He then told me he had received no other, but that Dr. F. had just put into his hands two or three letters which he had as usual opened and detained. Alas! if these letters had been sent they might have changed my mother's mind, and saved her and my family from two years of wretched contention with me, and exposure, and myself from two years' cruel and unjust confinement. They as well as I reaped the bitter fruits of surrendering their judgments to the pre-posterous and impudent claims to confidence of ignorant and charlatan practitioners; and of neglecting the complaints of a lunatic relation, restored at that time to a purer and truer sense of religion and propriety than they possessed, although not cor-rect in all his understanding.

For by what right can a doctor presume to pry into the secrets of a patient's conscience, who is not only a perfect stranger to him, but also a gentleman—to overlook the affections and the desires of his heart? and what right have his relations to presume on their authority to betray a patient's and a gentleman's feelings into such hands? They confess themselves ignorant of the nature of the disease they handle; they show themselves wilfully so, and it stands to reason that as far as the mind and morals are concerned, they cannot pretend to so much fitness as the relations of the lunatic; moving as mine do in a higher class, educated to finer feelings and to use much more consideration. They neglect their duties even as surgeons or as physicians; the dictates of common sense they make light of; let them mind their own duties at least, before they trespass beyond their line. But their impudent presumption is beyond calculation. If any particular kindness had been shown to me, if any persuasion, exhortation, or investigation, had been diligently used towards me, then to pry into my secret griefs or follies, might have been excusable; the zeal, however misplaced, was consistent. But ruined in body and in mind, I was left to help myself out of the dilemma as I could, and what is more, surrounded with every difficulty. When too, in spite of their cruelty and exposure of me, my constitution triumphed over riot and severity, where peace and indulgence were required; and my mind by its own efforts, shook off the appalling chains of de-lusion: these wise, clever, at least cunning men, heaped every obstacle in my way to health, in my return to sound society. Climbing out of the well into which they had thrown me, the stones fell down upon me, wounding and crushing me in my ad-vance, or hurling me again to the bottom.

The clergymen of the established church ought to have the superintendence of the mental wants and infirmities of the deranged members of their communion, and the two offices of physician to the body and physician to the soul, distinct in nature, should be equally respected. Sovereigns in this country, their ministers, and the people have been guilty of a great crime in neglecting this important distinction, and the hierarchy have betrayed their office. Yet who can wonder at that who knows how they are appointed? A respectable clergyman, however, unless he were entitled by the ties of friendship or of affection, would not presume to do by treachery or by compulsion, that which these men do without any title; and in spite of the remonstrances of their patients. There can be only one excuse for a doctor opening the letters of his patients, and that is when the patient is without friends and without relations who take any interest in him. It is obvious, however, that it is unjust that the doctor should at any time have a summary control over the patient's correspondence, and where a patient has connexions, that in many respects, interference in the privacy of that correspondence may be improper; whatever mystery may hang over the origin of the disorder of any individual, whatever absurdities or worse than absurdities he may write, his relations are the most worthy to be first trusted with that mystery, and they ought to shield those absurdities and irregularities from the ridicule and from the officious scrutiny of strangers. They ought to judge after inspection, what parts of the correspondence may be communicated to the physician, and this not without self-respect and the respect due to the character and to the misfortunes of one who cannot control his feelings, and who exposes the nakedness of his heart, in a state of exasperation and of delusion.

When I left the doctor's parlour for the last time I bowed to the old man and Mr. F. F. without speaking. I shook hands with the other son, he was not to blame, and had shown me kindness. The eldest of the two maliciously replied; "Good bye, Mr. ——, I wish I could give you hopes of your recovery." A vile and cold speech towards me, and as it regarded my two unfortunate brothers: but they deserved it. My relations with Dr. F. were compulsory. Thank God I knew that I was recovering, and knew their hollowheartedness; therefore I was more shocked at the possibility of such expressions being used to a patient who might not be able to endure them, than I was myself discouraged, or disinclined to act upon the judgment I had formed of their conduct and of their principles.

SOLI DEO GLORIA.

CHAPTER XXVIII*

LETTERS.

[The following Letters will prove the state of my affections at this time towards my family—which my illness at least had not altered. They are also, to those who will credit me, deserving of attention as evidences of the reality of one species of inspiration—I saw, as upon the paper, every word and stroke almost, before I wrote it. I do not contend for the nature of that inspiration.]†

S—— P——L, [Spencer Perceval]

Brisslington, Nov. 29th [1831?].

I HAVE many thanks to give you for your last letter to me, and apologies I owe to you for not having replied to it. I wish you, however, to think a little more of my situation here. I wish you to consider my case a little more spiritually. I wish for change of scene, or a change of residence—a change of circumstances. Not that I am discontented or dissatisfied with the arrangements in Dr. F.'s asylum, though not altogether, for I ascribe them in the greatest part to a most minute and benevolent consideration of our wants, mental and temporal; though I do not subscribe to the judgment that has concluded in favour of their adoption.

I should feel glad for the use of my little Greek Testament,‡ and Hebrew Grammar, Lexicon, and Bible.

*   *   *

* From this chapter on, the text is from the 1840 volume (see Introduction, p. xxi. The heading "Letters" occurs near the beginning of Chapter IV of that volume. G.B.

† Double brackets are used to indicate Perceval's parenthetical remarks, as differentiated from the Editor's additions. G.B.

‡ I asked particularly for my Greek Testament and a Concordance I had —from a desire to have some object of attachment by me, which I seemed to long for. My brother brought me a new Testament and a new Concordance, but I felt no delight in them, and refused them because of his conduct.

I should be glad to hear from you as minute an account as you can give me of all I spoke or wrote (or whether I wrote any thing during my state of derangement in Dublin or Bristol) to you or to others, as far as you know, particularly with regard to my conduct towards you in the chaise as we came along from Bristol here, or in Bristol, or in Dublin; and with regard to any confessions whatsoever, &c., which I may have made to you.

I wish you also to give me as correct an idea as possible of the opinion you entertained respecting me, when you left me here, as to my state of mind; what you thought me to be; as also when you came here in July or June. This in order to further correspondence; and also in order to assist in clearing my ideas in certain moods of mind, and to lead to further disclosures probably towards you and others.

I wish also very much for information with regard to my mother's and brothers' and sisters' opinion of me; as also with regard to their spiritual state at present, particularly with regard to the Row Heresy.

I wish also —— to write to me sincerely what he thinks of me, or what he inferred of my condition, mental, spiritual, and religious, from my demeanour, language, and conversation.

I pray you to beseech him to do it, with earnest prayer to be guided by the Holy Spirit.

I received the other day (the 25th) a beautiful and kind letter from poor E—— A—— Perceval.

The cause of my madness, Spencer, is this: That all things about me do appear to me so beautiful and so lovely, through the Holy Spirit, which is upon me and in me, and through me unto them, and in them or upon them and through them unto me, that I do not know how to behave myself to any thing about me* as I should do, in a reasonable manner: and I have an inward tormentor and an outward tormentor, harassing and tormenting, reproving me for (being a hypocrite) hypocritising before them; for loving them too much, and not reproving them in spirit, or in word, or in demeanour; and at the same time accusing me, and taunting me, and ridiculing me, and agonizing me in a worse manner, for being uncharitable in all my attempts to reason in any way so as to come to any conclusion whatever, with regard to

---

* My state of mind was perhaps like that of those of whom we say all their "geese are swans." It may have arisen from a disinclination to acknowledge other realities, besides the beauties of the objects which attracted me; but it appeared to me at the time to be sincere, because I had no quiet and time to reflect, and to detect what I was really thinking about, what were my real feelings.

their real worth, merit, or actual spiritual state. Moreover, in attempting to do a duty of any kind, I am immediately assailed with doubts, and fears, and scruples, and anxiety of heart and mind, and body too at times; so that my nature, or a hypocritical fear upon me, makes me find that my nature shrinks from doing it. At the same time I feel it right, and that it must be done; and I can have no peace of mind, or heart, or conscience, unless it is done; at the same time, in doing it, I load my heart and conscience with agonies of mind and spirit. Even as I was writing to you my eyeballs seemed seared, and knives to be in my eyes. I will explain to you the reason of this. Spencer, you might have saved me from much of my agony on board-ship, and on my miserable, melancholy, horrible, agonizing bed, in Dublin and Bristol. You do not know what insanity is; but you are a spiritual man; and you should have weighed every thought, every word, every motion, every feature, and expression of my features, in Dublin. All I remember of you is, that your conduct was most affectionate towards me; but you could have done more for me; for you believed the miraculous power of God Almighty to preserve his elect.

I threw* away the use or exercise of my judgment, or rather power of reasoning, or gave it up, or fancied that, and believed that, I had given it up, through horror (as I believe till this moment in part): a fear, alarm, and terror united, and yielding myself up to sloth. The exercise of my reason, it has now become apparent to me, or, I believe—I should almost venture to say—it has been revealed to me.—Pity me, Spencer, that I cannot write distinctly—my circumstances I feel and find, in the present state of my mind, most cruel.† . . .

After some delay, I procured paper to write another, a letter which I addressed to my mother. The foul copy runs as follows; but the one sent differed probably in many points:

Brisslington, December 11, 1831.

Dearest Mother,

I was very glad to receive your last letter, as I feared you might have been offended by my last, or have misunderstood my meaning, when I wrote to say that I found it painful to write.

The smell of your letters‡ has always brought me to a sound state of feeling, or rather has been a proof to me that I was in as

---

* I had written "through" instead of "threw," I observed upon it in the margin thus—"This is Lunacy. Inadvertence the world calls it."

† The part of this letter from "The cause of," was not sent if I remember rightly; and the beginning of it, perhaps, modified.

‡ My mother kept her letter-paper in a drawer with musk.

sound a state of mind as that I used to be in at Ealing and Harrow. For often I am miraculously, by which I mean, contrary to the common laws of nature, deprived of all power to smell at all.

I am not at all surprised that I am not yet in a state of mind to write coherently to you; nor have been restored to it, till lately, in any degree; as I have not been in circumstances or in society to which I have been at all accustomed; or which have been in any way suited to my habits of feelings or principles, as a gentleman—as a man of education—as a man of feeling—as a member of the outward and visible, or of the inward and spiritual church.

Herein I am compelled, in order to deal frankly and truly, and sincerely, to attribute some culpability to you, and much to poor Spencer; as you have, I conceive, heard, at all events, though you have not been (being afraid to judge for yourself) confessing to yourself, not only that it was materially likely to contribute to my discomfort, to wound and destroy my finest and most delicate feelings, (wherein I suppose you may have been consoling yourselves as a punishment, or eventually a cure for my former misconduct* in the parlour, the room in which I am now writing,) but that it was destructive in itself to the moral tone and spiritual frame of my mind. I feel confident that if you had confessed this to your Redeemer, you would not have been allowed to continue in error any longer respecting the unsuitableness of the society, manners, and manner of thinking of almost all around me, to the peculiar disposition of my mind, of which you, but still more Spencer Perceval was fully aware.

As far as I can at present understand it, I can hardly conceive any thing more damnable than Dr. F.'s plan in some of the details; at the same time they are to be pitied, for they do not consult scripture, but their own experience alone; and they do not know whose ministers they are when they depart from the truth, from ideas of meaning well.

---

* After what I have written, I need scarcely observe, that the idea of punishing lunatics is wicked and preposterous. I will not, however, shock the prejudices of *humanity*, and the interests of a certain class in society, by asserting this proposition too roundly. The idea of punishing *all* lunatics, then, is wicked and preposterous. I think society will agree with me that it should not be left to doctors and their servants to decide which. I suspect it will be found that women, old men, and children, are the best guards of violent lunatics, if their situation is respected. But if force is necessary, then two or three able men should be at hand to overpower the patient immediately, and to prevent the use of unnecessary violence, arising from the fear or spite of the person resisting him. There is a great difference between force applied to prevent an improper action, and blows given, or language used to correct the patient for doing that which his delusions tell him it is his duty to do.

[Here the spirit guided my hand to write some characters resembling the Arabic, and the name of one of my sisters, who had studied Persian when a girl; and I find these words interlined: I may say with Pontius Pilate, "What I have written, I have written."]

I have written a more full account of my feelings to Spencer, he will communicate to you my wishes with regard to my removal from hence; also with regard to my request to have a letter in pencil, written to me by Mary Campbell, which I used to carry about my person in Dublin, sought for, and I now earnestly request opened (if he will read it in diligent faith and prayer to understand and respect it), by him or D—— alone; and not show it to —— —— or to —— ——, and then sealed and taken great care of till I can receive it from his own hand, as I hope to see him soon, before I go to E—— [Ealing] or to my future abode.

To-day, as I was going to write to you, the domestic came and said to myself and to an old clergyman who was writing with me, "I want the ink, sir, if you please." He took my pen out of ——, I naturally, through the goodness of Christ Jesus to me, yielded it instantly, putting my pen into the inkstandish—for it was one of those old leaden things you see in schools, or counting-houses. I was afterwards reproved by my conscience for yielding it prematurely, as, if I was in a right state of mind I should have rebuked him in manner, or by word of mouth. If I understand the system of Dr. Fox's house now, we are allowed to go on as pigs till we come to a right state of mind. That is to say, the lunatic, under which term is of necessity included the idea of a person unwilling, except at intervals, or unable to judge for himself,—for some infliction of Divine Providence, which he cannot without divine assistance overcome, and therefore under the necessity of having others to think for him,—is at the same time under circumstances of peculiar perplexity to his understanding, because he is treated with a mixture of benevolence and insult at the same time (for I consider outward manner and innuendoes, and deprivation of personal liberty, and conveniences to which one has been accustomed, a more cruel method of insulting even than open violence, and personal rating and abuse)—is, I repeat, at the same time visited with all the consequences of his inability to reason for his own self, or (rather as it appears to me in many instances) for his Maker's glory, as if he had a finer and superior judgment and discernment than those to whose control and superintendence he is subjected; and this under a state of mind already too heavily laden with sorrow and oppression, and doubts and wounds, and anxieties, to be able to control his feelings amidst the rubs of general society; having usually a nobler mind, probably, than half the world of tergiversant, unreflecting hypocrites around him, he is made a lunatic because he sees consequences or difficulties in actions from which he shrinks, and which he considers himself unprepared to overcome, which the world are lunatically blind to, because they will not reason for their Maker's honour at all.

I say we are allowed to go on in a state of want even of personal liberty and clothing, till we are sensible of not being treated as we are at least accustomed to be treated; and then—being sensible that we are in a state of mind and body too, which requires some control and some restraint, and some deprivation at least, if not punishment—we are supposed to be capable of reasoning exactly as to how far we may be intended to consider ourselves entitled to those indulgences or necessaries of life, and to that liberty to which we have been born, as well as to find out in what spirit we have been deprived of them. Now pray do consider the blasphemous and damnable way in which you must, and Spencer must, and Dr. Fox must be thinking of lunatics, in considering us and treating us as reasonable beings, and shutting us up and dealing towards us under the idea—a being deprived of the power of reason: when I assure you that for a long time I considered it contrary to my conscience to speak at all, and unable to obey my Maker excepting in making use of the most extraordinary phrases and appellations; and it only just now struck me, with a force of truth, that my duty at least most evidently was to have inquired (supposing my conscience allowed me) of Dr. Fox, what was the intention of their conduct and arrangements towards me.

What led me to this consideration was the fact of having been led by my Saviour to consider whether I and the gentleman who was with me, were not in fact trespassing against good manners in making use of another Christian's property without considering whose it was (if the old clergyman was not considering it) for I was not; and whether it was not our duty to expect or to request to be provided with other means of writing, as I am in doubt now, whether I am not indebted to the domestic's bounty for using the ink and inkstand. This is the perplexity of feeling to which I am still, and have been often reduced; murdered as I have been at the same time by the consciousness that I am at intervals capable of judging minutely for mine own wants and those of others, and that I am consequently suspecting others uncharitably, sometimes, in consequence of inability to control my feelings in ill-humour, because in doubt and perplexity, wearied out of all patience: and myself suppose myself to be suspected of an indecent disregard to my own best interests.

This arises from what I consider in the world sinful in a system towards lunatics, who are often simpletons; damnable in the extreme, for it is a contradiction of the first principles of your reasoning concerning lunatics; it is an express violation of that rule, "do no evil that good may come;" and that other word of light to those who will apply it to themselves, *"all false ways I utterly abhor."* This is communicated to me of the infinite goodness of my God, whose servant I am, though I have been, I know now too truly, delivered over to our infernal enemy—in whose abodes of misery I am confined.*

December 12.

I have written this in hurry and agitation of spirits, and I hope you will excuse my disregard to order, method, and good writing.

I copied out part of this letter, and suppressed a great part of it before I sent it. On being about to send it by the post, I was informed that my first letter to my brother was not yet gone. I was then very indignant; for my circumstances were circumstances of great perplexity and suffering, and I longed to come to an understanding about them, and to be delivered from them. This must have been about the 18th of December, for I enclosed the above in an envelope directed to my eldest brother, with the following lines and date, so that my letter was detained at least three weeks:

* I allude here to the different kinds of inspiration I was sensible of, and I beg to remark again, that the whole, or nearly the whole of these letters, and those I sent from Dr. Fox's house, were visibly inspired to me,—that is, I saw on the paper, in different handwritings, the words before I wrote them. This is a fact; modern philosophy—that is, modern infidelity—may disbelieve or reason, as they call it, from this as it will; but I saw on the paper the sentences before I wrote them; and they were prompted so fast, and shifted so rapidly, that I had difficulty to choose which I would write—each spirit prompted me in a different style, and in a different handwriting. I can, therefore, now believe that persons may be able to discover, to a certain extent, the character or disposition of others by their writing. Let me observe that I find these letters, on re-perusing them, much more coherent than I expected; but the handwriting *is so minute, feeble, and irregular,* that my family might be excusable in disrespecting them; because the world do not respect so much what is written or spoken, as who writes or speaks it. But, whilst from an early age I have been accustomed to doubt the best man's word—I have always thought it my duty to receive, and examine the word of the humblest individual. A liar may speak truth; a wise man may utter folly—a child or a fool may speak wisdom.

DEAR SPENCER,

I enclose you this letter to my poor mother, and request you to ask her to return it to you to read when she has read it with attention. In it I make allusions to a letter I have written to you, which I intended solely for your private perusal. Dr. F. F. has considered himself authorized to open it without my permission, and in defiance of God Almighty's appeal to his conscience, which must have made him to consider what relationship he stands in with regard to yourself and me, as also what title he had to do that without my cognizance, which I had twice or three times shown him that I had reason for wishing him not to do. In the hurry of my spirits, not recollecting all that was in the letter, I told him that I was glad—and so perhaps I still might be in part for some reasons—at his having opened the letter, in spite of my having confided in his sense of gentlemanly feeling to do nothing, at least without telling me of it, or preparing me for it beforehand. I have twice since then requested him to forward that letter, for it cost me much to write at all upon the subject on which I have written;* to my surprise and indignation, and mortification, after twice having told me it should go, he has detained it. I am impatient at this state of control and restraint, as also of the society in which I have been forced to remain so long: and I beg that you will write to Dr. F., and desire him to forward my letter to you. I am anxious to have some communication with you by writing, previous to any personal interview consequent upon my removal hence; if not immediate. But I am resolved to send no other letter to you or my mother than the one I enclose to you, unless I am secure of private correspondence, except it be a mere verbal answer to your observations and inquiries.

I am thinking of writing to Edward, to ask him to accompany me abroad to Italy. I cannot express to you at times the acute agony and indignation which I feel, at the thoughts of my letter to you having been opened and read by any one besides yourself or D——.

Give my affectionate love to —— and —— and to little ——, and ——, and poor little L——, and the other little children, and believe me

Your very affectionate brother,
JOHN PERCEVAL.

Dec. 19, 1831.

---

* I cannot describe the pain of mind, and head of fire, with which I often wrote. Considering my situation it was not wonderful. The doctors, for these reasons I understand, often refuse pen and ink to their patients: if their treatment was really humane they might have reason; but I should perhaps never have recovered but by the means thus afforded me of controlling and concentrating my thoughts, and exercising my powers of judgment and discrimination.

DEAREST MOTHER,

I received your letter on Monday afternoon, and I am much obliged to you for having replied to it immediately. I am thankful to God Almighty and to you for your kindness in considering my probable anxiety about receiving an answer as soon as possible; more especially as I had written with much trouble of mind and consumption of time; and had besides given it to be delivered into Dr. Fox's room, on Tuesday afternoon, before the post left the house. I have reason to believe that he detained it, at least, one day; but I had also hopes that it would have reached you on Friday evening, by his own admission, which he made to me on Thursday, that it was gone. My agony of mind and my indignation is and was great at his having presumed to interfere with my correspond- ence at all: having previously shown my displeasure concerning this on another occasion. Of course, therefore, I was at times un- controllably agitated, by the idea and disappointment of not ob- taining an answer from you before the ensuing week; not only from your not having time, but perhaps from your thinking it wise and your duty to delay answering me, in obedience to some counsels of his, or hasty impressions of your own. For I have sus- picions, I think well founded, that he has tampered with the cor- respondence of my friends, at least with that of my mother, and my brother with me. At least, I cannot otherwise account for your mockery of me, and total, except in one instance, indifference con- cerning any communication with me.

I call your letter a reply to mine, as it is not an answer. I am thankful to you for the only communication which has yet been made to me, or, or likely to be of, any real importance or conse- quence to my tranquillity of mind even and body. I allude to that which regards your state of belief concerning the miracles wrought upon those who are the authors of what is called the Row Heresy. Grieved as I am that you should be doubting their divine source, and conscious as I am that my misconduct may lead you to doubt the sincerity of them, and the holiness of their . . . . ; and that the awful calamity with which it has pleased God Almighty to visit me, may be looked upon as the fruit of enthusiastic blind obedience and adoption of their principles, or to their system of doctrine and practice, instead of disobedience to, and doubtless want of reliance, in the counsel and admonitions of the Holy Spirit, which dwelleth in them and through them, and about them and in me; yea, even to their written exhortations. I—feeling as I do, though not yet as I should do, I—am nevertheless glad to be no longer in suspense with regard to the state of belief on this momentous subject of those who are most dear to me in the flesh. And I should have been glad if your communication had been more particular. It relieves me of a great burden, as I now know how I may account for much of your behaviour concerning me; and can reason with myself and hold communion with my conscience and my Creator in prayer or meditation, concerning your probable motives for silence on these subjects, and on the course which I may have to pursue. I should have been saved from much acute misery and anxiety, and perhaps might have been at E—— [Ealing] in a firm state of mind, if you had been allowed to do, as I am confident you or S—— [Spencer] would have done, if you had obeyed your own natural impulses of sympathy with, and attachment or tenderness for, the anxieties of an even ordinarily-gifted and religiously-disposed person. I loved your letters as they were— oh! pray consider it—the only tie which kept up any communication of idea, or feeling, or interest with my . . . , excepting S——'s [Spencer's] one visit, and one letter to me early in the year. But it was mockery of me, of your own self and of my understanding, my best feelings—of the only feelings which are really worth considering in the intercourse of—of one professor of Christianity with another, to write to me merely concerning family arrangements, addressing me only as a person clothed with natural affections, and that too, usually, as if I were under all the accustomed circumstances of ordinary society.

I should have been more happy still, if you had been particular with regard to giving me information, as well, concerning my sisters' individual opinions. I wrote to ask Spencer concerning their belief in the miracles, as well as yours. I fear you may think it unaffectionate in me, that I should not have written to ask you. If I had not previously written to him, and had more thoughts to write about to you than I can arrange or control, I should probably have done so, and preferred addressing the question to you.

My allusion to my sisters, reminds me of a remark I have made on your letter to me, that my sisters, as well as yourself had great pleasure in seeing by my letter that the powers of my mind, &c. are gaining ground. I think this remark proves to me, as I concluded also from other parts of your letter, that you have answered it without consideration. As I made an observation in it with regard to writing to I——, which I could wish that you had frankly alluded to and contradicted if not true, I ought perhaps to have asked explicitly a corroboration of it: it was a statement of Dr. Fox to me, that my sisters were not acquainted with my state of mind. I remember now that in a former letter you mentioned the family as participating in your joy and happiness at the receipt of my first letter. I wish to be particularly informed as to the truth of Dr. F. F— [Fox] having any authority from you to make such an assertion: considering it contradicted by your expressions in your last letter, I have refused him my hand and my confidence, and all communication with him that is not absolutely necessary, as I think he has been on this; and it leads me to suspect also on other occasions not acting in a straightforward, open, gentlemanly manner towards me; but under pretence, probably, of seeing whether I was exercising my own judgment, or to pry into the state of my feelings; condescending to leave the noble path of truth, by an unmanly, unjustifiable, cruel, and by what, when our relative rank in society is considered, I conceive an uncalled for and impudent falsehood. Nor is the wound inflicted upon the heart the only mischief to which I am exposed; but such untrue conduct is loathsome towards a lunatic, as he is already wounded with doubts and anxieties, which he finds himself often debarred from the means of solving, or relieving, or remedying the causes from which they spring; and I might have had (besides the horror of believing it possible, that my sisters were not prepared for, nor suspecting the awful blow which might come upon them unexpectedly, of hearing that their brother was in a lunatic asylum) not only to have debated with myself under all the disadvantages of a deluded and deranged mind, how far I was entitled, or in duty bound to take steps to inform them of it; but also without sufficient grace to endure the anxieties of all those measures being thwarted, impeded, or put a stop to, by the impertinence of those around me, by the inconveniences of my situation, through suspicion, jealousy, mistrust, contempt, neglect, or what is still more tantalizing, the misconceived prudence and benevolence of my relations, and of those with whom I had to do.

This is one among the number of gross insults and outrages, to which at times my holiest and inmost feelings have been entirely exposed during the state of delusion and lunacy, and perplexing conflicts between contending duties, in which I have been bound down by the Almighty. I am grieved to think that I am obliged to complain to you at all, much more that I should be reduced, by being no longer able to control at times my indignation or impatience of my position here, to complain to you in this manner. But remember I do not condescend to complain to you for your counsel, or advice, or opinion. I am sorry to do so; but after the manner in which you have, together with Spencer, left me, in a state of defenceless and broken-heartedness, to be taken charge of, and to be put under the control of, and associated with persons of a tone of mind less refined than that which I have been accustomed to meet with even in your domestics at Ealing; and as it appears to me habitually deadened to the consideration of respect for age, rank, or misfortune, and brutally ignorant of the habits of a gentleman; after you have left me either in ignorance,—which argues the want of true Christian love, and much want of natural affection,—or in slothful and negligent acquiescence to the counsels of Dr. Fox for a whole year, nearly in constant communication with such persons, as well as with lunatics of every description, but one, perhaps—that is, of high birth and gentlemanly manners and habits;—in constant communication, I say, besides exposure to their observation under every stage of feeling and passion, or apathy, or agitation, in despair or in hope, without permission, (I now have found to my confusion of thought, and amazement of understanding,) even if I had wished it, to have a private room for one moment—after, I say, having permitted me to be the victim of such a system of spiritual treatment, . . .

When I found that my family were still blinded by the Doctor, and did not respect my remonstrances as they ought to have done, I thought that it would be right to communicate with some mutual friend, who might convince them of and reprove them for their error; and turning about in mind whom to address, the spirits directed me to write to Mr. R. Ryder, my father's dearest friend: at the same time they intimated to me, to lose no time, as though they foresaw his approaching death, which took place, indeed, in the ensuing year. I wrote the following notes, but I doubted if it would be right to send the letter; shrinking also from exposing myself.

I have been now a whole year nearly Mr. R——, under circumstances of the most painful and trying nature, and such is my sense of them, that although I do hope to be delivered from them immediately, at least through your interference, I still think the persons who exposed me to them should receive, from some person to whose authority they may defer, rebuke and well deserved reproof. In a state of such extraordinary superstitious delusion and credulity, in a fancied spirit of inspiration from the Lord and from God Almighty, as to worship a common lunatic attendant, or keeper, of the most reckless, and to say the least of him, thoughtless character, publicly and privately, and throughout the fields and villages of this neighbourhood, as the Lord Jesus; and to adore another lunatic as the Lord Jehovah supremely omnipotent; besides committing a thousand other more foolish extravagancies; I have been deserted without compassion by my mother and brother to the control and surveillance of common lunatic keepers, and physicians, (Dr. Fox a converted or relapsed Quaker,) and I have been confined, under their system to a gloomy room, for a whole year, in the company of twelve or more lunatics, individuals, for the most part, of no rank, no birth, little education, no manners, and thoroughly dead to all gentlemanly and moral feelings, and I may say moral habits, to which I have been accustomed, to which I have been educated, and to which I have clung from my father's cradle until now.

I have been exposed, sir, I say, to this state of things, now nearly a whole year, continually, (without leave, or liberty, or permission to retire, even in my moments of acutest agony and consciousness of despair and degradation and lost station in society, to a private apartment:) to the insults of low vulgar keepers, and the mockery and derision of lunatic infidels and atheists. Had I been raving mad, or guilty of acts of malice, and unprovoked violence, extraordinary indignation against myself or my maker, or my attendants, I could have borne to have been treated with much more restraint if it were possible, and more personal violence than I have been. But a state of unparalleled delusion, and abominable hypocrisy, sottishness, stupidity, idiotcy, under which I groaned and struggled, and loathed and hated and abhorred my own soul; and panted and fainted, and struggled against the impressions of a horrible dream, against a something, nothing, a fanciful fear, which appeared to bind——.

I write to you not only for my own sake, but in hopes that you may yet have time spared to you by the Almighty to take into consideration and lay before a member of either House of Parliament, the——

Mr. R——r, I have had my head I assure you struck against the wall by one of the attendants here, and that repeatedly, with such violence as I should have been afraid to make use of myself towards a person in a sound state of mind for fear of driving him into a state of derangement and delirium, and on two occasions but on one especially with such force, βιᾷ τοσαυτᾷ, that I believed at the time that I could only be healed of a broken and fractured skull by divine and miraculous power. You may conceive our, or at least my state of helplessness and delusion, and simple humility, and obedience, which you will call lunacy and idiotcy, when I acknowledge to you, that though surprised at the time at such violence being offered to my person, I yet endured it patiently and thankfully, not only without a murmur or complaint, as wholesome *perhaps* to my mind, as the duty of the person who used it, in respect of his situation towards me and his employer—and as a thing to which my lunacy exposed me; *and never dreamt of its being my duty to complain of it to young Dr. Fox or old Dr. Fox.*

It was done to me I remember on two several occasions against the wall of a dark cell which served as the antechamber to two baths, and to which it was their custom in a morning to take me, and throw me in head foremost, during the cold winter months of last year. I was then as far as I can remember accurately, in the habit of resisting the men who came to take me to the bath every morning, as I believe in order to punish me. If they had struck me then, I could have accounted for their conduct, I thought I was obeying a fancied, nay a positive command from God Almighty to do so, in fear of the wrath of God, in fear otherwise of becoming deranged, in other words of hell-fire, if I did not do it—a command given me by inspiration, that is, I mean by the hearing of an audible and beautiful, and articulate voice sometimes about me, or within the room, sometimes by my bedside, sometimes in my head or skull. (In order that you may receive what I say as at least astonishing, for I can hardly expect you to *believe* it as yet; and that you may understand perhaps scripture more fully, and me too, or believe what I tell you to be possible and probable by comparing my words together, I refer you to those passages in scripture, where it is written that the word of the Lord came to Isaiah and Jeremiah, Ezekiel, Amos, and other prophets,) I say although I was obeying often, I may, in one sense say always, this voice, in seizing and wrestling with the persons who came to me, yet I could have borne with violence if they had resisted me then with βιᾷ, with force, for that was intelligible, and I could understand punishing the absurdities and apparently unreasonable conduct of a mistaken and misguided conscience; but usually, though overpowered by numbers, I was not struck on those occasions.

It may be that I was quietly refusing to put on my stockings in obedience to some spirit of delusion, of fun and frolic, or good humour; for I loved him with a love that I cannot express; for this too I used often to do in obedience to the word of God, as I supposed, to learn to be beautified by God's salvation, in obeying the spirit of agility and activity and lightness at the same time. I used to do it partly understanding and having heard from the same voice, that it was agreeable to and expected by my keeper of me or from me; supposing him also to be inspired, and to know my inmost thoughts: but I could hardly believe this delusion, though through fear of God's wrath and of hell-fire I acted upon it—for I feared Hobbs' wrath and anger, and impatience and impenitence, (and malice too, though I was not aware of this until now). I feared his impatience because I did not believe that he could bear patiently with conduct, which to me was worth the value of my soul and salvation at the time; nor consider for a moment that it ought to be borne with, and that however apparently wilful and unreasonable, and done on purpose to irritate or provoke, it might be reasonable in a lunatic; it is reasonable for me or a lunatic to say, that such patience, such consideration is due from a lunatic attendant on his patient.

It may be, that I was about in fact, or according to his suspicions, to have proceeded to an act of resistance in raving madness, or derangement; but was he entitled to proceed immediately against me, even if I were so, without first attempting patient or mild measures.

It may be that he was conscious that I was hypocritising before my maker—Was he to be my *castigator morum?*

It may be that he knew, or thought, I was affecting to do it in obedience to my conscience, but in order really to annoy and vex him;—but was he not to use reproof, or earnest exhortation, or persuasion, or entreaty?

Persuasion! I have hardly heard a note of persuasion unaccompanied with authoritative, insulting, or sarcastic reproof, and that from inferiors, since I have been in this house.

You may consider in the first place what is my indignation, now I am come to a more sound state of mind, at having been left under a state of things in which such treatment should have been possible or probable. What it might have been, to have been enduring the probability of such treatment from my superiors, or equals even from gentlemen—from my brother ——, or uncle ——, much more from my inferiors, and inferiors of the lowest description.

But what am I to conceive of a system of treatment which could expose me, me a man of honour and a gentleman, to the possibility, nay, more than that, the probability of such treatment? I add more, me, or any other human being, under a state of delusion and confusion of conscience, intellect, and judgment, under a state of complete destitution of religious feeling, at times, and of gross irritation, and want of all comforts. My lunacy was of a kind perhaps that tempted cowards to offer me this insult; and now when I look back upon it, I feel indignant and surprised that I did not, in my state of lunacy perpetrate, as I might have done, the murder of the individual who offered it to me.

From the above letters,* it is evident that my mind was still

* In a letter to one of my sisters I suggested, by command as I thought of my Saviour, that the drains at home should be cleaned, as a security against infection from the cholera morbus. I wrote also concerning some books I wished to be made a present of; and suggested that my netting-needles, &c., should be sent to me.

deranged when I wrote them; but there is no symptom of want of affection to my family, although that indignation which I felt at my exposure and betrayal to such treatment, occasionally finds vent, which, perhaps, even then ought to have overborne all other considerations; but which afterwards certainly broke out into expressions of hatred and revenge, when I found my remonstrances slighted, my word disrespected; a preference given to the opinions of those who had ill-treated me, and under whose power I was, whilst impugning their characters; and my person exposed to fresh violence and insult. It will be seen also from these letters, that in spite of the powers of mind I had, I was unable to come to any thing like a correct conclusion of the intention of the treatment used towards me; looking still on the result of a coarse and severe regimen applied heedlessly to all characters, as on a punishment to my individual case. The effects also of my seclusion and want of employment, may be remarked in my minute attention to trifling matters.

In answer to these letters, I received kind but short and commonplace answers from my mother. In the first or second of these, she refused me a private room, stating that the doctor's suggestions were to be attended to; this drove me in one sense mad, and filled me with alarm. From this commenced my violent and insolent demeanour to my family. In the next, a private room was ordered for me, and hints that other plans were being thought of: but by that time I was standing out on other rights, and so, unfortunately, I continued being irritated by the refusal of every successive demand, till it was too late to receive it as an obligation, and then I was taunted with being never satisfied.

These letters wounded my feelings by their style, which was such as might be addressed to a person in ordinary circumstances; by their neglect of passages in my letters, and particular remonstrances, and by their complete silence on any of my arguments: dealing with me as with a child, who had no option but to obey. But in this respect I learnt not till after my release, that my mother was bound down by her credulity in the opinions of the doctors; and even at times, by her fears of irritating them to do me a mischief, by expressing her opinions too openly whilst I was under their power. Had I known any of this, had any of these excuses been made to me, I should have been saved from much painful intercourse and altercation.

On the expressions used by my servant, respecting my trousers, I find the following notes and deliberation, written about this time.

—— —— trousers, or hedge —— ——.

Did he mean to insult me as a gentleman, under his power and control?

Did he mean to insult me as a lunatic, deeming me a hypocrite or coward, irresolute and despicable?

Did he mean to insult me as a lunatic, to try me, to wound my feelings as a gentleman, or as a minister of the word of God? believing it his duty.

In the first place, how could I proceed? Could I complain to Dr. Fox and expose myself to his revenge and cruelty.

I had to condemn you (my brother) before Dr. Fox and Dr. F. Fox, for putting me under such control. Such a scoundrel about me.

Was it my duty to rebuke one, who was only tempting me to reprove him, and so spend my breath in vain?

How could I bear it; yet how could I endure it unrebuked?

I believe it was because he saw that I disliked it, and loved to hurt those feelings of delicacy which I have yet remaining?

I should have reproved him, and warned him of complaining to Dr. Fox.

Why did I not?

1st. How could I reprove, having been a gross sinner and idiot here, and being in punishment for my offence; knowing too that I was a disgusting object of compassion for hypocrisy.

2d. I was in delusion, and thought him to be the Lord Jesus Christ, and how could I rebuke the Lord?

If I had acted as a man of courage, I should have forbidden him to make use of such language again. If as a natural man and a true Englishman I should have knocked him down. This was my real duty perhaps. Then I should have been respected by God Almighty, but strangled by the man, or put into a madhouse for ever and ever.

[A Letter from Dr. Fox, Senior]

Brisslington House, Jan. 30.

MY DEAR SIR,

I would not have troubled you with writing had not age by interfering with my powers of speech prevented me from expressing myself as clearly as I could wish; and from uttering those feelings that your recently excited state would naturally elicit.

If you have any power of reminiscence, consider to what a degraded condition of mind you were reduced only a few weeks ago. Should I at that time have been justified in allowing a correspondence with persons not of your own family?* Many of your companions, like you give me letters addressed to people whom they had never known. I receive such letters and they are satisfied. But it would be worse than madness in me to suffer them to proceed except to their friends. This rule therefore is not confined to your case. I told you however that I was glad to consider your state of mind improved, which enabled me to address you more as a reasonable being; therefore to deal candidly with you, I must without any judgments on its contents, send every thing you write for your mother and brother's approbation. Could any thing be fairer? but you give it a different interpretation and allow your mind to run into a state of exasperation badly according either with a soundness of understanding, or with the Christian principle of humility and forbearance.

What you mean by reviling Hobbs I don't understand—he was placed to wait upon you because he was gentle and considerate. Has he at any time been obliged to resort to power: I believe it will be found that violence and erroneous obstinacy on your part first provoked it. I must own that it not a little surprised me, that you, as a humble follower of Christ, would think of him, or any other as your inferior. Do we not know that God is no re-

---

* I do not know to what period Dr. F. alluded: unless it was a time when I ate my bread and butter with pepper, &c.; but I think this was a long time previous to my writing at all. This remark is directed to a complaint I had made concerning letters to very intimate friends, whom, I think, at the age of twenty-seven, I was fully at liberty to write to, and they competent judges of whether I wrote improperly, without a lunatic Doctor's interference, and much more fit to be entrusted with my opinions. Upon this pretence a lunatic is deprived of all assistance: and the more surely the more he has cause to complain of his relations, whose delicate feelings are not to be wounded by the suspicion that they are doing wrong, though they are murdering him by inches. *I never gave* Dr. F. a letter but to my earliest friends. Lastly, supposing it to be true, as the Dr. so absurdly assumed, that his patients *were satisfied* at their letters being received, though they received no answer; yet that was no argument that I should be satisfied, who was exercising my reason.

specter of persons? [yet I never saw Mr. Hobbs sitting at Dr. F——'s dinner table.] The apostle declares in the seventeenth chapter of Acts, that "he has made all nations of one blood."

Though owing to the accident of birth, the artificial state of society and the advantages of a more refined education, you may think yourself his superior, you must not forget that we shall all be called to give an account of the talents committed to us.

The effect of this letter on me at the time, in consequence of the subtlety and cunning mockery which runs throughout it, gave rise to the suspicion, that the doctor intended to provoke me to acts of violence, by puzzling and by innuendo, and by showing how he could blind others. There is so much religion and plausibility in it, and at the same time so much contradiction and clever confusion. Even now that suspicion still affects me, whether I am to consider that Dr. Fox was acting wittingly, or that from the habitual and unchecked practice of imposture he knew not what spirit he was of. He who pretended to be preaching on the ways of providence, talking on *the accident* of birth—he who refers to the New Testament, casting reflection on the artificial state of society, when in the same Testament we are informed, all authority is from God—and whilst he clung to all the personal advantages of that state.

He again, respecting my education, or pretending to do so, and yet confounding my ideas as if refinement of education made distinction between individuals only in thought and not in reality. He officiously reminding me that I was to give an account of my talents at the judgment-seat, when all I had then to do was with his lunatic asylum; as if one of the talents I had to give an account of was not my judgment, and God knows a mild and temperate judgment it then was, considering my state—of his horrible system of treatment. Let them who are interested in being deceived, be deceived. The letter goes on—

In respect of your threats of revenge, I am not the least afraid of it; although I do not wonder that you consider those as your enemies from whom proceed any repression or control. [This was NOT the case, for I supposed myself to need repression and control for a long time after this.] But religion will be a mere mockery if you can profess to retire and wait upon your Maker in prayer, when destitute of that love which betokens a disciple of

Christ. [This is in allusion to my having remarked on the inconsistency of his system with the duties of meditation and prayer; in which, by my plainness, I took Satan in his own net.] If however, you shall continue to view us in as your enemies, still *"fas est et ab hoste doceri,"* I recommend you therefore, to cultivate the fear of God, which will so influence all your thoughts, words, and actions, that you will think more favourably of all mankind, and of your sincere well wisher,

EDW. LONG FOX.

The men under whose authority I was placed, both this year and after, have ruined my temper and mind; so that I appear against them even in my writings at fearful odds! for they have all the composure of secure duplicity and cold-blooded malignity, of sound skins, and of sound humours—whilst I am full of sore and angry feelings, and bear the marks of their ill conduct about me; but if the fear of God ought to make me think more favorably of Dr. Fox, I am indeed a lost soul and spirit: once I scarcely knew what it was to utter an oath, but these men made it familiar with me to curse and to blaspheme. He ought to have written—the fear of the devil—which will so influence all your thoughts, as to make you *speak* more favorably of all mankind, and of your sincere well-wisher—whatever may be your opinion. To the above letter I began to write the following reply. It was written according to inspiration, that is, I saw the words on the paper before I wrote them; they appeared in capital letters, but much more beautiful than I could print them. Also, if I recollect right, they did not change so swiftly as on other occasions; so that I had more time to copy them down: whether this was owing to my having more confidence in my cause, and more practice in seizing them, or to my being now in a private room—at any rate it was owing to more quiet and confidence of mind, so that the mirror was not so ruffled or so broken.—

[Draft of Reply to Dr. Fox]

SIR,

I have received a letter from my mother this afternoon, in which she notifies to me her intention to have me removed to another asylum. I write to you, therefore, a few words, in answer to your letter to me, which I should otherwise have delayed doing to another day. I shall prosecute my appeal to the laws of my country for personal liberty from that asylum also, if God permit; or, at the least, for leave to choose my own physician—unless—

I acknowledge, sir, that my sense of the injuries which my person has suffered under your treatment, which now that the cloud of delusion is burst through, under which God Almighty confounded my judgment, I know to be unlawfully inhuman! together with a daily further discovery of the awful consequences which your course of management has produced upon my everlasting happiness, has excited in my mind not only wrath, but fury. But if you use the word excited to hint that my indignation is lunatic or unjust, I deny it—I deny that I could be in a sound state of mind without feeling and expressing it; though, being a lunatic, I dare not—for fear of misconstruction, and often feel that I cannot express it through the control of a superior power, I cannot express myself as I should, as I can when I have time in seclusion to reason with myself.

I regret and ask your forgiveness for having uttered my sentiments to you in an unmanly, malignant, and I fear disrespectful way. But I wished to be upright and sincere, and that you should not leave my presence without knowing that revenge is my object, which I mean by all lawful means to pursue. I hope the Lord would punish me if I shrunk when called upon to do so, from confessing one of the attributes of human nature to be mine also.

This letter I had not time to finish. I told Dr. Francis Fox, however, that I would write from my new abode; this was the only promise I made that I remember breaking; but during the next year I had enough to do, and I reflected—that advantage might be taken of my expressions, and that it was not fair that I should be writing, in my state of excitement and agitation to men, who take advantage of every violent expression and of every singularity to alarm a patient's relations, and to keep him in a situation from which they ought to take every fair opportunity of releasing him, by reason of the very nature of his disorder; whilst in the eyes of society, and in their own eyes, I doubt not, to a certain degree, they are acting for the security of society, and for the individual's security.

"FATHER, FORGIVE THEM, THEY KNOW NOT WHAT THEY DO.— AMEN."

CHAPTER XXIX

My affections ever remained towards my family such as they previously were. If by this term is meant an honest desire to serve them, to meet them on friendly terms, to hear of their being well and happy, they ever have done so; but I resented the ill-treatment and barbarous usage to which I had been exposed through their neglect of me; and to which, in spite of my remonstrances and my appeals to their affection, I was still subjected. This breach became widened by continued injustice, and this resentment naturally found expression. Moreover I considered it my duty, if religion be true, to convince them of their error, that they might acknowledge it to the saving of their souls. It gave me agony of mind to reflect, that if there is an hereafter, they might die unconvinced, and in an hereafter alone first acknowledge when it was too late to repent, the extent of their iniquity. If I could not convince them by argument, I conceived it to be my duty then to procure their correction by the judgment of a court of law: and I conceived this to be a duty I owed to my countrymen, and to myself for my future protection. If I considered this my duty in order to obtain their correction for the injuries I had sustained, still more did I recognise it as such, and as the only path left for me to pursue in order to recover my rights; yet, God knows, how my heart ached and my spirits sunk, in spite even of my desires of vengeance, to be at variance with my relations, and to think of being compelled to prosecute my own mother. Here, too, I was in a straight. The doctors gave me no credit for having any feeling, nay, they spoke evil of me, saying my feelings were perverted—

then—that agitation, that suffering, that disorder produced by the conflict of different feelings, those of duty—and those of affection —of love to others, and of self-respect and fear for my safety, must necessarily be attributed to a deranged intellect; since they took no account of the proper and true causes of it. How cruel it is to be exposed to the judgment of such infidels; how shameful of the legislature, of an aristocratical legislature to allow of it!

But of what avail is it for a man charged with insanity to argue against any calumnies; however gross, however absurd, they are believed of him, even because they are contrary to reason. Their calumny was also very prejudicial, and acted very cruelly upon me, because I am of a turn of mind, that whenever ill is spoken of me I always direct my thoughts inward, to examine my disposition if it be so or not, and to try my feelings. Thus I lived continually suspecting and watching over myself—weighing my emotions on the recollection of my home, my friends, and my family; and, although I found kindly and affectionate feelings arise, almost doubting the reality of them, through the bold lies told and accredited of me, till my patience was exhausted, and perhaps passion, anguish, and perplexity, triumphed over every respect and every attachment, and all decorum in my manner of thinking.

But although my affection, at least my affectionate disposition, still remained the same to my family, I do not deny that my writings often broke out into very sarcastic and violent expressions. I could not always overcome my exasperation. But even then I was frequently influenced by a spirit of bravado and defiance of the doctors, to whom I knew my letters were subjected for inspection; I was determined, if they declared that my anger at being confined, and at my treatment, was a proof of my madness, that they should have evidence enough of it. I was incapable of truckling to any system so detestable, to any power so hideous, as their power. Even a deeper motive lay hid under all this violence of expression; and this may perhaps by many be deemed an insane motive: I knew that, of all the torments to which the mind is subject, there is none so shocking, so horrid to be endured as that of remorse for having injured or neglected those who deserved our esteem and consideration. I felt for my sisters, my brothers, and my mother: I knew they could not endure to look upon what they had done towards me, to whom they were once so attached, if they rightly understood it; that they could know no relief from the agony of that repentance which comes too late, gnawing the very vitals, but in believing me partly unworthy of their affection; and therefore I often gave the reins to my pen, that they might hereafter be able to justify themselves, saying he has forfeited our respect, he has thrown aside the regard due to his parentage and to his kindred—he has deserved our contempt, and merited our abandonment of him. I state my feelings as I recollect them; I do not pretend to justify them. It is impossible to suppose that recovering from severe illness, after revolting treatment, in shocking circumstances with every spiritual and moral and mental want, recreation, and amusement neglected—passion may not have broken through; but it is difficult to say, whether or not in allowing it I did not act wisely: where nothing was to be gained by other behaviour—however decorous and respectful.

So far, therefore, was it untrue that my affections were alienated from my family—except by the immediate sense of wrong—that I regarded them almost with a romantic attachment, at the same time I considered it to be my duty to stand up honestly and independently in defence of my rights, and in claiming the attention nature pointed out as due to and required by my situation. In like manner the charge was equally false—that I ever doubted the affections of my family to me: I felt deeply the very great injustice and absurdity of this charge. It was very unjust because, although recovering from delusions, although without scarcely any evidence of real care and true affection on the part of my kindred, I did not hesitate to ascribe all their neglect to misconception—to impotence of mind—and to credulity; I never questioned, before or after my removal from Brisslington, that my family maintained the same honest affection for me that they ever did, and that I did to them; only at Brisslington I conceived that I was looked upon as worthless—*having deserved it*. It was absurd, because if I disbelieved my family's affection towards me, to what end could I be writing to them. That the doctors invented this of me is not surprising or astonishing; it was their interest so to do. I might wonder at their impudence, as my letters were certainly full of testimony of my real feelings in this respect, whatever might have been their virulence and violence in one particular; but their success shows that they have not learnt the trade of dupery for nothing, and that they know the extent of human folly only too well. That my family should adopt the delusion they thrust upon them surprises, I acknowledge, and continually perplexes me; for, although I repeatedly denied it, in express terms rejected it, and carefully explained that redress for my sufferings was all that I desired—that I respected and loved them still, and that my anger against them arose solely from my treatment, not from my attributing false motives to them —the charge was constantly repeated. Did they not read my letters, or did they deny my words to be true, though they repeatedly deprecated the idea of questioning my honour? Or did they suppose that I was deluded, and did not know my own sentiments; ready to believe all evil of me, but no good? Or did they, as I imagine, read my letters indeed, but with no attention, alarmed at my accusation, and piqued by my addressing them in a-tone of superiority, whilst attacking their judgments, seize only on those passages which justified, in their opinion, my continued confinement? Did they, with all their affection and all their attachment to me, seldom or never let that affection and that attachment have fair sway over their conduct and upon the operations of their minds, when reasoning and acting in my behalf? This is my suspicion. I should think that my letters could never have been read by them: certainly they could not have been read with due attention.

Here again let me assert, that even the violence of my language, which was seized upon as evidence of my distrust of their affections continuing the same towards me, was often indulged in, actually with a view to wounding and exciting those affections to make some exertion on my behalf; because I found that there was no chance of success in addressing their reason: I thought they might do from passion and resentment of my condemnation of them, and apparently cruel rebuke, what their spell-bound judgments would not consent to; that they might risk, for the sake of proving that the stigma they supposed I cast upon them was undeserved—what their own fears, and the whisperings of the doctors would not otherwise have allowed to them. So far was I from doubting their affections, that I relied upon them to the uttermost; confiding in them, and as far as my family were concerned, in them alone; and trusting that they would endure through all the expressions of my contempt and aversion, on account of their dealings with me.

I also found it a relief to my mind, to be able to say that there was some excuse for my relations' conduct towards me; for that which I found most insufferable, was the sense or the idea that I was treated with complete injustice, and without any cause of offence. Here again I state my feelings, that others may benefit from my experience. I do not justify them. It appears to me, and it appeared to me even then singular, that the foresight of disappointments and contradictions should not enable me to bear them with fortitude when they came; and that the consciousness of a good cause, and of a perfect heart, should not be a better defence against oppression, than the idea of having in some degree retaliated. But, without deciding the great question, I recollected that the scripture speaks of God himself as mad, at the rebellious conduct of his people; although he foresaw that rebellious conduct. I reflected therefore that I ought not to be surprised, but that had my foresight been perfect, I should have foreseen not only the sufferings I should be exposed to, but the feelings that they would excite in my bosom.

I am far from pretending that I am more than a man—or that I have any pretension to be a perfect man, in the regulation of my passions and of my desires; on the contrary, I despise myself. If I often cursed the hour in which I was born, if often bowed down with grief—with pain of body, and pain of mind—I blasphemed the very nature of God in my affliction, hating reason; not merely because reason was against me, but because I could see no reason for it. If I felt, at times, that the Almighty and man and the devil were against me, and that I struggled alone and hopeless, against the powers of goodness and of evil, and man their instrument— if I was desperate enough to offer my soul to Satan, to escape from that horrible confinement and seclusion into which I had fallen, by my credulity, and the abuse of my faith in the gifts of inspiration, still less can I pretend to say, that there were not moments when I hated and devoted to destruction all those who were bound to have protected me, and through whose abandonment of me and cruel neglect, I had forfeited my self-respect, in falling out with my Creator and in rebelling against the desire to love his holy name. But these were moments, moments of conflict in privacy; and to these feelings I seldom gave vent, in my correspondence with my family. And whatever they were, they arose from my confinement, and the arbitrary and insolent manner I was dealt with, not from the disease that was pretended as a cause for that confinement.

I have a further remark to make, that had it been in my power, I would have steadfastly declined altogether corresponding with my family. I protested repeatedly against being compelled to carry on my correspondence with them, and desired that I might be allowed to communicate with my friends, in order that one of them might act as a mediator between us. I knew that I could not avoid being guilty of many inconsistencies, writing to them familiarly at one moment, in respect of our relationship and mutual affections, and with coldness and indignation at another, in respect of their conduct towards me, so contrary to such affections. I expressly remonstrated against the unfairness of my being forced to write to them, because I knew that I could not avoid using strong language in declaring my resentment against them, and that that language would be produced as evidence against me. In like manner, and for the same reasons, I did not wish to see them.

CHAPTER XXX

HERE it may be useful to make an observation which regards lunatic patients generally. The doctors generally say that the presence of their friends is hurtful to them. I am informed this is often the case at the commencement of the disorder; and if the disease is connected with remorse of conscience, or with dread of ruin being brought upon the patient's family, nothing is more probable; for then the bewildered conscience finds the objects of its care and duties changed at times into tormentors. Thus in a splendid passage of one of the Greek plays, Orestes exclaims to his sister, "μεθες μι' ουσα των εμων Ερινννων."* Even without any ostensible cause, this *may* take place; because lunacy being the *perversion* of the understanding, it is possible that this perversion may take place in the apprehension of the objects of our affections. It may arise, not from any particular repulsion of the relations, but from a general repulsion of what is evil in mankind, or even of what is good; for the mind sometimes—I hazard the conjecture —repels what is beautiful in the creation, and endeavours to destroy all traces, and to refuse all impressions of it, touched with a remorse at its disobedience to the mild government of the Creator: so it is written in Revelations, that the wicked will cry to be saved from the wrath of the Lamb. This arises, I have found, not from dislike to, or want of desire towards what is beautiful, but from the pain of body which accompanies the mental conflict on seeing it, which springs from a complication of feelings,—desire,

---

* The quotation is from Euripedes' Orestes, line 264. After a lucid interval, Orestes starts to rave, hallucinating the Furies. Electra throws her arms around him, but he screams: *"Loose me! You are one of my Furies."* G.B.

regret, hopelessness, remorse—I cannot at present define. Ingratitude, I suspect, is at the root of all. Sometimes the mind repels and dislikes that excellence which, without being beautiful, corrects the passions and self-will. Now whether there is manifested a repulsion of any particular excellence, or of evil, whatever contention of mind may arise thereupon, may be supposed in many instances, to be aggravated by the presence of relations, especially by such excellence or evil being recognised in them. For, however faint, the honest sense of duty remains which commands us to respect our parents and their connexions, and, unfortunately, in ill-regulated minds, the command to obey frightens and agitates— and passion once ahead, scared and wounded by what violence it has already exercised—exasperated with itself—desperately and blindly dashes on. This too is often to be attributed to apathetic or disrespectful behaviour on the part of the persons who are being addressed. Now, whether a lunatic expresses his predilections or his dislike, whether that dislike is of disrespectful conduct towards himself, or only of an evil disposition, discernible in the individuals addressing him, we must recollect that they are often unable to control their passions, and give way to exaggerated feelings. Their condemnation or their approbation may be just, and yet their language and manner exceed the bounds of temperance and decorum. The world, on meeting any one to whose character of countenance, or to whose demeanour they have a particular aversion, can control or disguise their feelings, their sense of fear, if not of duty and forbearance, their hypocrisy, if not their modesty and long-sufferance, check their utterance—their action—the expression of their features;—but the lunatic cannot perhaps do this, he has no sense, or little sense of prudence, or of duty, or a false or true idea of God's wrath may prevail, and he hazards at once the open and decided avowal of his disgust and abhorrence. If for this reason alone, how evident is the impropriety of confiding them in any way to any man, or set of men so unreservedly as to enable them, if tempted, malignantly to punish them with impunity for a merited rebuke. But to the point on which I am writing, how evident also is it that they should not be exposed to express these violent and condemnatory emotions, disrespectfully against the faint remonstrances and leadings of a better and a gentler feeling, towards those to whom they owe particularly affection and regard. Nevertheless, let it be remembered, the separation of a lunatic from the objects of his natural duties and affection, *can never be justified unless proof has been obtained that the disorder is connected with them*—or unless the relations should use too much indulgence, or in their exercise of kindness, and in their benevolent conduct forget self-respect, and the respect due to the misfortunes and character of the wretched being they have to deal with. For kind language and demeanour are often repulsed by the lunatic—because they are offered in a manner which compromises the dignity of those who would show it, and that of him who is expected to receive it. BUT NO PLEA BUT NECESSITY WILL EXCUSE THE ENTIRE ABANDONMENT OF A RELATION BY HIS FRIENDS; they cannot be excused for not going OFTEN to see and look after him although he may be unable to bear the sight of, or to express his gratitude to them; still more should they visit and stay with him when he is recovering.

But when the lunatic doctors say that the presence of friends is hurtful to lunatic patients, they are not aware of one fact,—at any rate they do not acknowledge it,—that the violent emotions, and disturbance of spirits, which take place on their sudden meeting with them MAY arise from their being overcome by a sense of their relations' conduct towards them, in neglecting and abandoning them to the care and control of strangers, *and from the treatment of the doctors themselves*. The doctors naturally do not acknowledge this, for if they are acting from stupidity, their pride refuses correction, and will not admit the suspicion of being wrong; if they are acting with duplicity and hypocrisy, they necessarily preserve their character, and cannot in consistency confess that there is any error on their part—who can expect it of them? You cannot gather grapes from thorns. Nevertheless, it is true. There is, also, another truth the doctors are not aware of, which again is not surprising, for they are ignorant of every knowledge that ought to make them fit for the office they presumptuously or covetously undertake—namely, that lunatics often do not know their own minds; and when their simplicity or imbecility has allowed them to be placed in circumstances for which they are not prepared, nature struggles with or breaks through the films of stupidity and delusion, and entirely deranges them, or finds utterance in vehement, and uncontrolled, and unexpected language. Thus it is, that the doctors may be deceived and mistaken in their calculations. They talk to a lunatic of his mother, his brothers, and his sisters; they tutor him into the idea of his being rightminded when he hears of them with unmitigated pleasure and satisfaction; they neglect the man, and only think of the relation; his simplicity and imbecility adopts their views, and echoes their sentiments; his weakness yields and submits; they suppose now that he can endure the sight of his friends who are longing to see him, they write to say so; the sorrowing but unreflecting relations eagerly come down—the afflicted object of their concern is ushered into their presence, and then ensues a dreadful scene of disappointment, agitation, and perplexity. The outraged feelings of the patient either find vent in a sudden torrent of menace, of sarcasm, and of abuse, or, unconscious himself of the cause, he finds his self-possession give way, and he rambles away incoherently, mingling expressions of wrath, terror, pity, and affection, running upon all subjects disorderly, and dwelling upon none.

Even if the patient were then able honestly and decorously to express his feelings in intelligible language, and with becoming dignity, his frame, shaken by violent emotion—his broken speech— his pathetic action, the vein of poetry that would run through his discourse, would cause him to run the risk of being condemned, and hurried out of the room as a confirmed and raving madman: much more his violence or his incoherence. The friends stare at the doctor, and say—how is this? The doctor replies, he was mistaken in the lunatic's being able to bear the sight of his family, and ascribes all to delusion. They are too willing to admit this apology, rather than incur self-condemnation, and, perhaps, admit their error, conscious, at the same time, of their helplessness, which, by the deficiency of their property, may be irretrievable.

These reflections I made first at Dr. Fox's, in 1832, upon observing the conduct of a tall, middle-aged, black-whiskered male patient, who was walking, at the time, a short way from me, in the kitchen-garden, when the young doctor or the servant told him in a very coaxing manner, that he brought him a letter from his mother, or that his mother was coming to see him. The impropriety of the style of approach to a grown-up man of about thirty years of age, and the imbecile, childish grin of delight with which the patient received the information struck me, the more particularly as I was at that time in a state of great indignation at the conduct of my mother and of my family towards me, and I knew that the doctor insinuated in consequence that I was, *for that reason,* not of sound mind. I perceived that the patient was not exercising self-respect. All the conduct of the same kind that had been pursued towards me rapidly passed over my mind, and I saw that the system of the doctor was, as he would express it, to win the attention, or touch the mind through the affections, but in reality to entangle the patient in a snare; to make him confess, by thinking only on his parents, that he was satisfied with his treatment, and so to get him quietly out of his wretched abode, and ensure his silence on the enormities practised in it, or his being disbelieved, and treated as a madman, being contradicted by his own words—if ever he ventured to utter the resentment of a correct understanding. I saw that the doctor was the dupe of his own system. He was overlaying the sentiments of manhood and of justice, in the bosom of the person addressed, by undue appeals to his tenderness and to his filial duties; he had thrown the meshes of affection and of a superstitious sense of a child's obedience and respect to his parents, over the honour, the honesty, the fortitude, and the resignation of the man. I saw that if the individual in question was restored to society, he must re-enter it as a simpleton, but that, probably, the force of his character, and the voice of nature would tear asunder the false ties by which he was being bound down, and these not being under the controul of what men call reason, that he ran the chance of being confined for life as a madman.

This may appear an extraordinary digression, but I introduce it to show, that many persons confined as lunatics are only so because they are not understood, and continue so because they do not understand themselves. Acknowledging their affections, and palavered over to obey their affections, they yield themselves up wholly to them; not discriminating, not listening to the inward monitor, which commands them to recollect what is due to their own rights, and to their own independence, and to their own honour. By this means their conduct is inconsistent; and when they are admitted into the presence of the relations who have neglected them, they become deranged and disordered through contending feelings. My case was different from this: the doctors would fain have made me, or have found me such a simpleton as one of these. But I knew my rights; and I did not know how to lie. There was no danger to be apprehended to my understanding from my meeting my relations. I understood my position too well: but knowing that position, and my correct feelings in consequence, knowing also that my family were blind to their real position in respect of me, and could not make allowance for these feelings; whilst I was not afraid to meet them, I expressed my reluctance and my indifference to do so, previous to their having made me any apology. This I felt due to myself, on account of the embarrassing position in which I knew I should find myself, if they came to see me, full of their wonted cordiality, unable, through irreflection, to believe that I could really be offended with them, and finding me stern as a rock, and cold to their addresses. I felt this also due to them, to prevent any indecorous language on my part, to which I might be provoked by the cruelties and the difficulties of my situation, and give way through the weakness of my health of body and of mind. For I knew my strength, and did not wish to try it beyond its power; and though, willing if necessary, to meet my relations (and to embrace them if they admitted their error), I could not do so, so long as they disrespected my complaints; and I thought it imprudent to allow, and unjust, that I should be tempted before them to abusive language, by their callousness and unbelief, when I was certain such language would be converted into a justification for further confinement. This state of mind I often expressed in my letters to my family; and upon the same principles, I often deprecated and remonstrated against being compelled to correspond immediately with them. And I declare to God that I was of sound mind in this respect, for no man is fit to correspond with persons he is offended with, upon the topics of complaint, but through a third person, particularly not one so cruelly confined as I had been and still was. It was unhandsome and unjust in my family not to attend to these remonstrances. Of Dr. Newington's conduct I cannot speak with becoming dignity. He knew that he was sowing the seeds of discord between son and parent, brother and sister, and brother and brother, and yet he continued to degrade himself to accept office as the restorer of peace between us, on grounds incompatible with my religion, my honesty, and my honour, or to be as my gaoler for life if I did not accept them. Surely there is no villany greater than that of these men. Yet, "who hath believed our report?" to whom is the iniquity of this system revealed?

Begotten in love to woman, and not to man, I have great difficulty in arranging my ideas, to confess that I felt excessive embarrassment in commencing my first letters with my family and my friends, and to explain how this was occasioned. But I found it painful, not to know how I was looked upon; not to have any light from which to judge in what tone, or with what expectations, I might properly address them. This may have been a morbid feeling, but I was ashamed of the origin of my disorder, and felt that I deserved condemnation, and it was extremely painful. Suspicion haunted me that my family had not abandoned me without a cause—that I had not been treated in so cruel and abasing a manner, but from contempt; and my respect to them revolted from the idea that they had neglected me as they had done, to save themselves from the trouble of self-examination, and of inquiry and reflection as to the best manner of dealing with me: as well as from the perplexity they might be under in attempting to take care of me themselves. Besides, my habit of mind was one of self-accusation, in a great degree a diseased habit of mind, which has been increased by the severe mental conflict, and inward suspicion, and investigation of myself, occasioned by a long denial of justice to me. For it was difficult for me to be satisfied that I, recovering from lunacy, could be right, and my relations and those in authority over me entirely wrong. More especially when I reflected upon the character of my relations, and knew how they had loved me. Low-spirited originally, and now from illness, I lived self-condemned, and self-despised, and conceived that others thought of me in like manner: I was encouraged in these thoughts by my circumstances, and by the ferocious conduct of the keepers. Could any people have subjected one whom they respected and valued to the brute force of such ruffians? Could any beings have deserted one whom they loved, to be tied up hand and foot, day after day, in such society? When, too, my judgment had been corrected, there still remained a doubt on my mind, whether a just God could have dealt with me so, or allowed me to be so dealt with, without himself despising me; for indeed letting alone my bodily injuries, I have been used mentally and morally very cruelly. I am afraid no man will give credence to my sufferings, for my character and my dispositions have been so marred and so changed, I have now so little resolution that I hardly know myself. *Heu! quantum mutatus ab illo.* Now, according to a man's character the generality of men adopt their behaviour and think nothing wrong to those—who shew no seriousness, no reflection, no sense of decency, no piety, no self-respect. But I was not such an one when I was placed under the sole charge of lunatic doctors, by the religion of my family and of my countrymen. But my experience has necessarily engendered levity and fitfulness.

This entire ignorance of the opinion others might entertain of me became the more painful when I knew that the style of my letters might be weighed as a proof of my state of mind. So that, if I addressed others too confidently I might disgust them, as unconscious of the discredit I had brought upon myself, and of my circumstances; if I was too lowly in my appeals to them, I might appear weak, unable to control my feelings, and of unsound judgment. But this uneasiness on my part was unnecessary. My letters to my friends never reached them—I was cajoled, they never went further than Mr. Newington's house—and my relations seemed to exercise as little reflection in their style and demeanour to me, as they had done in the selection of my treatment. Whilst outwardly manifesting nothing but pity, and commiseration, and hopes of my being again soon with them, and regret that my state only rendered it impossible; they took no pains to inquire whether that was true, and to give me a fair hearing before unprejudiced persons; they followed the steps the least likely to restore me to them, and such as rendered it impossible for me to be with them again upon an honourable footing; and, at length, I so despised them, that I grew reckless as to how or what I wrote to them, or what they might think of my writings.

I cannot say what I feel at my correspondence having been always left subject to the inspection of my physician; I am astonished, I speak as a man, at the indelicacy of my family—at their want of respect to my honour and to their own; I am astonished that I, recovering from derangement, should have been more sensible and reasonable in this respect than they were, who quenched sound feeling in obsequiousness. But I desire others to reflect how disgusting it is for lunatic doctors to challenge, and for relations to allow them this title. What! Mr. Newington to be the keeper of my conscience—to be the meddler in secrets between my Maker and myself—which I might feel compelled to divulge and yet only confide with propriety to a minister of religion, or to relations, or to friends! I obliged to confide my feelings and desires to a stranger —feelings which it required even great delicacy to communicate properly to my nearest connexions!—or to be compelled to hold my peace in doubt, mistrust, or difficulty! By what authority do these men exercise this power—a power which even a clergyman, if he were a patient's guardian, would not be entitled to; on what grounds can they claim a confidence, which ties of kindred, or of friendship and respect, can alone confer? What is the result of their so doing?* That a patient cannot return to a really sound

* I had reason bitterly to deplore this system of meddling with correspondence on a late melancholy occasion. Being compelled to submit to it, I remonstrated against it. The consequence of it was, that one of my cousin's letters to me, and one that I had accidentally sealed and forwarded, did not reach their destination; and two letters I afterwards wrote were detained and returned, for reasons, in my opinion, very inconsistent and contemptible, considering the urgency of the occasion. Thus a delay of three weeks took place at a distance of fifteen miles; and not being able to come to a decision, from want of information, I was restrained from repeating a visit which, if made in time, might have strengthened and encouraged my relation to have still endured his confinement. On receiving, also, the last letter he wrote, my mind very much misgave me, and I was tempted to write back immediately, that I was determined to get him removed to another dwelling; but I feared no such letter would be delivered. I was to blame in putting any trust, and in deferring too long my return to see him.

state of mind; or else he must forego all useful communication by letter with his relations: since the very conditions these men force their patients to submit to, they can only be excusable in submitting to from insanity or dulness equal to their doctor's stupidity. These are like owls set to judge over the sanity of larks and nightingales. These are like swine or sloths set to judge over the manners of greyhounds and fleet coursers. The reasons given for this interference are, that the patient may write something improper to his relations; but since highly important letters may be destroyed, who is to be on this plea the judge? and if he does, is it not equally improper for the doctor to see the writings? Therefore on this plea the letters should be burnt without reading. This is absolute prudery—an affectation of delicacy, and of respect for the feelings, on the part of men who prove that they have little or none. Surely, as far as the patient is concerned, he should be saved from the apprehension of having exposed himself before a *stranger.* The second reason is, that the doctor may know the state of the patient's mind, and require some clue to his disorder; and it is of a piece with all their charlatanerie, to affect a great care where they have no business to meddle, and to take the very course to disturb the peace of their patient's mind under pretence of restoring it.

In addressing my friends, I was under another difficulty, besides that of not knowing in what attitude I ought to approach them: I feared to let them know too much of my situation, lest, even if they were disposed to communicate with me, or to come and visit me, whilst under the charge of a doctor—they might feel it too delicate a matter to interfere in, if they were at once informed of my dispute with my relations, and abandon me to my fate, without inquiry, except from those whose judgments were perverted.

Part of a letter to Lady C—— [Carr], from Ticehurst.
DEAR LADY C——,
I had determined not to remain here at all. But though nothing will administer true comfort to my mind, but consciousness of being no longer under control and observation, I am content to remain here until I am admitted to be of sound mind by Dr. Newington, or till he at least can remove your anxieties for my personal safety—provided I have permission from Dr. Newington, through

or without your consent, to proceed now to London, in order to take legal advice as to proceedings against the Drs. Fox, and to have the opinions of medical practitioners who are acquainted with my former state of mind, as to my actual —— or ——.

Part of another letter to the same, not sent.

MY DEAR MOTHER,

Thou usedst not to leave thy carriage beasts to the uncontrolled care of thy servants; nor even thy cattle to that of thy gardener and thy cowherd: thou deliveredst up thy son, in heart—spirit—soul and body, to strangers, and thou committedst him, even as other parents have also their children, the noble and the delicate of mankind, to the entire management and brute authority of hinds. Can I pardon Sp——r? Can I pardon you? Even a sportsman keeps his racehorse with its kind tenderly, and the drayhorse with its kind; neither is a strange dog turned on a sudden into a kennel with other hounds. I, because I was unable to judge or act for mine own self—because I was deprived through lunacy of power to articulate—and by the hand of Almighty God of command over my spirits, even in private, was, and am still degraded to fellowship and company with the low—the profligate—the infidel and the profane. I, a gentleman! Childish imbecility has been made the excuse for treating me with indignity, contempt, and oppression; and as though I was devoid of all feeling, I have been compelled to witness the mental and bodily agonies of those whom I could not relieve. Ay—I have seen them strangled, shaken, and beaten by ruffians, whom, if it had pleased Almighty God that I should have had at that time half the reason and determination that I have now—as Moses slew the Egyptian—I would have prayed for courage and strength to cast them with violence on the stones, to rise up again no more: except that prudence restrains me, because I cannot fly like him from the wrath of man, nor escape perpetual imprisonment. I say, I was given over in weakness, in helplessness, and in nervousness, to be harrowed by the sight of a menial attendant throttling a poor young lunatic gentleman till his face was bloated with blood, and his eyes started from their sockets; whilst a humane butcher spares even the cattle appointed for the knife, the sight of their fellow creatures' agonies.

Again, I repeat, can I pardon you and my sisters—my elder brother—no!

I had my head thrown back against a wall with such force as made me imagine my skull was split cross-wise. A force which no man would have dared to use to one who could apply to the law for protection against assault with intent to stun or render lifeless, with reasonable hope of being relieved: and such as I should have feared of making use of towards a sane man, for fear of deranging his reason. Such is the treatment the son of a noble family is subjected to in a lunatic asylum. These are the hands his mother's affection delivers his soul and person into. You plead example, and call that an excuse. I mentioned ———'s conduct as an instance of similar cruelty, negligence, selfishness, and oppression; but neither are the cases parallel, for he knew the state of his daughter's mind by experience, and had I believe attempted to heal and reclaim her. Thou wast content to banish me from town upon hearsay; and abhorredst the idea of Sp———r bringing me up to Ealing, and lately to town: and prevailedst on him not to write to me those communications which alone could relieve my heart, and bring any comfort to my love. My misery might have been alleviated by your affectionate compassion, indulgence, and consideration—and by the solicitude of my sisters, and my confidence in them—in their attachment, secrecy, and deliberation. C—— being a lunatic, could not, I conceive, endure her mother's preciseness and scrutiny, nor perhaps her father's severe authority.

I am not now surprised at accounts I have heard, if I remember correctly, of lunatics living at variance with their relations and friends. Can I return to my mother—can any Christian gentleman return to his relations—after they have proved by their actions, their no less hatred for their son's spiritual glory, than contempt for his personal comfort, and neglect of his bodily welfare? consigning him from their immediate superintendence to the care of, and control of, ay, intercourse, ay, continual intrusion and company, of menials. I say, can I associate with my mother after this? If I value the blood that was poured forth for my soul's salvation, can I have sympathy with any of them?—unless you all acknowledge to me personally, your deep sense of shame at the enormous guilt you have incurred by such reckless indifference, I cannot. My affection must yield to higher considerations. Nay, the good of her own soul, my duty as faithful witness of awful truths, prevents it; and I conceive where a lunatic has not those or better motives, a sense of his own natural dignity, and the duties he owes to his Creator, to assert his claim to respect, as any authority in society, and—

God forgive thee, my dear mother, God forgive thee; even the share of guilt thou must have had in those awful expressions of my wrath and indignation, which were torn out of my heart by the cruelty of my situation, which I pray you to forgive me for as disrespectful to you, to your infirmities of age, and to your authority; though in doing so, I caution you not to mock at yourself as doubting their sincerity (they are fearfully true), or that they are fully justified by my torture. The Lord commanded me to write many of them; most of them I saw written on the paper, in faith, for me to copy, and the Holy Spirit, in whom I have hoped and trusted——.

In a paper written about this time, I find the following reflections on the illness of my cousin ——, above alluded to:—

I used to think of —— as older than me—as one to whom I could be of no service—of whose disease I knew nothing—of whose disposition I knew or remembered very little (query—cared to remember?)—of whose mental affliction I knew nothing.

I had want of hope to be of service to any lunatic. I said to myself, disease is beyond my power to cure or heal; and I did not know how far —— was affected by disease, or ill-health. I did not think, I believe, of delusion; or, if I did, conceived, from ridiculous stories and exaggerations, that they were incurable but by accident.

I had fear of, or respect for, or reverence towards, my uncle. I knew the family and he had wished to conceal it from me altogether; therefore I suspected ill-will towards any inquirer, or feared to wound his feelings.

Delicacy also prevented me. I knew some part of the disorder—apathy, and deadness to shame, or contumely . . . might be one. I feared . . . and brokenheartedness about some misdemeanor, which her friends might not trust to me.

But when I came to a right state of mind, and sound state of feeling, and wished to be of use, and to use reason with myself how to be so, I conceived her delusions might be healed by remonstrance and reason, and attention to the word of the lunatic, and belief of his word, and of the reality of the delusion to him; and by not calling it imagination.

[*Reply from mother.*]

Ealing, March 5th, 1832.

DEAREST JOHN,

Your letters make me quite miserable. It is most painful to me to be obliged to refuse you what you so earnestly desire, and which yet it is my duty to you not to grant. You are not in a fit state to be allowed to come to London. Your wish of prosecuting Dr. Fox for his conduct to you is a sufficient proof of it—if there was no other. Believe me, *my dear child,* I can have no wish to detain you an instant longer in your present situation than is necessary for your recovery. It will be our greatest happiness to have you well and able to come amongst us again: *and you will then be the first to acknowledge what erroneous views your illness has made you take of our conduct to you.* You are evidently so much improved lately, that if you can but make up your mind to remain quietly in your present situation, and dismiss as much as possible all irritating subjects, I cannot but hope, by the blessing of God, that we shall have you restored to us in a few months' time. But at present, as it is evident that all I can say in reply to your letters only tends to irritate you the more, I must decline after this making any answer to any letters of reproach that you may address me, and I beg that you will not write to me any more till you feel more kindly disposed to me.

I am afraid from what you say, that I must have missed a letter, in which you asked me to send you something, &c., &c.

The remainder of the letter was on family topics.

Part of a letter begun in answer to the above.

MY DEAR MOTHER,

In your letter to me, you say, that I am not in a fit state to be allowed to come up to London; "your wish of prosecuting Dr. Fox for his conduct to you is a sufficient proof of it, if there was no other." This makes me hope that you are acting under a mistaken view of my case altogether, and indeed no wonder. If you will refer to my letters you will see that I do not wish to come up to town to prosecute Dr. Fox: it makes me fear that you have not received a letter which I wrote to F——, nor read my other letters with attention. In my letter to F——, I expressly——

But the longer I dwelt on the above letter of my mother to me, —her summary decision that my desire to prosecute Dr. Fox was a proof of continued insanity; her assuming that I had no cause for irritation, and declining to write to me any more until I wrote without irritation; her presuming that my views of her conduct were erroneous—when I recollected all I had already gone through, from her neglect, when I looked upon the horrible consequences of such a resolution of her mind—a long, perhaps a perpetual imprisonment—or my being obliged to deny the truth, and to lie against my conscience, I could not keep patience—her expressions of sorrow for my situation, or of a desire to see me restored to a sound mind, &c., &c., came to my understanding as the keenest and cruellest mockery—though I willingly believed she did not know whose instrument she was in so writing—and I reflected even on her addressing me as *her dear child,* instead of her dear son; considering it a proof that she did not respect my character. I then wrote in the following style—if not the following letter verbatim. Soon after this, feeling that I could not command my feelings respectfully towards her—I declined corresponding with my mother directly, and as I could not procure the mediation of any friend, I addressed my sisters:—

March 6 or 7, 1832.

Lady C—— [Carr],

I received your letter this afternoon; it is dated March 5, Ealing. I will answer it *seriatim.* In the first place, my letters *must* make you miserable, and in the second place, I am glad of it, and of your confession—because either you are lunatic and made miserable by nonsense, or they carry weight, argument, and terror with them.

Time will show whether or not I am a lunatic in wishing to prosecute Dr. Fox. I will not waste argument with you on this subject. You have succeeded in preventing me coming to London; whether or not now it would be of use to my lawsuit to come, I do not know; I have been delayed now come Friday four weeks since I left Dr. Fox's; and four weeks and three days since that treatment was left off for which I intend to prosecute Dr. Fox; of course, therefore, the attestation of my medical friends, to my state of health and of mind, such as it then was, can no longer be so valuable as it was.

How far the law may require such attestation I do not know; but if I fail in my lawsuit through want of it, I shall certainly make the punishment of the law fall upon you, or Sp——r, or Dr. Newington, whichsoever it may concern, if I can: and not only so, but even if I succeed in my prosecution of Dr. Fox, I will endeavour to make you sensible—all three of you, in the legal way— that I am not to be mocked at; unless I receive an apology.

I am a lunatic. But for that very reason I will make you wince at daring to oppose me in a legal, reasonable, natural, and consistent course to obtain lawful and just ends. You do not respect my disease. This I ought to expect from you, but you add oppression and injustice to one whose illness makes him prone to suspicion: whose illness!—no—but whose sense of the unnatural behaviour of his family, has at last made him prone to suspect evil even in good.

Since I have been a lunatic, I have not dared to make an appeal to my Maker in prayer, for fear of mocking; four times I have endeavoured to do so, and one of them is for your death by the cholera morbus; or for your more confirmed lunacy. Any tidings by which I may hear of the authority you abuse, being conveyed even to S——r's [Spencer's] indolent, self-sufficient, and superstitious hands, I may add, hypocritical, will delight me; but I revoke my prayer, for I can wait for an opportunity with patience, in hopes of a bitterer revenge, and of making you taste more deeply what it is to have mocked at the voice of reason and the word of life in a lunatic and contemned son. In fear you should wrest these words to my temporal hurt, I explain them again, by repeating, that I will seek no means of revenge but what the law makes secure or lawful, and human nature certain.

I will teach you one day or another, if God spares you or me, to know that it was your duty to have attended to my first demand for a private lodging; and that ever since I made it, you have known no other duty in respect of me, except to mourn over your whole conduct towards me in placing and leaving me in a lunatic asylum.

Gray hairs are an honour if found in the way of righteousness. I would respect your age if I could—but I cannot—and yet I hope I do in some sort.

As far as any thing in my disease hinders me from coming amongst you; you all know that nothing at all has ever prevented that, but your own unwillingness to bear that load which you, to whom it was natural to endure it, cast-off to be borne by strangers: nothing, I say, has prevented it but *that,* from the commencement of my illness; and now, you know also, all, that nothing in me prevents it but your own unwillingness to acknowledge your own brutal hypocrisies and my reasonableness. You fear the word of God in me—"Dear Mother"—too much, I know, to bear my person in a sound state of mind.

I shall probably still endeavour, if I can, during the next fortnight, to obtain by law what you refuse—leave to go to town for legal and surgical purposes—though, as I have said, I fear that my legal object is defeated by the obstacles which *you* have thrown in my way, besides others. If it is, I shall then wait, in the patient hope of future satisfaction, till I either obtain my release through the condescension of Betty Newington and Dame —— ——,* and then avail myself of their own sagacity and sense of duty for their brilliant manifestation before the legal and public tribunals of my country, as a pair of the wisest old women breathing; or, till I have sufficient courage to appeal to the law for my final emancipation:—but enough; I am losing self-possession.

As far as I can see—I mean, if I do not succeed in the course I am pursuing, in arousing some of spiritual or other friends to a sense of their duty to me;—I shall probably be compelled to go to Ealing, or to Sp——r's house. If so, I must endure it patiently, till the wisdom of the age be satisfied at last that I have determinate principles of thought and action. I hope you understand my words, but I fear not. But I can't help that, you know; it is your own fault.

Reflections written about the same time.

Because I became a lunatic, the persons around me threw aside consideration, all gentlemanly, all humane feelings. I was not treated with common civility or humanity, or common equity.

God b——t their souls.

God d——n their eyes.

God confound their judgments, for ever and ever.

I was not considered to have the wants and common feelings of a brute beast—no—or to need the necessary sustenance even, or exercise, or use of my bodily limbs; neither was I washed or cleaned, or allowed to dress myself, or dressed by others.

Neither have I since been treated as I deserved. I have been treated with inhumanity, want of consideration, misplaced severity and laxity.

For the inhuman, the unchristian, the barbarous, the disgusting, the degrading treatment which I have seen English gentlemen endure in that asylum, and which I have endured in my own person, would have made me melancholy. ——

I publish this fragment as a specimen of the exasperation pro-

* I do not think it right to publish this language without an apology. May God pardon those whose cruel treatment and neglect exasperated me to make use of it, and him who indulged in it. I must observe, the letters I sent were very much altered from these foul copies.

duced by my treatment. I have a few other fragments as passionate, but I need not shock my readers unnecessarily. I wrote them down to preserve them as memoranda of my state of mind. I am confident that no honest man will pretend, as the doctors do, *that* passion and violence as a justification for confinement, which were produced by confinement and contradiction.

Part of a Letter from my youngest Brother.

Tuesday, March, 1832.

MY DEAREST BROTHER,

I must apologise to you for not having answered your letter yesterday; I got it on Sunday afternoon, but I was so much engaged, &c., &c., &c.

I was very much pleased at receiving your letter, though I was grieved to think you should have thought that we had acted unkindly to you. You little know, my dear John, how much we have all been afflicted at your dreadful calamity, and though the measures taken by your family may not appear the best, and what you would have wished, still I think *that the event has proved, that they were not altogether to be condemned, as, with the blessing of God, you have, under them advanced most considerably to your recovery:** which, I am sure, it is the earnest prayer of all of us, may be speedily accomplished.

If you knew the anxiety of my mother and my sisters, as well as of Sp——r [Spencer] and the rest, about you, you would not accuse any of them of apathy and want of compassion; and I must say, that, as far as I am able to judge, I do not see that there is any just ground for your accusations.

I remember hearing at the time, that the presence of relations was of all things to be avoided, as being very prejudicial to the recovery of a person in your state, and the same objection was offered to letter-writing; and that opinion coming from persons skilled in the care and remedies necessary for your malady, it would have been wrong, I think, you must allow, to have acted against it. I just offer these remarks in great haste, to show you

---

* This passage whilst it was a proof of the simplicity of my family, and of their innocence in one sense, in another sense proved to me the indolence of their minds in reasoning concerning me. They took the first thought that came to them without examination; it was very difficult for me to bear and to unravel their sophisms. The spirit of the passage is false, not the letter. I did recover *under* Dr. Fox's management, but it was through the mercy of God and a strong constitution, *in spite of* their barbarities.

that, under these circumstances, I, for one, never felt it necessary or proper to go to see you or to write, which latter I most likely should have otherwise frequently done; and knowing that Sp—— went down occasionally and as often as was conceived good for you, to see that you were comfortable, &c., which I always then understood you were, I did not feel the same anxiety of looking after you myself which I otherwise should have done. You have put a number of questions to me, which if you think necessary after this, I will answer; but I hope you will see from what I have said, that though you were placed with Dr. Fox, you were still anxiously regarded and felt for by all of us.

I cannot recollect any place like that you describe about Slut.* I have no more time, so must conclude, with best love from Beatrice, and hoping and praying that you will continue recovering till you are quite restored, which God grant.

Believe me, dearest John,
Your affectionate Brother,
E. PERCEVAL

Extract from another letter from the same, dated March 23.

In answer to your letter I received the other day, the first time I received the sad news from Ealing of your great calamity was at Birmingham, and I was a little prepared for it, having been told by my sisters that they anticipated something of the kind; and I attributed it to your excitement of mind on religion, and I was not acquainted till afterwards, when I was in London, that you had been ill in Dublin before, which Sp——r [Spencer] gave as the immediate cause. I then also heard that Sp——r had heard of Dr. Fox's establishment, which was strongly recommended; and at the same time heard that those asylums were reckoned more favourable to cures than private ones: and I trust, my dear John, that it will prove so in your case. I never thought of proposing your removal to a place near Nottingham, as I never for a moment supposed you could be under better care; and the moment I heard from Ealing that through your letters you complained greatly of the treatment you received, I at once said that you should be removed, as I conceived anything that would fret or give excitement

---

* My brother had lost a favourite terrier bitch, named Slut, and I took a great deal of interest in his loss. Whilst thinking of his loss I saw two or three visions as of inns or turnpike-gates, at which I was made to understand he might have lost her, or might find her. I wrote to my brother to ascertain if there was any truth in these visions. His answer helped to cure me of my delusion.

to a person in your unhappy state must be injurious. If I continue writing I shall lose two days' post, so must conclude, my dearest brother, hoping soon that it will be in my power to see you, which I shall certainly take an early opportunity of doing, if I hear from you that you wish it, and I can get leave to go down to you. May God bless you with speedy recovery, and that you may be once more able to join us, is the sincere prayer of your very affectionate brother

E——.

Of all the letters I received, these showed the best feeling. Still I thought they were not conceived as they ought to have been. I think I did not express any wish for my brother to come and see me; but I let him know that I considered it his *duty* to come and look after me; that if he did not consider it his duty of himself to come and look after a *lunatic* brother who needed protection, and to have his treatment by strangers superintended, I could not *wish to see him* as far as I was concerned, though to see him well and happy would give me pleasure. There was nothing at this time to prevent me joining my family, but their not acknowledging that they had done wrong; so that I might live honourably with them, and honestly.

About this time I wrote certain questions in a letter to my mother, which were unattended to; this and the delay of several of my letters, by neglect, for about a fortnight, caused me much impatience and anxiety. I subsequently addressed the same questions to my second sister, who replied to me as follows:—

March 26.

My dear John,
Your letter to me came by the evening post on Saturday, under the same cover with the one to F—— about Nixon (the Cheshire prophet). I could not begin to answer it on Saturday evening, because Lady N—— was with us, and I was obliged to put it off till to-day. And first I must assure you that my not writing to you before did not proceed from either indolence or apathy; but it was thought* better for you to have but few correspondents, as writing seemed to agitate and excite you;† so mamma decided on being

---

* Without reason.

† This conclusion was adopted without inquiry or judgment, as to the nature of the writing and the cause of excitement.

your sole correspondent from this house, in which decision, as in every other that she has made concerning you, she was guided only by an anxious wish to do what was best for you.* I gave her your message about answering her letter when you had time. [Here follow notices of several articles I had desired to have sent to me—amongst others the dressing case, by the refusal to send which, I ascertained that my family apprehended I might be guilty of self-murder. It was partly with a view to ascertain this awful truth that I sent for it. My family had no just grounds for such a suspicion.] I now come to those questions to which you desire to have positive and plain answers. First, as to the private sitting-room at Dr. Fox's. There was no stipulation made for one originally; but Sp——r [Spencer] says, that his impression was that you would have the use of your bed-room for that purpose—and D—— says that from the appearance of the room he should have judged that it had been fitted up and furnished with that intention.† At the same time I should say that Dr. Fox expressly told S——, an opinion which I know is not only his, that *mixing*‡ with other patients was very beneficial; so of course, mamma's knowledge that you did so—would not have occasioned any remonstrance on her part, as long as you expressed no dissatisfaction§ on your part with the arrangements; in fact it was no subject of discussion between them till your letters complaining of it arrived about Christmas. She then went to Dr. Fox to beg that you might have a private sitting-room if he saw no objection to it, and also, as she I believe

* She appeared to herself only to be so guided.

† Can any one believe that a gentleman—and my brother is truly a gentleman—would so treat a gentleman grown up, and of the habits of society and of conduct such as were mine, in so absurd and puerile and degrading a manner? Can any one believe that the room thus spoken of, was a room with bare white-washed walls and scanty bed-room furniture! Yet how many do the same?

‡ I cannot understand, nor do I believe this. I have found *the occasional* sight of a lunatic patient's errors have corrected me, or set me on my guard against similar ones: but if "mixing" be advantageous, surely the doctor and my friends should have distinguished between that and *constant communication* and society.

§ Therefore, as long as I was stupid enough to continue in unbecoming and unhealthy circumstances, for aught those guardians of mine, who were of sound mind, reflected about it, I might have been allowed to continue. But when I began to exercise sound judgment, that is, when I needed their care no longer, I with difficulty obtained a hearing to my complaints. My mother's first letter to me informed me that Dr. Fox refused me even a private sitting-room, and that she must be guided by his judgment.

explained to me some time ago, took other advice as to the expediency of removing you from Dr. Fox's establishment. This answer to your first question, answers also your second as far as relates to her knowledge of your being all the year exposed to the company of lunatics. But you say, a set of vulgar lunatics and servants. Now with respect to the lunatics— Sp——r [Spencer] was told by Dr. Fox that they were classed in three sets according to their rank, and that the different classes though they mixed among themselves, which, as I said before, was considered beneficial, did not mix with one another excepting sometimes one of the second class, if a good player, joining with the gentlemen in games of skill—bowls, billiards, &c. &c. Of course the first-class accommodation was engaged for you—but it was never said that that class did not admit persons of lower rank than grandsons of Earls or members of noble families in any degree, or even than the *élite* of the gentry. And as you know that in society you are liable to meet people by no means your equals in rank, and still less, perhaps, in cultivation and refinement of mind, whom yet you could have no possible right to object to meeting and receiving as gentlemen, so of course that distinction between the degrees of gentility and of refinement could still less be made in an establishment like Dr. Fox's, where the line can only be drawn between the higher, the lower, and the middle classes, and he could not refuse to admit as gentlemen, those whose friends were willing to pay for the accommodation of gentlemen; though at the same time the difference between individuals, especially in refinement of mind and of feelings, must be still more perceptible under their unfortunate circumstances than in the ordinary intercourse of society. Then with respect to the servants, their attendance *of course** was indispens-

* I observed my family whenever they asserted a proposition against me which was not true in letter or in spirit, always introduced it with the words *"of course;"* this style of speech I know to be a proof of want of reflection; and I recommend all those who reason with such phrases to examine the sentences to which they attach them. I replied to this letter, sentence by sentence, but all in vain, as follows:—The attendance of Dr. Fox's servants was indispensable, but it was not "of course" indispensable that I should have had their society all day, if I had been placed in proper circumstances: the servants were necessarily vulgar, but it was not *"of course,"* that they should have been so low and vulgar as they were, even if no gentleman could have been prevailed on to accept the situation. Being subjected to the regime of Dr. Fox's first-class patients, "of course" I was treated like them, but it did not follow, that "of course" I was to be contented with the wisdom of those who subjected me to that regime, without inquiry, and kind consideration of my particular disposition and habits. Being in the world, I did mix "of course" with many men of

able, and it was equally *of course* that they must be vulgar. Your next question is marked "two," respecting an operation performed on you by Dr. Fox's orders; whether it was with or without her sanction, with or without her knowledge? previous or subsequent to the performance of it? also what cause was assigned for it by Dr. Fox? This question my mother answered in one of her letters to you; but F—— says it had been forgotten, and the answer was inserted in a little corner of the letter, where it may have escaped your notice. Mamma never heard of any operation from Dr. Fox, except once bleeding from the temporal artery when you were considered to be in a state of plethora, of which by the way Sp——r, when he had visited you in the spring, mentioned that you had the appearance—a more than usual redness and fulness about the face. Mamma did not hear of the operation from Dr. Fox till after it had been performed, and was then told by him, that though more painful than bleeding from the arm, you had borne it patiently, and that it had so beneficial an effect at the time as to be followed by a lucid interval, in which you expressed a strong hope of your recovery.* We afterwards heard from D—— when he had seen you in the autumn, of an operation which had been performed on your ear, and which was rendered necessary by blows, which you had given yourself in chapel. This second operation I think you alluded to in one of your letters to mamma after Christmas, as you mentioned one which had been rendered necessary by blows received. To this day mamma has not heard of any other operation

---

uncongenial habits and education; but there is a wide difference between the occasional intercourse and interchange of respects and civilities with such gentlemen, when duty or unity of pursuits, or feelings of gratitude, bring us together, and the being huddled with them in one prison for fourteen months, without distinction, or where distinction in one's favour is painful; and it did not follow "of course," that because I might be thrown during a voyage into the heterogeneous society of a steamer's cabin, that I was to submit to such society, as my drawing-room and dinner companions for a whole year, without just complaint.

* The conduct of Dr. Fox in proceeding to this operation without my mother's approval was very improper. If, too, I had attempted resistance, as I was tempted to do it, it might have been highly dangerous. I feel much offended at the separation of the temporal artery, but my objections would be treated as prejudices. I recollect on one occasion after an operation, saying quietly, that I hoped I should recover, but with no distinct idea of what I meant; on the contrary, I leant my head on this occasion in the bosom of my servant, calling him my saviour. I cannot help thinking this to be a very unfit operation to be performed on lunatic patients: as the operations of the mind depend upon the regulations of the breathings and of the pulses, and on the wholesome flow of the blood through the system, which must be for a time impeded, till nature has re-formed a channel.

whatever having been performed on you, either from Dr. Fox or from any one else.

[The rest of this letter was on many family matters.]

I find the following fragments of letters I wrote about this time, or perhaps later. I retained these sheets because I did not think them of a proper nature to send to my sister.

[*Part of letter to sister, F.*]

These are some of the principal injuries I received, and I cannot wonder at any inhumanity which might occur in that asylum, when the very basis of the treatment consists in the very cruellest and blackest cruelty which can be adopted towards human nature, whilst it is forced upon the objects as solicitude and anxiety for their lives and their eternal welfare. God knows, as I lift my hand and my eyes now to Heaven, I would rather have perished with your tender leave, by my own hands, by cutting my throat, by hanging, by drowning—in any way—than have gone through the fearful ordeal; which, whilst it exposed my body to insult and injury, and my person to degradation, hardened my heart, and ruined my soul. I know no other possible excuse for confining me in a public lunatic asylum, but fear for my own personal safety, or for that of some other. God knows I never attempted to do myself any injury, but under the fullest impression that it was for the benefit of my soul, and in expectation of being raised to life again, if I should accidentally happen to kill myself. Was then the care of my soul or body your object in selling me to strangers of no worth, and of whom you knew nothing. My *body* as well as *my health* has received injuries from neglect and violence, and mistreatment, of which the effects are still felt by me, are outwardly visible, and are preying upon my frame; *but enough*—I cannot write for very indignation.

Here, too, what am I doing? Whilst my brothers are living with their wives in town, I have not for a year and two months seen a woman's face with whom I could converse freely. If my brothers choose to wear the mask of Christianity in town with their wives, whilst they have treated me as they have done—let them. But then let them, whilst praying, I suppose, with their wives at home, remember that very word of life they prate so wonderfully about; which at the beginning declares that man was not made to be alone; and not expect me to endure unjust imprisonment with patience—and let me tell them that excommunicated from Christian society, and from Christian consolation and advice, I have human passions and human feelings; and let me tell my family too, that if they in their compassion for my soul, have thought fit to banish me from their bosoms, and to prescribe to me retirement, under pretence of management, I consider it much like preserving lobsters alive to put them into boiling water; and with my mother's kind leave, I would rather take care of my soul and body my own way, in obedience as far as I can to the light which the word of life throws upon the path which is conducive to the well-being of my life (which you all seem to have made *wondrous light* of indeed); and as I am neither enabled or willing to obey the precepts of St. Paul, or St. Peter, St. James, or St. Jude, for the sake of *the branch!* I will obtain that society by money which has been refused to blood! if so be that she will be so kind as to write to Dr. Newington to let me go about my own business. If she does not, God knows if I can wait in patience; but if I can I will—but in hopes of other things than you all expect for.

I am no madman now, though I may be a fool for writing so freely. If I am no Christian, you may, as I said before, thank yourselves, whilst I laugh at you, and ask after your progress in *Divine grace!* Thank God, I know now a little who is who? and what is what.

Farewell poor F——, —God grant you and all *good* sense; and preserve me in a *good* understanding, which having been restored to me—I hope not to throw lightly away. Give my love to my mother and sisters, and believe me

Your truly affectionate brother,

JOHN.

I send you enclosed the flower—but I believe *you* know it. I wish I was a good botanist.

Part of another letter to my family, full of remonstrances.

What prevented me from enduring HERE what I endured at Brisslington? Only that, thanks be to God! I was *not* in the state you supposed me to be in. Thanks be to God! I was then in the same capable state of protecting myself as I am now! though not so strong, and able to make myself feared and respected by the servants and manager of this asylum. Had it not been for this I should not probably have escaped from Bristol usage here, which I have seen myself employed to another (elderly) gentleman, and know by the handwriting of another lunatic gentleman that *he has* either endured or witnessed.

What thanks then do I owe to you? or where are your proofs of anxiety and kindness? None, and no where. I demanded a private lodging, and a servant of my own choosing? You go to the expense of 300 guineas for another lunatic asylum, and leave me to have any rough ostler Dr. Newington chooses to put about me.

I told you I was able to take care of myself—what do you do? You show my letters to Dr. this, that, and t'other, in London, who know nothing of me or you.

What did you reply to Spencer, who originally wished me to have been brought to Ealing? That you would not hear of it, it was quite out of the question.

Was it not your duty *then* to have seen in what state I was, your ownself. It was.

Was it kind to refuse it? No, it was not.

Was it not Sp——r's [Spencer's] duty to have travelled with me by easy stages up to town, and to place me in your neighbourhood? It was.

Was it not your duty in December to have sent down Sp——r [Spencer] or D—— [Dudley] to me, and for me, to bring me to town, that you might see yourself in what state I was? It was.

Has it not been your study to do so all along, since my dispute with you? Yes, it was, but not altogether. Because why? Because I have shewn you that I have great indignation against you all, for your conduct towards me; and you might reasonably think it indelicate to force me into your presence, or perhaps dangerous to my feelings.

What, however, is my demand now? Not to return to my family, for I say the truth, that I hardly *care a curse* if I never see the sight of you any more, *excepting* E—— [Ernest] *and poor* F—— [Frederick]! but I wish for a private lodging—and, so long as you choose to pretend that I need confinement—confinement IN PRIVATE.

And what is your duty now? To desire E—— to obtain leave of absence, or to make F—— call upon me to travel up to town, to be reconciled with you all, if you will confess yourselves *sinners* against my saviour; who desired me at Dr. Fox's to think of you; and to command your cleaning out the garden drains,* for your own safety and security—and to suggest schemes for *improving your idea of a crane* at the lodge gate, to prevent infection. Of whose kindness and goodness you took no account, nor did you relieve me by one prayer or one note of thanks-giving, in reply to him as the author of my care, but only to me; neither did you try from thence to draw out the cause and motives of my delusions, in order to heal me if possible. But you left me, a prophet of the Lord, bound by his affliction, amongst blaspheming and infidel lunatics.

---

* This alludes to imaginations I had at Dr. Fox's respecting preserving my family from the cholera morbus, on which I thought earnestly, and *in which I still believed* as a species of inspiration at this time.

CHAPTER XXXI

ACCOUNT OF ESCAPE FROM MR. C. NEWINGTON'S MADHOUSE,
AND REASONS, &c.

Copied verbatim from a manuscript written at Ticehurst, soon
after the occurrences narrated in it.

Dr. Newington's Asylum, April 26, 1832.

HAVING for the last nine weeks or more been a resident in this
asylum against my own will, and considering confinement in my
case altogether unnecessary.

Having also peculiar objections,* of a solid and justifiable

* These objections are, first, that I AM A GENTLEMAN, and *in affliction*, the
first ALONE makes *my sense* of *confinement cruel*, being, as I am, constantly exposed to meet other patients or their servants whenever I leave my room, and
constantly when I go out or come in from exercise, as also when out walking.

Secondly. That there is no fastening to the water-closet door so that I
have seldom or never been there without being intruded upon suddenly by
one or other of the domestics. *This* I have only once mentioned to Mr. Newington, or twice.

N.B. I do not object to this precaution in a lunatic asylum, though I
suppose some fastening might be contrived which would secure a patient's
feelings of delicacy and modesty from being insulted, and yet, if necessary, be
opened by a stratagem from without side.

Thirdly. I object, and have informed Mr. Newington of my objections
since the first evening I have been here, to my having a man servant to sleep
in my room with me.

It is a filthy and stinking, and indelicate insult to my best feelings, besides
this I consider it *unwholesome.*

I think it also an inhuman and unnecessary regulation in any lunatic
asylum for any person who objects to it; for the servants of *two patients* might
sleep in a room between each of the patient's rooms, with doorways into them.

Fourthly. There is an offensive practice in this asylum of leaving the nature, to public confinement, and to other regulations in Dr. Newington's establishment, extremely offensive and indelicate, and such as no gentleman ought to be subjected to longer than his madness renders *absolutely necessary, nor indeed in my opinion even then.*

---

excrement of the patients in the pan of the water-closets for inspection, at the same time that they have not sufficient ventilation. This I have not yet mentioned to Mr. Newington, because it is *beastly,* and yet I know he is aware of it.

Fifthly. I object to having my walks for *recreation* spoilt, by the attendance of a common hind close upon my heels.

Sixthly. I object to the general deportment of the servants of this asylum as being at the least rude, I have also no bell in my bed-room or sitting-room; and though these things may both be highly advantageous to a poor lunatic, I object to them *both,* as rendered unnecessary by my re-establishment in good *health.*

Seventhly. I object to the annoyance of hearing them and the patients whistling, singing, fluting, fifing, fiddling, laughing, talking, running, and even occasionally dancing in the passages and wrestling.

Eighthly. I feel a *desire* to *seek society* which I am suited to, and I consider it necessary for my advancement in good health. I have confidence *in my resolution* and *habits* to follow it only in moderation, and to leave it, if by chance necessary.

Observation. I deem it is *insane* conduct on the part of a physician, as any insanity can be in a patient, not to *persuade* his patients and to *prevail upon* them to re-enter society suited to their habits, as also not to recommend their friends to place them where such society may be *easily procured.* I know in *some cases* grief alone compels a person to retire from the world, but also it is injurious to a person to indulge that propensity too long. I know also that *lunacy* makes a person unfit for the society of his superiors, and often of his EQUALS, and as his *fits,* although only occasional, may return irregularly, he cannot be trusted, except where his eccentricities may be tolerated, when they are not of a kind to produce evil; but I consider any system of cure, which pretends as its BASIS *on all occasions* to separate a man or human being from the society he has been accustomed to, unless at the very commencement of his affliction to be impious and madness as well as empiricism: in the very second chapter of the Bible; in the eighteenth verse our Maker expressly says of man, "IT IS NOT *good for man* to be *alone.*" I conceive that my Creator knows what is best for His own work, moreover this word has never been contradicted by my own experience, but *mad doctors* neglect the *word of life!* and follow their own *conceits* in insisting upon a *regimen! !*

Ninthly. I object to the situation of Mr. Newington's asylum as very cold, and this partly owing to its lofty situation, partly to the cold clayey soil and other causes; the windows also and doors admit cold currents of air, so that I am compelled to sit with my feet in the fender, or over the fire-place to keep my feet warm, a dangerous and unwholesome remedy!

Having mentioned these objections to Dr. Newington and my family, by word of mouth and by letter repeatedly, in order to obtain my release.

Having, also, expressed to my mother my willingness to consent to be confined still, in a private family, or private lodging, and also to Dr. Newington my readiness to submit to his control, if he could find lodgings for me in any *warm* farm-house or cottage in the neighbourhood, provided that he would allow me to sleep without a man servant in my bed-room.

Having been asking of my mother a private lodging ever since the 29th of November, 1831, as indispensable to my more speedy recovery and comfort.

Having considered it also necessary to my more speedy recovery to seek the society of my equals, since the middle of March, and having mentioned this also to my mother, and Mr. Newington.

Having received no satisfactory answer from my mother; but letters from herself and two of my sisters, by which it became *evident* to me that they did not carefully read mine, nor consider my arguments.

Having also had the misfortune of having seven of my letters to my family at home, and three to one of my brothers at Derby, miscarried.

Having moreover received no answer at all to about forty-five other letters, addressed to different friends in order eventually to procure legal advice.

Having in all written above sixty letters to obtain my release, with no success.

Having also demanded leave to proceed to town to see *my dentist,* Mr. Cartwright, not having been attended to by one since I last left London in 1829, or 1830, and being also afraid to trust a country dentist, or indeed any other than Mr.—— or Mr. Cartwright in town; and having been refused permission to proceed to town for this purpose by my mother and Mr. Newington.

Having been also refused the same permission, both by Mr. Newington,—at the advice of Dr. Mayo, owing to my nervous state of body and general health,—and by my mother, at a time when I was particularly anxious to obtain the medical certificates of two surgeons and one apothecary, my acquaintance in town, to *that*

VERY state of mind and body, which I attributed chiefly to my having been forced, *contrary to my written request,* to make use of the cold bath and shower-bath, during the winter of January, 1832, when in a delicate and already excited state of mind and frame; for which I purposed to prosecute the Drs. Fox, in order at least to expose their treatment to the scorn and hatred it deserves.

Having also given my mother and Mr. Newington, as a reason for my proceeding to town, my wish to prosecute Dr. Fox, and the necessity of obtaining the advice of a legal *friend,* not to commence *immediate* prosecution, but to take such *steps* as *might ensure my ultimate success*: having been refused this request by Mr. Newington, although I offered to go up to town with any one of his domestics, and to return in three days if my mother chose, or the keeper thought me injured by the sight of, and by communication with my friends.

Having given Mr. Newington solid reasons for my not anticipating a relapse, which is the only objection he gave me at that time for my not proceeding to London; and now* "for my not having a private lodging in this neighbourhood."

Being also subject to various other inconveniences, privations, and mockeries of my reason, *impertinences,* and *insults,* and neglects.

Having also waited NINE weeks for the arrival of the visiting magistrates in vain, who are my *only* protectors! and feeling that they after all are holding an office for which, in one sense at least, they appear to be not responsible; fearing also that they might not pay attention to my arguments, but act from prejudice and suspicion, without being culpable before the tribunals of my country which others already have done; as well as mistake my reasons, and having no other means of obtaining release.

Having also, in vain, asked for Mr. Courthope's direction, he being on a tour, or party of pleasure.

---

* Except, *nota benè,* one notable reason, that he thinks it right to keep me with something to hope for! that he thinks my hopes of benefiting by more privacy will be disappointed! *Ergo,* it is imprudent to try it, as if forsooth following a reasonable course to pursue a *probable* and healthy end, was like a gambler throwing his last stake, or a general sacrificing his best troops at a venture.

Having also no *legal assistance,* nor any offered to me but that of Mr. Newington's own solicitor.

Having moreover applied, in March, to Captain Wetherall, magistrate, of Paixley, Ticehurst, for his opinion and protection, and having only received *good wishes* as an answer, and the assurance that he had no authority.

Having, also (if my memoranda are not incorrect), addressed a letter to *Mr. Courthope,** on *the 13th of April,* to which I received no answer.

I resolved to endeavour to effectuate my own escape, even at the risk of my own life and limbs, or at the expense of another's blood; being as I conceived illegally, cruelly, and also unreasonably CONFINED; but besides exposed to treatment in that confinement which was offensive, unbecoming, indelicate, and not to be put up with any longer with patience, and, therefore, a continual irritation to my mind, and cause of *ruin* to *my soul;* viz., a temptation to fretfulness, anger, wrath, impatience, impenitence, vindictive feelings; and also of great injury to my moral system, being only in company with my inferiors, and exposed to the intercourse of ill-educated hinds, over whom I have little control.

On Tuesday, April 17, I attempted to put my resolution into execution according to a plan I had been before thinking of; having an opportunity by my attendant seeming to dose on a carpenter's stool. Two dogs barking as I passed through a farm-yard, alarmed some peasants working in a field through which I had designed passing; this impeded me, and occasioned my servant's obtaining sight of me, who came up to me as I leaped into a lane.

His words were, "Ay, now, you'll come along, back again." "Not for those words," said I, "at any rate I will give you a start, so here goes." I commenced running down the lane—he pursued; but feeling that I had not breath, nor probably strength enough to run so long as he could, and also fancying that he was gaining ground of me, I saw that my only chance was to get into the fields, and escape, if I could, in the woods, by his losing sight of me. I

---

* Directed to Mr. Courthope, at Ticehurst. Mr. C. received it, but I do not know when; he gave me no answer till he came to visit the asylum on the 17th of May; he had been in the country some time previous to the visit.

saw some bars, which, in my confusion, I thought to vault over, but when I had lost my time to consider them, I found them too high. In endeavouring to clamber over them my servant caught me by the skirts of my coat.

He had before pursued me with words, saying, "You have dropped your watch," "Ah, I'll make you pay for this when I catch you!" &c. He now held me between his arms, pressing me with his breast closely against the bars, when he recovered his breath a little, he began, "Eh! now you'll walk back, or else I'll make you. Eh! you thought I was asleep—I wasn't though! I knew what you were about. Now come along back, or else I'll make you! Pretty behaviour this for a gentleman! Aren't you ashamed of yourself? I'll teach you to run away from *me*—come along back?"—"No, I won't," said I. "Won't you?" said he. "No, not by your making—not by you alone;" and I begged him, bantering, to leave me, and go back for his coat. "Not without you," he said. Then I proceeded to try my strength at wrestling with him, and having laid hold of his neck, was tempted to throttle him, but my stomach revolted at the idea—which I had seen practised on patients at another lunatic asylum, and I said, "No, I won't do that." I also perceived that he was stronger than I was.

As he however attempted to force me from the bars, or to keep me there, I endeavoured to wrestle with him, but he seized me by my neckcloth and soon had me on my back on the ground. He there shook me, not however very violently, by the neckcloth, three or four times against the ground, as I still refused to return with him. He kept vomiting forth his fury in threats, "Ah, I'll have you in the straight waistcoat all day for this! You shall never come out again any more! You shall be locked up all the day through. I'll manage you! They shall put you into the dungeon!" "Dungeon!" said I, "I didn't know that there was one."—"But there is though. They shall put you in along with the madmen; now come along back." I told him, "Now, Rolph, or what is your name; hold your tongue, and listen to me, I will speak to you. I consider myself illegally confined here, and justified in attempting to take your life, or to knock you down, in recovering my liberty; which I would do now if I were strong enough, but you have the broader pair of shoulders. I am an Englishman, and love my liberty as well as you or any other man; and besides think that I might recover my good health sooner elsewhere. I counsel you, therefore, to let me go; for by the Lord, I will hold you responsible at law, as well as Dr. Newington and others, for my illegal detention, if it is illegal; in that case, my day is yet to come. You know the old proverb, 'Every dog has his day,' or, 'My day now, yours to-morrow.' I warn you therefore, to be careful what you do, and to use no unnecessary violence to force me to return, nor to attempt it, but to let me proceed."

A bricklayer's labourer having come up, who was sent after me by his master to assist Rolph, I told him to leave me alone, that it was no business or affair of his at any rate; and I threatened to prosecute him also for an assault against my person, if I could, when I recovered my liberty; telling him also that I considered myself unjustly confined, and asking him how he would like imprisonment his own self. I also warned him of a passage in Proverbs, "He that passeth by and meddleth with strife that doth not belong to him, is like one that taketh a dog by the ears." As he, however, was not rebuked by me, I told him, "then I will not return home without your having assaulted me, that I may prove your interference in a court of justice."

Accordingly I resisted the two men till I was again thrown on the ground, and afterwards only walked home in their custody.

On my arrival at home, I met Mr. Newington, who ran up to meet me. He took me by the hand; I believe I was rather nervous, but collected; he remonstrated with me upon what had taken place, and argued with me. I laughed a great deal at his manner and his reasoning, but I told him I should certainly attempt my escape by force, if I could, as I had already warned him.

He told me I was mistaken in my legal opinion that I had a right to take away another's life, and justified in doing so to effect my freedom.

I answered, "In that case I am wrong; but you, sir, are no lawyer, and I must have legal opinion. But," said I, "at any rate, sir, I will not attempt the life of another till I am satisfied by a lawyer that I have to right to do so."

He told me he considered it his duty to confine me. I told him I also had a duty I owed to my God—to escape from unjust confinement, if I could, under circumstances which I could not bear.

Mr. Newington told me, "There, my good sir, you are in a delusion." This was his duty, if he thought so, and noble and candid! I replied, "We differ in opinion, we must leave it to others to decide."

Other conversation of more importance took place; but referring to other matters, lawsuit, &c.

In the same evening he returned to my room, saying to me "Well, now sir, what am I to do? Your servant told me that you attempted to strangle him, and he is afraid to sleep with you, and so are all the servants of the house."

I interrupted him, seeing what was coming, and said, "Then, sir, that will just do; you know I do not wish to have any one to sleep with me, I have told you so, long ago and often, and it is one of my objections to continuing under your care."

He said, "No, that will not do, I must have you fastened in your bed, or two servants must sleep with you, one is afraid to sleep with you alone."

I said, "That is, sir, to offer me an additional insult for no reason; but I must submit to it, I suppose. Why should I not, however, have my room to myself?"

Mr. Newington.—"You'll try to effect your escape, sir, during the night."

Lunatic!—"How so, sir," said I, "I cannot fly through the bars, and you know it: besides there is a bolt, as you also know, outside my door, which can be bolted."

Mr. N.—"Ay, sir, but you'll try to break through the walls of the house."

Lunatic!—"How can I, sir? What! do you think that I can do this with my earthenware pitcher and glass decanter? No, sir; but you are now a lunatic yourself, and are mocking me, and determined to insult my weakness."

Mr. Newington paused a few moments, and then said, "You must be confined in your bed, the servant won't sleep with you otherwise."

Lunatic!—"What does he fear, sir?"

Mr. N.—"Why, you'll get up in the night and strangle him, or something! You'll try to effect your escape!"

Lunatic!—"How can you think that, sir, possible? You know in the first place that I am locked in, and in the next place he is stronger than I, and there are about half a dozen young hearty fellows within call on each side of us, how can you think that I could attempt any thing so foolish?"

Mr. N.—"A sudden impulse may seize you. You ran away,— I thought that you would never have run away."

Lunatic!—"You know that it was no sudden impulse made me run away, but that I have given you warning that I would attempt it long ago, and I have been conning over my plan ever since I was here."

Mr. N.—"It was an act of folly and madness."

Lunatic!—"No, sir, it was an act that required forethought, dexterity, courage, fortitude and resolution, and enterprise."

Mr. N.—"Well, sir, I must have you confined; none of my servants will sleep with you."

Lunatic!—"You know, sir, I neither want them, nor need them;" but, said I, "perhaps if you will allow me to make my case known to the female keepers, one of them will have no objection to sleep with me unconfined?" This I said in fun, for I saw that reason was useless.

At night he attended himself, kindly enough to see his own ridiculous and unreasonable precaution carried into execution, for fear I might be tempted to further acts of violence. When the manacle, however, was on my arm, he conceived that I could slip my hand through it. I did not answer him, for I thought him too absurd to be reasoned with; but I asked him if he was not afraid the *iron would melt* during the night:—the one seemed as probable as the other to myself.

After having tried about six or seven bolts, one was deemed sufficiently tight to ensure my safety, and I was left, to be put into a fever by its confinement through the whole night. Mr. Newington told me that many patients requested to have the manacles put on. I answered, "I hope they like it," and thought such people are surely made for these houses.

Mr. Newington also, during the day, threatened to make my man-servant sit continually in the room with me. I insisted upon this not being done, as he knew that I could not make my escape through the iron-barred window; and that I was perfectly capable of being trusted alone, having been so now eight weeks or more in his own asylum, and one week also and some days allowed to sit *alone* in the asylum which I quitted to come here; I also added, "Besides this, sir, my door can be bolted outside, if my servant will stay within call."

Next morning I went out walking, as he had resolved, with two attendants. I find this unexpectedly a great relief to me (as they are occupied with conversation between each other, which distracts their attention from me), and to my feeling of annoyance at being alone with a being who cannot behave to me respectfully, and yet whom I feel called upon at times to make some observation to—very likely through *lunacy*.

In the afternoon I wished to go again to see the labourers at work, which is the only amusement I have here; but I find an order is now given that I should not go there, now that *my way of escape is discovered!* and that I am doubly guarded.

Mr. Newington also has refused me leave to walk off his premises in this beautiful country. This is another precaution in which he is *only* justifiable by the supposition that I am a lunatic, and likely to do myself or others injury off his grounds; or at liberty. It is true, there *are probably* more *chances of escape* in my being amongst the woods and farm-houses, than on his grounds; but he must suppose me a madman to attempt to escape by stealth or without assistance from two clowns both my superiors in strength and courage, and swiftness, and knowledge of the country.

Mr. Newington also had informed me, on Tuesday, that by an Act of Parliament, I was defended by two things—the appointment of magistrates to superintend these asylums, and the existence of a commission in town to prosecute lunatic physicians and others for the unjust detention of lunatics:* and I told him that this altered my relations to the government of my country very much in my opinion, that I should therefore hesitate long before I at-

* This I found afterwards was a complete falsehood.

tempted to escape from the asylum by violence, and that I should not attempt it at all until I had further information and legal advise, unless as sure as I could be of succeeding.

I therefore considered his forcing me to be attended by two keepers an unnecessary precaution, and intended partly as an insult or act of tyranny to *punish me* for having attempted to escape: whereas, he ought to have punished his servant for allowing me so fair a chance. But I am thankful that it is rather a blessing than a punishment.

I consider the fears of his servants, and his own, of my being capable of so wantonly cruel, desperate, and useless an attempt as to strangle my servant at night, to escape from the house, if pretended, as insulting me, if real, as lunacy; so also with regard to my being able to get my hand through any of the bolts he put upon me, this was absolute lunacy, uncontrolled and unreasonable fear, proceeding to an act of wanton tyranny!

On Monday night, April 23, I desired my servant to ask the butler for another manacle to my wrist, as the one I had on was so tight it hurt my wrist. The butler came up shortly without one, and told me, "That I couldn't really be hurt by it surely, for Mr. Newington put it on himself, and he is afraid that you will slip your hand through another," or words tantamount. I told him, "Mr. Hervey, you are both mocking me and giving me the lie. I don't care for Mr. Newington or any one else. I desire that you will walk out of the room." "No, sir, I don't wish to give you the lie; I am sure I didn't give you the lie." "You have, Mr. Hervey, in spirit at least if not more, so I pray you leave the room."

On Tuesday night Mr. Hervey brought me a new bolt by Mr. Newington put it on himself, and he is afraid that you will slip pretty well.

On Wednesday, the 25th, I went out walking, only in the afternoon, the forenoon it was cold and rainy: during the week I had practised myself in running to gain wind. This afternoon as I was passing through one gate from another to complete my walk round the grounds along a back lane which passes through the grounds, the servant told me, "Sir, I have orders from my master to make you return through the same gate, and not to allow you to go down that lane any more." I said to him, "Nonsense, who gave you those orders?" "Mr. Newington, sir." "D——n Mr. Newington," I answered, and proceeded to walk down the lane. "Mr. Newington has desired me to prevent you, sir; therefore, it is of no use." "I don't care a d——n for Mr. Newington," I replied, "he is an old fool!" and I proceeded to run down the lane; it proceeds to the back of his asylum, and is not three hundred yards long. The servant overtook me, and threatened to force me to go back. I said, "No, I insist upon going on." He told me, "No sir, it's of no use, you can't overcome me, it's no use trying." I told him, I must try one day or other, so I might endeavour as well then as later. He struggled with me some time, but as I found him apparently stronger, and I had no great object in view, I said, "Oh, very well then, if I must not go that way"—he let go of me—"let us try another," and I made full speed for the turnpike; he overtook me, however. I again wrestled with him to try his strength, but found him at least one third my superior.

We had a good deal of conversation; and I walked with him into the grounds, here after proceeding through the garden* on to the broad walk, I broke off the conversation, by saying, "well then let us run here at any rate," and set off at an easy pace as I had previously used to do; "No, sir, you must not run any more, I have orders to prevent you from Mr. Newington!" "Nonsense," replied I, "I will run when I will, and walk when I will at least." I ran again to try his speed; he overtook me decidedly, and insisted on my walking, and walking in. "No," said I, "not unless you make me, neither will I walk; I have my exercise to take, and if I choose to run I will run, if I prefer walking I will walk."

It ended in my wrestling with him to prevent him forcing me in, at last he carried me neck and crop. During the afternoon I did not see Mr. Newington, I believe that he was unwell, but the servants of their own forethought and resolution sat with me in my room. I did not object to this; for though I did not feel prompted to do any mischief, if they thought that I was a lunatic, they were justified in taking precautions against it. But I observe

---

* The little fruit-garden at the east entrance.

that its continuance unjustly, that is unnecessarily, is likely to tempt a person to acts of violence, who has other many serious causes for complaint, which he feels unjust, malicious, and oppressive.

The same conduct being adopted towards me by the servants on the morrow (this day the 26th), I inquired if they had any orders to do so of my friend Rolph, as I thought it unnecessary, for they knew I was not lunatic, but perfectly calm, and peaceably striking on my pianoforte during the most part of the evening, also studying, and teaching one of them to spell and write. *But I find that Dr. Newington has given orders for them to continue in my room!* This I consider as an additional provocation to resistance and an insult, and an act of oppression. I hope however it will be discontinued to-morrow.

But, moreover, yesterday evening, the butler, Mr. Hervey, came to tell me, "Oh! sir, Mr. Newington hopes that you won't mind having another person to sleep with you to-night."

"Mr. Newington," said I, "knows my mind well enough upon that subject! I have already told him that I object to having one man in my bed-room! it is not necessary, and he knows it. But I must consent to what I cannot prevent." I then said, "but if it must be so, I hope you will give orders that I may have my window open two or three inches." "I don't know, sir, whether Mr. Newington would like that, sir!" "I do not know, sir," said I, "whether Mr. Newington likes it or not, I know that I do, and as he pretends to consult my wishes, that is my wish, which I desire may be attended to. I consider it unwholesome." "Oh, sir, but you have the ventilator." "What ventilator do you mean, Mr. Hervey?" "*The chimney!* sir." "That is no ventilator, however, sir, as I see I cannot have this wish," I pointed to the doors out of repair, and my sofa not covered fit for a gentleman's sitting-room, "perhaps your master will be so good as to put my room into decent order at least, which I have requested some time ago. That at least is one of my wishes, if he is pleased to consult my mind."

I cannot but express my opinion, that this too is an act of tyranny and wilful provocation, I am thankful however that I have not yet been provoked to any act of violence by it, having had prudence to delay at least what I purpose doing if it be persisted in, *i.e.* to pour water upon the beds of my servants when night comes on.

It cannot be for safety or precaution, it can only be a malicious affront, and perhaps purposed by design to provoke me to some further acts of violence, which may be misconstrued and attributed to lunacy; at least, I do not think myself unjust in this suspicion, for I already have one servant in my room, I am fastened by a bolt on my wrist, attached to a chain covered with leather to the frame of the bed, and servants sleep in all the rooms of the passage, which runs by my bed-room door; it is therefore a design to retaliate upon me my opposition to his folly out of doors, by fresh folly within! to provoke me to folly, perhaps to some unguarded expressions, and to break my spirit.

Mr. Newington called on me this (Thursday) evening about half-past nine o'clock. The butler who was with me left the room, Mr. N—— appeared to me to be proud, haughty, wrathful, malignant, and also, I grieved to see, unwell! he stood by the mantelpiece, and I shook myself as I rose up from the sofa, on which I was reading, half dozing.

He asked me how I was, I told him very well, and asked him how he was, observing his ill health, mentioning that I heard that he was ill, and was sorry for it, we were then silent for a few moments, and he asked me jocularly what had happened the day before; I was resolved to take up the matter rather warmly and seriously, and asked him if he had given orders that I should not be allowed to take exercise, running if I preferred. "Why no, why do you wish to run? you should not run, it's bad for your state of mind, it heats the head, it calls the heart and lungs, &c. to an unwholesome action for one in a weak state of bodily health, it makes the blood to flow fast, rise to the head (or word of this kind) &c. &c. &c." I attempted to argue with him, rather in anger, but as he stopped my mouth, and it appeared to me, probably, if not evidently, his intention to jeer at me, I desisted.

He at last desisted speaking; when he was done, I then said, "I wish also to know sir, why I have an additional man-servant in my room, and why my servants are desired to sit in my sitting-room with me."

"Because sir, we didn't know what you might do yesterday. If you had behaved well you should have had your servants taken out of your room! You did not behave properly yesterday."

"Sir," said I, "you know at any rate that I was fastened in my bed up stairs, and therefore could do no harm, for I could not get loose. Your intention has been to insult me; but as the Lord lives (my frame trembled with wrath), I will make you and others repent. With regard to removing my other servant sir, it is too late to talk of that now, I have often spoken of it, too long for me to value, or rely upon what you express to have been your intentions."

He said to me, "Come, don't put yourself into a passion, there is no use in your being angry, we'll deal as awkwardly as others did to you elsewhere; so don't put yourself into a passion:" before this, he had spoken to me something about law and solicitors, and I told him that he used very big language; but that I believed that I was right after all, in spite of his superior information; he continued his jeering, threatening manner, and I continued for a sentence or two to speak with warmth and vehemence, but fearing that I might be misrepresented, I suddenly left off and sat down.

He continued, saying, "Besides, sir, I have heard other things since these two last days, I have heard things which you are not aware of." This appeared intended to lead me into foolish remarks, so I took no notice of it, but sat down and spoke to him afterwards in indignation at what I was made to endure. He again told me that I must learn to be patient, and jeered and insulted me, so I desired him to leave my room, he said he would not, and hesitated; then I said, "I believe that it is the hour of bed-time in your asylum sir, and I will desire my servant to show me up stairs." I then called the servant, and after a few more sentences, I bowed to him and wished him good night.

Friday, twelve o'clock.—Mr. Newington called on me, offered to shake hands. He followed me into my room, telling me to forgive and forget was my duty: he had brought a letter and parcel from my mother.

The parcel was on my pianoforte! We had some conversation, in which I mentioned still my dislike to being prevented taking exercise as I wished; but I expressed my sorrow at having disturbed any gentleman by running when taking exercise, if I really had done so, which I did not believe. I told him that I thought I had run only when out of sight, but that at any rate I would take care to do so.

I did not satisfy him, nor he me. He told me, one patient, a gentleman in a cloak, had observed me running, and asked him if I was not deranged, and that that gentleman was a first-rate scholar, and had gone through, I do not know how many books of mathematics in a shorter time than any one else! I did not of course mention to Mr. N—— my reason for running.

He next told me, that yesterday he had been to travel upwards of forty miles. I understand, to have a consultation with Sir —— Tothill and another physician, concerning another lunatic, a gentleman who had been residing in a cottage with two keepers, had been visited by two physicians, or by one twice a week, and having only seen those three faces, wished naturally for more society. He was coming to Dr. Newington's at his own request! If so —poor fool!

I seized the moment to offer to Mr. N—— in fun to make an exchange of prisoners, but it was to no purpose. The additional man-servant did not sleep in my room this (Friday) night—the servants continue to sit in my sitting-room.

CHAPTER XXXII

HAVING proceeded thus far, I must now again interrupt the Diary to approach the most difficult, and in a scientific point of view the most important part of this work. So difficult, that I acknowledge I have hitherto shrunk from and feel unequal to the task; and I suspect that this has been a great cause of my delay in bringing it to a conclusion. I began about this time (April 17, to May, 1832), to declare that I was of sound mind; I will endeavour to explain how I became so, and to show at the same time, the origin and nature of those delusions under which I laboured, and under which I was destroyed. In doing so I shall make known spiritual or mental phenomena, which will hardly, I am afraid, find credit; but I bear testimony to them with an honest and upright heart, striving only to express myself accurately, and to report faithfully what I have experienced. They who give credit to me, will find, perhaps, the foundation of a new system of metaphysical and moral faith and practice. My first and chief difficulty will be so to order my ideas as to be intelligible; my second, so to describe what I have witnessed, as not to be turned to ridicule. I fear I may fail in the first, for even the memory of the past is very painful to me, much more to dwell upon and arrange the ideas that present themselves to me. I am conscious too, that I am exposing my own follies and my dulness of apprehension.

Having adopted at an early age the opinion that the religion of Jesus Christ was a true religion, I resolved to look to the New Testament alone for a knowledge of the doctrines of that religion;

and I was confirmed in my purpose by the suspicion which arose from comparing the conduct and expressions of society with the standard of faith and practice contained in the Scriptures, that the style and tone, the thought and practice of modern Christians were not correct.—At the same time being aware of great and repeated faults in my own conduct, and being as I thought unable to find in my own mind any sense of the fear or love of God, of the reality of heaven or of hell—but fancying that my life was not regulated by any such ideas, I was unable to decide whether I might not be mistaken in my suspicion, seeing, or imagining that others whom I condemned lived so much more regularly than I did, and with so much more propriety, and having to censure all whom I respected. Continually accusing myself of being without faith, and of being full of insincerity—I suffered extremely; for who was I, that I should find fault with others? Yet the Scripture to which I clung, seemed to condemn both them and me.

In those Scriptures I found the promise of miraculous gifts by the Holy Spirit to those who had faith, and I could not agree with the received opinion of the church, or admit that there was any reason why those gifts should not be now received,—but want of faith; and in the habit of churchmen not to believe that they were any longer possible, or to be expected, I saw excellent reason for their not appearing, as they were gifts to faith and not to unbelief. I do not now allow that I was wrong in this view of Christian doctrine, for though I acknowledge it is written that gifts of tongues, and of prophecies should fail, when that which is perfect is come —yet let me ask any sober and unprejudiced man, is the present divided and degraded state of the Christian church a state of perfection? or does he suppose that the bare establishment of Christianity is that perfection alluded to by the apostle?

I used then with great fervency to apply to our present wants that beautiful prayer, "Oh! Lord we have heard with our ears, and our fathers have declared unto us THE NOBLE WORKS THAT THOU DID'ST in their days, and in the old time before them, oh! Lord arise, help us, and deliver us for THINE HONOUR."

At the commencement of the year 1830, I was proceeding to the continent on a visit to one of my brothers who was at Ghent.

It so happened, that I was very anxious whether I should cross from Margate to Ostend, or go to Dover, to join a friend and from thence with him through Calais and Dunkerque to Belgium. I was alone in the coach on my way to Canterbury, and I knelt down for guidance, unable to determine for myself, and I prayed in an agony the Lord's prayer. Whilst praying, I saw a vision of three countenances in travelling-caps, which succeeded one another. At the appearance of one of these countenances I shuddered with horror; but my mind became troubled; I was astonished—I seemed to doubt at which I had shuddered—I became disturbed, and it seemed to me that in consequence of my being so puzzled and doubting, the vision was taken away.* I resumed my seat in the coach, wondering and stilled. I resolved at length when I left the coach at Canterbury to go by Margate. I got into the coach at night; we were delayed a great deal by the snow, and when daylight came I saw in the coach with me two young men with travelling-caps such as I had seen in my vision, and the features of one of these young men, who was a German, were exceedingly fair, mild, and regular, with yellow hair, such as I had seen in the vision. I was puzzled, when seeing the vision, to know whether I had shuddered at seeing this young man or at the sight of another; and I had thought to myself "Can there be any evil in one so beautiful?" And again I suspected I had offended the Almighty by supposing there could be evil in him. When I made acquaintance with my young fellow-traveller, I found that he was a well-disposed, honest, young Calvinist, who, though young, had thought seriously. I looked among the other travellers by the coach for the third cap. No one wore any thing resembling it; but after I had descended, in the morning, into the cabin of the steamer, a very strange and singular man came down, and I recognised on his head the other cap I had seen in the vision. This gentleman, from the moment he entered, made use of the most horrid oaths, scarcely opening his lips without one, until I ventured to reprove him, and, after a short argument, he gave up making use of them, for he was a gentleman, and we were on good terms afterwards. I was subsequently informed that he had been of unsound mind. He was certainly very wild.

* Compare Isaiah xxx. 15, and xxxii. 17, 18.

I have an impression that I saw, on another occasion, a similar vision, of which I do not recollect the particulars. I remember well, however, when on the point of leaving the army, and uncertain whether I would go to study at Dublin or at Oxford, being at my mother's house, I knelt down in my room, and prayed fervently to be directed rightly. I then saw, in a vision, a friend of one of my brothers whom I had known at Harrow School, sitting in a library with book-cases in it, in an arm-chair, at a table, and dressed in the cap and gown of the University, opposite to a fire-place, which was on my left hand between us, and with whom I appeared to be conversing, and who, during the conversation we were holding together, referred to a large folio volume. I said to myself, "Good God! that is H——, only his hair appears to be darker than it was at Harrow." Upon my arrival at Oxford, I found that this gentleman was at Brazenose College, and having gone one day to have certain points connected with the University oath explained to me, I found him sitting exactly as I had foreseen in the vision, and made the observation to myself, that his hair appeared darker than when he was at school; upon which, if I recollect right, I suddenly remembered the vision, and I became troubled, not knowing how to proceed, or how to direct the conversation, in the course of which he referred to a book, indeed, but to an octavo, not a folio volume. I have since questioned in my own mind, whether this discrepancy between what I had foreseen and what had come to pass did not arise from my trouble of mind and disobedience to the spirit which should have guided me in my conversation;* for it appears to me from experience, that the Almighty can indeed foreshow future events that may happen, but that the fulfilment of the details, or even of the vision itself may in some cases depend on the will and conduct of him to whom it has been manifested;† for it is evident, if any man should foresee that he should arrive at a certain place, and see or do there certain things, if it is at all left to his will to have those things fulfilled, he may thwart the counsels of Divine Providence, by immediately leaving or passing through that place. The prophecies concerning Jesus, if they are true, could never have

* Psalm iv. 4; xlvi. 10. Isaiah xxx. 7.
† I Kings xiii. 9, 19. Jonah i. 3. Numbers xxii. 12, 20, 21, 32.

been fulfilled unless his will had worked with that of the Almighty. For this reason, also, it may be, that the prophecies are generally so obscure—known only by their fulfilment.

There are many persons who esteem themselves very clever and very philosophical, who will be inclined to shut this book and turn upon their heel, at having such *trifles* laid before them; but to these persons I would observe, that such conduct is not sound, or consistent with a truly philosophical spirit; and if they will examine themselves, perhaps they will find that the spirit in which they walk, think, write, and converse, is either a spirit of irony and cynicism, designed to prove the faith and understanding of others, or a spirit resolved to reject all evidences concerning phénomena of the human mind with which they are personally unacquainted: as if the blind were to refuse to believe that there was such a thing as seeing—the deaf, that there was any thing like sound. Now I too am, I hope, a philosopher, not in conduct, perhaps, but in inquiry after knowledge; and I know it is folly absolutely to reject those evidences to a fact which are to be found dispersed throughout all ancient histories, and which are given also by modern authors, showing that whether by divination or by inspiration,—that is, whether by divine permission or by divine appointment,—certain men have been enabled to foretell or foresee future events. I esteem those persons very unphilosophical, who, sitting down to inquire into the nature and attributes of God, or, as they would rather hear, of the powers of the human mind, resolutely shut their ears to the representations of others, and to the testimony of antiquity, respecting qualities unknown to them: in the same manner I should think myself deserving of much ridicule, if I were to determine beforehand to reject all the information which I might find in the traditions of the Chinese, the Hindoos, and the Egyptians, and to adapt all their chronology to the system of the Jewish and Christian Church. Surely, as in the one case, when we find three countries so distinct and distant from one another, as China, India, and Egypt, possessing each a history whose origin is, and, if the facts are true, must be antedated to the deluge many years, if not generations, it is more reasonable to suppose that Moses may have been in error, or may be misunderstood, than to sit down and compress the events of centuries into the lapse of one generation, and reject what we cannot reconcile with our chronological table as fabulous: so, when we find writers of all nations and all religions, from Moses and Homer almost to our own times, bearing witness to the foretelling of future events, it is more reasonable to suppose that such a faculty is inherent in man, and to seek out the rules of an obsolete science, than to dismiss all these records from our minds as fanciful and untrue.

There are others who may be disposed to turn to ridicule the homeliness, if I may so call it, of the visions which I have recorded, —to them I would call to mind the vision of St. Peter, when he saw all manner of flesh and fowl descending before him in a sheet;— to others who may say, "But of what use were these visions? they could not serve as a guidance, but only as an assurance afterwards that the persons who saw them had been following the counsels of Divine Providence;" I would reply, that that assurance is a source of great peace to a troubled mind, and that this lesson may be derived from them,—that in the ordinary conduct of human life, the exercise of the understanding is sufficient to direct those who are desirous to serve their Redeemer.

After these visions, which made me more disposed to listen to the accounts which reached me of certain miraculous gifts to individuals of the church of Scotland, in the neighbourhood of Row, and Port Glasgow, in Scotland, when I had been some time at Row, attending meetings of these persons, a power came upon me of chanting words of Scripture, and words of spiritual exhortation without premeditation. I also felt myself impelled to address persons whom I did not know before, with passages of Scripture that arose in my memory; on one of these occasions, without my being aware of it, one of the party was a young lady, to whom I had promised to communicate the result of my investigation into the truth of the above miracles. About the same time, when I was at the manse of Row, one day the spirit of Mary Campbell, one of the inspired persons in the neighbourhood, seemed to come upon me, and directed me to leave the room in which I was staying, and to go to my own room and kneel down in prayer; this was the first time that I felt myself guided, and yielded myself to be guided as by visible or palpable spirit. At the same place, and in Dublin passages of the Old Testament were applied to me, which I turned to by the direction of a spirit, in which I was threatened with the most dreadful punishments, and with madness* if I were not faithful to the guidances which were given to me; again in Ireland, when I was attending a meeting in behalf of a Bible society at which I had promised to speak, my hands were guided to seek for passages in the New Testament, which I opened in a consecutive order in support of the line of argument I designed following. Later, in Dublin, I had warnings of evil of another kind, and when I was ill, my hand was guided to write in a style unusual to me. Then, also, I often yielded my limbs to be guided by influences which came upon me, which seemed to me like walking in a new life; on one occasion particularly, after my friend Captain H——— had rebuked me for my room being in disorder, I was very much grieved; and when he had left the room, a spirit came upon me, and in obedience to it I began arranging the room and putting my clothes in order in the wardrobe. On another occasion, whilst I was undressing to go to bed, I was taught to assume graceful attitudes of different kinds, chiefly of adoration—and at one moment to understand myself in spirit to be as St. John the apostle, at another as Judas—and this depended upon a turn of thought, to me unintelligible—at which I became so alarmed and troubled, that the spirit or influence guiding me seemed to vanish—and I exclaimed or chanted sorrowfully, and by inspiration—"Oh! where is my beloved gone?" When I was likened to St. John the apostle, I saw my countenance and form in the glass fair and bright—but when I was likened to Judas, my face was dark; whether this arose from any internal operation of the mind, by which the visual organs were affected, or, from my face being accidentally in the shade without my observing it, I do not know; the first is most probable; because afterwards I saw the countenances of others thus change from light to dark when in the same position relative to me and the light; but they appeared more black, and I was then

---

* Jeremiah i. 17; and Deuteronomy xxviii., particularly ver. 28, 29.

more weak. I have seen large pier-glasses in England and in France which make the reflections from them appear black instead of fair —they who have looked into them, and noticed the fact, will understand in some sort the effect of my experience.

Only a short time before I was confined to my bed I began to hear voices, at first only close to my ear, afterwards in my head, or as if one was whispering in my ear,—or in various parts of the room. These voices I obeyed or endeavoured to obey, and believed almost implicitly; especially after my mind was entirely deranged; I understood them to be the words of the Lord or of his Spirits. Afterwards, when I was very faint and ill, I saw visions of various kinds, the countenances of my friends and relations now white, now red as in flames; venerable countenances with flowing locks and silvery beards—the hand and arm of death stretched over me, and processions, beautifully delineated, like those of the ancient pagans.

Those voices commanded me to do, and made me believe a number of false and terrible things. I threw myself out of bed— I tried to twist my neck,—I struggled with my keepers. When I came to Dr. Fox's I threw myself over a style, absolutely head over heels, wrestled with the keepers to get a violent fall, asked them to strangle me, endeavoured to suffocate myself on my pillow, &c., threw myself flat on my face down steep slopes and upon the gravel walk, called after people as my mother, brothers, and sisters, and cried out a number of sentences, usually in verse, as I heard them prompted to me—in short for a whole year I scarcely uttered a syllable, or did a single act but from inspiration; though I now know that scarcely one of the things I said, or one of the things I did, was I intended to perform.

During this year, also, I heard very beautiful voices, singing to me in the most touching manner—and on one occasion I heard the sounds of the cattle lowing and of other beasts in the fields, convey articulate sentences to me, as it is written of Balaam. On another I was threatened terribly by the thunder from heaven— in short, nearly all sounds that I heard were clothed with articulation. I saw also visions, and the same day that I heard the cattle addressing me, on looking up into heaven, as I was leaving Dr.

Fox's premises, I saw a beautiful vision of the Lord descending with all his saints. During the same year, I also saw the faces of persons who approached me, clothed with the features of my nearest relations, and earliest acquaintance, so that I called out their names, and could have sworn, but for the immediate change of countenance, that my friends had been there. As they were walking at some distance their stature also changed.

I recollect that even at the height of my delusions I refused to obey these voices on several occasions, when by obeying them I was afraid of taking away the life of my attendants—for instance I was often desired to push a man named Hobbs backwards into an empty bath, but I was afraid to do it, lest I should injure him. I also often through disappointment and rage through fatigue and despair of comprehending them, rebelled against them, and refused to do any thing; choosing melancholy, sulkiness and inactivity, or my own will. On another occasion being desired to throw myself over a steep precipice near the river Avon—with the promise that if I did so, I should be in heavenly places, or immediately at home, I refused to do so for fear of death, and retired from the edge of the precipice to avoid temptation—but this last was not till after repeated experiments of other kinds had proved to me that I might be deluded. For I was cured at last, and only cured of each of these delusions respecting throwing myself about, &c. &c., by the experience that the promises attendant upon each of them were false. When I had fairly performed what I was commanded, and found that I remained as I was, I desisted from trying it with any sincerity, and soon left it off.

I was tempted to do these things very often from hearing the voices tell me that my fellow-prisoners were suffering for me, and that if I did so-and-so I should relieve them; but at last I was warned a change would take place in my situation, and when the voices one day said to me, "Mr. —— is suffering or suffocating for you;" another, or the same voice added, "to think of, or to reflect on with shame and contrition too," or words of that kind; then my mind began to have peace, and I began to breathe again. I knew I had been deceived—and when any voice came to order me to do any thing, I conceived it my duty to wait and hear if that order was explained, and followed by another—and indeed I often rejected the voice altogether: and thus I became of a sudden, from a dangerous lunatic, a mere imbecile, half-witted though wretched being: and this was the first stage of my recovery.

This took place in the cricket season about six months before the end of the year 1831, and the consequence of it was, that during the day I was released from my fastenings, though not at night for a long time after. My limbs being more at liberty, having more exercise, more occupation, more amusement,—my health and tone of mind soon made rapid advances towards restoration—and though afterwards I once struck my keeper and one of the patients, it was from ample provocation, and not from delusion or insanity. From this time, in truth, I needed nothing but observation, and not coercion.

During the time of my greatest infirmities, I also called my keepers and others by various names, and some by the names of my brothers or sisters, some I addressed as my father; this last was either on account of some resemblance in the features or in the dispositions, or on account of their age; I also called the keepers by inspiration, Honesty, Sincerity, Simplicity, Joviality, &c., according to their characters—though I did not then comprehend my own manner of address, and I knew not that I was in a mad-house;—but after I began to recover from my frightful dream, to become alive to the dreadful reality of my position, I understood both things and persons to be really what they were,—though not always, nor for some time; for long after I worshipped one of my keepers as the Lord Jesus—even a few weeks before my departure from Dr. Fox's.

It is curious, and it is contrary to the theory of the doctors, who deprecate all excitement among their patients, that every dispute and struggle I had with those controlling me, served to strengthen my mind and to dissipate my errors. Particularly that occasion on which I struck the keeper Hobbs, upon his attempting to collar me and to force me to come and be shaved. I cannot recollect accurately whether then I had already begun to doubt the truths of Christianity—but I had begun to reason with myself how often I had been deceived through life in adopting upon trust the opinions of others, and in following the fashions and habits of society; and I determined, when I was released from confinement to do nothing whatever which I could not prove reasonable, and among other things, as more consistent with nature and reason, I resolved to wear my beard and long hair; I had no sooner come to this resolution, than the voices I used to hear taunted me with cowardice and subserviency to those around me in not putting it into instant execution, on account even of the filthy manner in which I was shaved; and I was made to feel, that I was guilty of gross ingratitude to my Saviour in not insisting upon my right to do this in spite of any opposition that might be made to it. The consequence was that I replied in thought to these voices, "we will see if it is so," and I was soon after engaged in a desperate struggle with the keepers in support of my right, in which one of them wilfully dislocated my thumb, and another knelt on my belly, and seized my throat to suffocate me into submission. My spirits were completely aroused by this affair, and I gained a self-confidence, and a liberty of thought for a long time lost to me; the absurdity of my Saviour having desired me in such circumstances to expose myself to such disgraceful treatment was self-evident, and my resolution became the stronger to exercise a great control over myself, and cautiously and steadily to resist being led away again into any situation of difficulty by these voices. Still, however, I fancied the voices were holy, sent to try and to instruct me, and that I was bound to respect and pay attention to them; but I was no longer afraid of being led into any danger by obeying them, though I thought that I might expose myself to ridicule. For this reason I was desirous of being placed under observation, and I should voluntarily have sought retirement, and have submitted to the control of a physician or clergyman, if I had then received my liberty; and in this state of mind I continued, in this respect, for two or three months afterwards. The reason of this was that many of the guidances I received proved themselves by their results to be true and reasonable, so that I could not doubt but that they were benevolent and divine; but often when I had submitted either to the directions of a voice, or to the motions of a spirit to a certain extent, I found myself left in the lurch, and unable to understand further what I was to do; and this in circumstances of great embarrassment, likely to excite much laughter and astonishment in those with whom I had to do. For instance, I have been often desired to open my mouth, and to address persons in different manners, and I have begun without premeditation a very rational and consecutive speech, but in a singular, and as might be styled original manner, but in the midst of my sentence, the power has either left me, or words have been suggested contradictory of those that went before; and I have been deserted, gaping, speechless, or stuttering in great confusion. Conceiving at that time that the inspirations I received were true, but that I misunderstood them, I imagined that I was to blame, as the voices told me I was, through affectation or insincerity, or want of faith; that it was still my duty to attend to what I heard; and that if I were in quiet circumstances, and in private, I might at length discover the mystery of my difficulty in comprehending what I was to do or say; but I judged that it was impossible to do so without many failures, and that these might expose me to great contempt, I was therefore desirous that these failures might not take place in public. The letters I wrote from Dr. Fox's asylum will serve as another example of what I mean. I may say that every syllable of these letters I saw by illusion on the paper before I wrote them; but many other sentences also appeared besides those which I chose; and often these sentences made light of or contradicted what went before—turning me to ridicule, and that ridicule goading me to anger and madness, and I had great labour and difficulty to collect myself to seize those that were at all consecutive—or not too violent—or not too impassioned. This was extremely painful. My readers will find in these letters a great deal of sense and forcible writing, mixed with a great deal of weakness and imbecility; thus the inspirations and guidances I have received have been often good and becoming, and therefore I conceive, in the sense in which the term is usually employed, divine; often they were defective, and much my judgment ought to have rejected, and probably would have rejected in calmer circumstances. But I was in a room with other madmen—continually interrupted by the entrance of one servant or another—liable to impertinent questions—how I was getting on with my letters—to threats of having the pen and ink taken away if I did not get on faster—and to have my paper snatched up to see what I had written. Oh! my Countrymen! Oh! Humanity!—Oh! *Christianity?* Pshaw!

CHAPTER XXXIII

THERE were two or three other delusions I laboured under, of which I hardly recollect how I was cured—one in particular, that I was to lean on the back of my head and on my feet in bed, and twist my neck by throwing my body with a jerk from side to side. I fancy that I never attempted this with sincerity, because I feared to break my neck; and I think I left it off chiefly from being weary of attempting it, partly from being fastened down until I had grown out of the delusion or some other had supplied its place, partly from the fear of being still more confined in bed, as I once was, with a strap over my breast. Not long ago I threw myself, scarcely thinking of it, into a similar posture, and began throwing myself about; when, recollecting myself, it seemed to me as if I did it in some degree for relaxation, as a man stretches his limbs when yawning, in some degree to promote perspiration, being sensible of a dry and feverish state of the skin. But when I was ill I did it by command, and with the idea of miraculous benefits ensuing. I was also desired to suffocate myself on my pillow, and in various ways; this I never could perform, and I gave it up, weary of attempting it.

I suspect that many of the delusions which I laboured under, and which other insane persons labour under, consist in their mistaking a figurative or a poetic form of speech for a literal one; and this observation may be of importance to those who attend to their cure. I was led to it at Dr. Fox's and it was very useful to me. During the progress of my recovery there, I kept watching minutely all my experiences, and my conduct, and that of other patients, comparing their cases with my own, and drawing such conclusions as in those painful circumstances I was able: I did this also with the desire of being able to remove the delusions of others. If any one knew how painful the task of self-examination and of self-control was, to which I devoted myself at that time, every minute without respite, except when I was asleep, in order that I might behave, and with the sincere desire of behaving becomingly; they would understand how cruel I felt it afterwards, when I required my liberty for the further pursuit of health and of strength of mind, to have it denied to me for fear of my doing any person any bodily harm.

Keeping my mind continually intent upon unravelling and understanding the mysterious influence I was under, I one day saw an old gentleman who had been in China pluck a privet-leaf, and declare that it was tea; the same used to smear his face with red clay, calling it paint. I thought immediately thus—the spirit speaks poetically, but the man understands it literally. Thus you will hear one lunatic declare that he is made of iron, and that nothing can break him; another, that he is a china vessel, and that he runs in danger of being destroyed every minute. The meaning of the spirit is, that this man is strong as iron, the other frail as an earthen vessel; but the lunatic takes the literal sense, and his imagination not being under his own control, he in a manner feels it. In like manner, when I was desired to suffocate myself on my pillow, and that all the world were suffocating for me, &c. &c., I conceive, now, that the spirit referred to the suffocation of my feelings—that I was to suffocate my grief, my indignation, or what not, on the pillow of my conscience; that I was not to abandon myself to my feelings, but to control them, as others did theirs around me. Here, however, let me observe, that I suspect the health of the mind and the health of the body, particularly the operation of the lungs, and of the heart, and the state of the blood, to be essentially connected. I believe the healthy state of the mind depends very much upon the regulation of the inspiration and expiration; that the direction *"animum rege"* has a physical as well as a spiritual sense; that is, that in controlling the spirit you must control your respirations. I will instance, in support of this, the stupid appearance of many deaf people, who usually are unable to breathe freely through the nostril, and keep their mouths wide open; a habit very common amongst idiots. I will instance, again, the stupifying effects of a bad cold. Now the voices I used to hear during my illness at Dr. Fox's told me that that state of mental perfection they required me to attain to, was dependent upon the proper command of my heart and my head, and, if I recollect rightly, of my conscience, which I was made to suppose dwelt in my bosom. I was repeatedly desired to "keep my head and heart together," not to let "my head go wandering from my heart,"— that "if I kept my head and heart together," I should do well; but that this third power, which, if I am not wrong, was conscience, ought to regulate both, if I would be perfectly happy. I understood very little of what I heard at the time. But now I conceive that the voices when they told me to keep my head and heart together, meant me to think on what I was in need of, or desired; of those subjects or objects my heart and health dictated to me, since the head may be occupied on subjects which are repulsive to the heart, or out of time, and out of place, and out of character; as if a parent who had a family of children craving for food, were to go idling to a fair to look at puppet-shows—as if a man who had an important appointment to keep, were to lose himself, and all memory of it in reading a novel. It is evident, however, that a man may keep his attention upon his desires with the thought only of gratifying them; and such a man may be of sound mind according to the ordinary sense of the terms, and yet have no thought of his relative position in society, or in the creation. Here, then, conscience comes into play, to know whether the emotions of the heart are just, and how far they ought to be indulged, and reflection taken to allay them; and if I may be allowed to say so in a matter many make light of, others may think fanciful—I question whether the operations of the conscience and reflection can be conducted but through the medium of the lungs filling the chest at proper intervals, according to the degree of passion of the mind, or of action of the body. Should this be the case, and should a well-regulated breathing be essential to bodily health and mental restoration—it is possible, that the effecting of this mechanically even may give much relief. I have certainly found it so—and I cannot help suspecting that this secret, rudely understood, was known to Dr. Fox, or to his servants—otherwise why should one of the servants have strangled me, at my request, with the strings of my waistcoat; why should throttling and strangling when resorted to subdue a lunatic; why did one of the servants, with an iron bar, keep my head under water in the bath for a long time? And may not the virtues of the cold bath and shower-bath in the cure of lunatic patients reside principally in this, that they cause such a violent panting—such a sudden and, I conceive, often even dangerous and improper action of the heart and of the lungs? I cannot help thinking that there was in the madhouse of Dr. Fox some practical though ignorant apprehension of this truth, and therefore, whilst I give the above figurative interpretations of the delusion that I was to suffocate myself, I do not positively assert that, in this instance, there was no truth in the literal application of it, any more than that it was always suggested by the same train of idea;* far from it.

For I recollect during my recovery at Dr. Fox's, I used to place myself in the different positions I had formerly occupied, in order to retrace my thoughts, and see if I could account for my feelings —on one of those occasions I sat down in a niche, into which I had been fastened, in the bow at the end of the common room. I experienced then an extraordinary sensation of suffocation, *and I found it was produced by the position of every object and of every*

* To make my ideas more clear, let me sum up my arguments or propositions thus: That a healthy state of the mind is identical with a certain regulated system of respiration, according to the degree of bodily action; that the exercise of reflection or of conscience, in the control of the passions or affections of the mind, is concomitant with, or effected by a proper control of the respiration— quiet when the mind is quiet, accompanied with sobs or sighs when otherwise. That the mind and the blood being intimately connected, the health of the body depends also on this healthy regulation of respiration, promoting a proper circulation and purification of the blood; that, consequently, the effecting respiration by mechanical means, without the control of the muscles by thought, is profitable to the health of the body, and also to that of the mental faculties, although they may not be, at least distinctly, occupied by any ideas; in the same way as, if several printing-presses are worked by machinery, it may be necessary for the perfect state of that machinery, that all the presses should be in motion, although some may have no types under them.

line in the room being oblique to my visual organs instead of square; and I have no doubt this sensation caused the idea continually to haunt me when I was seated in that niche, where I passed whole days pressing my nostrils to a wooden ledge, that served to support the arms, as in an arm-chair.

Moreover I have remarked, that when my mind is most disturbed, I breathe at that time violently and rapidly, and with difficulty through the nostrils, and I have observed in the glass, when I have been exasperated, my nostrils compressed above and dilated below, and quivering rapidly with the violence of my breathings—reminding me of a bust I have seen somewhere of Achilles. The spirits also which I conceived to speak to me, used to direct me to control my breath, and "to breathe gently up one nostril down another." I have often found too, that when I am depressed or agitated by any passion, a deep-drawn breath will change the whole complexion of my thought and the tenor of my desires.

I am afraid that these details will appear tedious and frivolous: but on a subject, on which medical men are evidently so ignorant, and, usually, so thoughtless—and nearly all others are desperate, because they deem it beyond their comprehension, I hope I may be excused in entering upon these minute particulars, though they are but lucubrations on the operations of a deranged understanding—still that *was* a deranged *understanding*.

The following are further illustrations of the idea that the lunatic mistakes a poetic train of thought for the reality. I was told repeatedly that such and such persons were my mother, sisters and brothers, &c. I conceive the idea was spiritual or that they resembled them. I was told that I was not in England, and I believed it; I conceive, indeed I know* the meaning was, that the

* In the year 1833, at Sevenoaks, I received early in the morning a letter from a Colonel Austen, a magistrate in the neighbourhood, in answer to an application I had made the previous evening to him. In it he mentioned, that on receiving my note he had immediately left his dinner-table to answer it, and that he would take an early opportunity of seeing me. In every respect it was such an answer as a magistrate and a gentleman should give to a person in my situation, and the first example of kind and immediate attention that I had received. The moment I had read it I exclaimed of a sudden, "Now I am in England!" and then I recollected and knew the meaning of my former delusions.

treatment I was suffering from the system to which I was subjected, was unworthy of England. I was told to wrestle with my keeper: this I conceived so extraordinary that I hesitated; but the spirits told me "they intended me to wrestle with him in civility;" and I suppose I was meant to expostulate and remonstrate with him.

I remember, however, that the spirits, or voices of invisible angels, as I fancied them to be, used to sing to me at one time, "wrestle with Herminet Herbert" (that was the name applied to my keeper, Samuel Hobbs); at another—I must hope to be excused for mentioning it—"kiss Herminet Herbert." Both these commands were to me so extraordinary and unusual, that I could not undertake either, until scared by superstitious fear, or cut by feelings which I fancied were those of compunction for doubting and disobeying the goodness of God, and conceiving that I could be wiser than he who ordered me. At last I obeyed, in trust that it was my duty to do so, and that good would come of it, though I could not understand how. I do not recollect, however, having ever kissed the servant, and seldom did I try to do so, because my feelings of delicacy were stronger than my fears of bodily harm, which did not prevent me from often attempting to wrestle with him. Seldom, however, if at all, did I actually wrestle with this man, though I did with others stronger than him. I used to seize him by the waistcoat to do so, understanding from my spirits that it was what he wished me to do; and yet, not finding him meet me as if he had any desire to grapple with me, I was usually puzzled, and desisted. He was also, though a slight man, of a peevish, hasty disposition, more ready to strike than the others, and his language was often truly horrible. Perhaps this may have added somewhat to my irresolution: but I conjecture that the very fact that he was slighter and less powerful than the other servants, making him a more reasonable match for me, was the cause that I did not persist in wrestling with him, because the acts of lunacy are preposterous and *un*reasonable.

For this, again, is one species of lunacy, to mistake a spirit of humour enjoining an act which is an evident absurdity, for a spirit of sincerity, or, as the French say, to take it *"au pied de la lettre;"* as if a father were to say to his child in fun, "Now, run into the puddle,"—or, "Now put your fingers into the fire,"—or, "Now, put yourself into a passion," meaning the very contrary, and the child were to take his words as if meant in earnest. So I was ordered to throw myself head over heels over stiles—to throw myself to the right, and left, or flat on the face on the floor or upon gravel walks: these forms of thought may have been meant as absurdities, for me to do the very contrary: they may also, however, have a spiritual meaning, comprised in these words,—recollect yourself—remember where you are, what you are about, what you want to do, and act accordingly.*

If there is any guilt in lunacy, and lunacy is not a total deprivation of power to understand and interpret commands of this nature, I should say it is here that it is manifested; for it is written, "that no man is tried beyond his strength;" and the absurdity of such commands as I obeyed, was perhaps proportioned to my degree of understanding at all times. Of this I am not sure: I used to suspect it when I began to recover; and I thought very ill of myself, and believed that I had been very wicked; perhaps it was so: but, when I was most low-spirited and cast down by these thoughts, and had so deep a sense of self-distrust and degradation, that perhaps I might never have recovered a sound understanding, that is, spirit to claim the respect due to my situation, if that state of mind had continued, I was mercifully relieved (to myself it was mercy, to him it was barbarity) by witnessing the gradual destruction, and degradation, and exposure of a fine old man, who was placed in exactly similar circumstances to mine own.

I saw him enter Dr. Fox's asylum in every appearance of a sound state of mind: I mistook him for a visitor, a friend of one of the patients. The rude replies of the servants soon convinced me of my error. A fortnight after, the aged gentleman—a merchant of the city of Bristol—besmeared himself over with the red clay in the yard, calling it paint, and became the annoyance of every

---

* As further examples of this kind, I may mention the case of a very powerful man in Mr. Newington's asylum, who told me he was as weak as a child—he looked like a castle. Another gentleman at Dr. Fox's, on my remonstrating with him for tormenting an old Quaker lunatic, who was affected by *pavor lymphaticus*, replied to me "he believed God Almighty had put him there to amuse him;" and this he said not in joke, but in sober seriousness.

being in the common room in which we were sitting. A few days more, and he was fastened, as I used to be, in a niche, on a hard seat, the whole day long, with a belt, to the wall, and in a straight waistcoat, his face red and inflamed, his grey head leaning forward on his bosom, his eyes unable to meet the look of any other servant or patient. Gradually he became more loathsome, and when his meals were brought to him he "gobbled" them down— I can use no other expression—with pitiable and revolting voracity, without attention to order, to cleanliness—without respect to any object or person around him. This was a picture to me of what I had been; and I said to myself, "Surely, then, this sad state may be the necessary effects of the situation in which we are placed! Surely the lunatic's conduct, however profane, may receive at least extenuation, from the barbarous circumstances in which society connive at his being placed!" and I gathered courage and hope. Till then I had accused myself, and I had sickened at the thought that I had sacrificed reason and self-control to my gullet —to the pleasure of eating and drinking the fat meats and the sour beer that had been set before me. For at my meals, morning and evening, the voices I used to hear flocked about me like bees, and every one, in the tones of some relation or of some friend, begged of me in turn to refuse a piece of meat for her sake, to leave my bread for his sake, and so on. Then, when one voice told me to refuse any thing for her sake, another came to desire me to eat it for her sake, and I was bewildered. I suppose that I was hungry, and that I enjoyed my meals; I could not understand why I should be advised to refuse them. The servant stood by me, jogging me, offering me morsels, saying, "Come, Mr. Perceval, make haste; why, you won't be done all day." At length, if I refused, my meals were taken away or I was rated and scolded, and had them forced down my throat: I therefore, at length swallowed every thing that came within my reach, without compunction and without discrimination, and often as if it were very humourous to do so: and then I accused myself of selling my soul for a sop of bread and tea, or for a slice of bread and mutton—of sacrificing my immortal happiness for the sensual pleasure of guttling; and this, as I then thought, in a glorified body.

But now I reason thus—whenever I had most to think of, when-ever my thoughts and hands were most occupied, I became, I sup-pose, nearest to a sound state of mind, and consequently most aware of my situation, most distressed at my weakness, and most confused at my exposure, yet still in a manner unconscious of these feelings; for I am sure that the human mind has a double action; that of sense or sensation, and that of acknowledging, noticing, or defining its sensations, just as an absent man will walk up and down stairs to look for his pen or pencil, and at last find it in his hand or behind his ear; just as men, when occupied in thought, often rise from their chair and proceed to a table, or to a drawer, or to the garden, unconscious of their motion, until in a manner they awake, collect themselves, and feel what they wanted. So the lunatic is not entirely without sense, but his mind harassed by other painful thoughts, and intent upon them, appears insensible to the shocking situation in which he is placed. But, it being neces-sary to a sound state of mental and moral feeling, that all or that many of the faculties of mind and body should be called into play at one time, and above all things that the body or members should be occupied,—when such an occasion arrives, he becomes more sensible to his disgraceful and painful position, but without con-trol over his feelings or thoughts. So when I was at meals, my hands being employed, and when I was to be shaved, having to compose my features and person for the operation,—having to recollect myself,—I became more aware of my real position, my thoughts being called out from myself to outward objects. I have no doubt also that the recollection that I was often deprived of a knife, and not allowed to use my own razors for fear I should hurt myself, contributed greatly to my mental sufferings. But I could not command myself, the trial was too much for me, and I became a noisy and gluttonous buffoon, drowning, and flying from, sense in boisterous exclamations, and in the hasty devouring of my food. If I had been in humaner circumstances, probably this would not have been.*

---

* The lunatic doctors appear to think that patients do not *feel* their position: now, I know that many lunatics are extremely sensible to ridicule; this sensitiveness is, indeed, one of the phenomena of an unsound mind; and

But when the voices I heard desired me to refuse such a piece of meat for the sake of one friend, to eat such a piece for the sake of another friend, they commanded me to act so in the first place spiritually, that is, to revolt at eating such food in such a place, in such circumstances, served in such a manner;—to shew, in eating, a sense of my situation, and of my ill treatment; but in the second place, to eat in humility and in thankfulness, what was *necessary* for health and maintenance. Thus, persons who are in grief often cannot, that is, *will* not eat, and women when offended will leave their meals, shewing a high spirit. Often, also, since my confinement, I have felt disposed to leave my food, but I fear for my health, and I have swallowed it as it were against myself, thinking on these things; but at other times I have regained self-possession, and found my mind at liberty, by pausing and drawing a deep breath, sobbing or sighing, as the cloud of former recollections has passed over me.

Thus, lunacy is also the mistaking of a command that is spiritual for that which is literal—a command which is mental for one that is physical, and so I conceive when I was commanded to kiss and wrestle with Herminet Herbert, the intention was to cultivate such and such dispositions to him, not practically to put the words in execution.

Why I called this man Herminet Herbert I do not know, neither can I explain or define my understanding of the term, only I was told on my inquiring of my spirits the meaning of the words that I knew it very well, and I then endeavoured to explain them thus with reference to the Greek and German languages—"Herminet"—the messenger, herald, or interpreter*—"herr," the Lord—

I know that lunatics are very much pained and embarrassed by exposure under their misfortune, and I suspect that this is common to all. But they are not able to bear up against the feeling, and therefore fly for relief to boisterousness and impudent boldness, or sink from it into an apathy and passiveness, which is supposed to betray absence of feeling, when it really betrays incapability to meet such feeling. I have noticed in another volume my having been, during the progress of my recovery at Dr. Fox's, completely thrown off my balance by the fear of meeting strangers; but it was not until I reflected, that I knew the cause of my own silly conduct.

* The keeper of the *key* of a door, or a mystery.

"bert," I could by no means translate, and the voices told me it meant "of hell," and I understood that Herminet Herbert was a familiar style by which souls under punishment might term the Lord, as a son calls his father "governor," or a debtor, his prison, his "palace," or "castle." I have found since, on referring to an old dictionary, that the word "herbert," or "*heer*-bert," signifies Leader, or Lord of Hosts.* The name, like many of my thoughts at Dr. Fox's madhouse, was, or seemed original to me. I had no clue to lead to it; other ideas were, I have no doubt, suggested by my position, by the manners around me, and by the language of this very servant. I believed I was to be dissected alive, and cruelly butchered, and often he used to rate me saying, "I'll cut your guts out,"—"I'll cut your —— —— out!" Who would imagine that such language was possible from a keeper of a *lunatic asylum* to a gentleman! But so it was; and if my readers will only consider how a lunatic is abandoned, and reflect upon human nature, they will know how guilty society is, and that these things are only too probable.

I remember, also, that when I was ordered to wrestle with Herminet Herbert or to kiss Herminet Herbert, the voices explained to me, that I was to take each of these directions in a contrary sense—ironically. That is, when I was desired to kiss him, I was to wrestle with him, or strike him,—when to wrestle with him, to kiss him; but I disobeyed, and then I was told I disobeyed through cowardice,—that I was affecting not to understand and, in consequence, losing all patience: at last I knew not which was which; and then the voices said, that my understanding became confounded through my hypocrisy. Moreover, I often heard the command, "Wrestle with such a one, if you will," "Strike such a one, if you will," "Do this, or that, if you will;" but, when I became more healthy, the form of address ran thus: "Do so and so, if you will,—be obedient to a spirit of decision or precision," or—"be obedient to a spirit of mockery and derision,"—and the like. When I discovered this, I became more orderly, supposing that I might choose and study in what spirit I might act or behave.

* Properly, the glory or the brightness of an army.

I conceive, therefore, that lunacy is also a state of confusion of understanding, by which the mind mistakes the commands of a spirit of humour, or of irony, or of drollery; that many minds are in this state; that, perhaps, this is the state of every human mind—that it certainly is the state of every mind in certain moods. I mean that in the operations of the human intellect, the Deity, if not always, yet often intimates his will by thus jesting, if I may be allowed to call it so, with his child—with his creature; that in the misapprehending or perverting of this form of address may consist original sin; or that such misapprehension or perversion is the first consequence of original sin (if such there be) pervading and making false every future deliberation, and conception, and action. Hence, I imagine, it is, that those who profess religion are often so hypocritical—for the true hypocrite is he who, like the Pharisee, fancies himself religious and is not. Wherefore, also, Jesus companied with publicans and sinners; because amongst those who profess least, true and good feeling is often most prevalent. Hence, I imagine, also, arises the great mystery spoken of by St. Paul, "That which I would, I do not—that which I do I allow not;" "my mind lusteth against the flesh—my flesh against the spirit;" because the mind of man, fallen from a state of grace, thinks in a spirit of humour, as if that spirit were a spirit of truth; and when the mind, thinking in a spirit of humour, supposes it is forbidden to touch, taste, or handle, then, in reality, nature desires the contrary; and when the mind appears to command any thing to be done, then, in fact, nature desires it not to be done. Hence it is also that we say "We don't care," "It does not signify," "Never mind," and the like, in matters which are really of the greatest, perhaps of eternal, moment. Certainly, this law of contradiction exists, and it has been noticed by other writers besides St. Paul, even in its physical effects. By Ovid, somewhere, writing on the passion of Love, and by Martial, in an Epigram I must only allude to. I guard myself from saying that this is an universal law, lest I lead myself or others into error. But do we not know how often, as boys at school, we have disobeyed orders, and done things merely because they were forbidden—do we not know that the surest way to make people read a book is to say that they ought not to do so? Do we not often meet persons of whom it is said, that they are of so perverse a disposition, that you have only to desire them not to do a thing to make them long to do it—to request any thing of them as a favour in order that it may not be done. I acknowledge I do look upon this as a discovery in the operation of the intellectual faculties of much importance, for which I am thankful. Others have noticed the fact—I have been enabled to give a solution of the fact—a solution, I suspect, if rightly considered, to a great degree, of the mystery of iniquity. Sin then is a misapprehension, a shadow, a mockery.

Those who have the conduct of little children, will find great pleasure and benefit, in attending to this rule, particularly if they are of a fractious and passionate disposition. Children should be respected, not only as our children, but as little temples of the eternal spirit—and temples in which the operations of the mind are more pure, and more orderly—in which the moral sense is more perfect, than in vessels which have been bandied about in, and polluted by the world, and wherein the mental machinery is deranged, and clogged by disorderly appetites. Servants set over them, will order them abruptly to leave their little sports—hurry them here—frighten them there—snatch things out of their tiny clinging fingers; by doing so, the order of nature is disturbed, time is not given or method employed to let their wills chime in with those of the person set over them—they become cross and ill-humoured, crying, passionate, and violent. But I say yield to them that they may yield to you—watch the moods of their minds, and according to their dispositions, or to the humour they are in, play with them; in the manner you conduct yourselves to them, play with them as a skilful angler will play with a fish that he has just struck, and would safely bring to land: is not the prize worthy of your attention?

What more shall I say, lunacy is a confusion of the understanding—but it is also the emancipation of the mental faculties from the control of a natural but often erroneous, that is, already confused judgment; so that the talents become free which have before been cramped, and those discover themselves which were before smothered. Lunacy is like drunkenness; only that it is worse and more lasting: and many poets, many painters, many singers, many actors, and even orators, have never spoken, acted, sung, designed, or written so well as when they have been intoxicated; because inebriety overturns the natural judgment, which sets right for wrong, sweet for bitter, and with it the sense of many improprieties, which embarrass speech and action. Now the judgment of man was intended, with humour, to control and moderate—but being sinful, it is liable to spoil every thing by affectation and hypocrisy, and to fetter, oppress, and mislead. When the power of judgment is taken away, then passion and feeling take the lead, and splendid diction, splendid action, splendid delineation follows; but such as a sober mind still condemns as needing correction,—which, however, the critic himself often cannot apply. I think, therefore, that by the observation of the operations of the mind, under such circumstances, much spiritual and even *physical* knowledge may be obtained, because I am convinced that the mind is a piece of excellent machinery. Like to a musical instrument, whose movements we are yet to discover how to regulate, by certain fixed and, if I may call them so without offence, mechanical laws. I am witness that there is a power in man, which independent of his natural thought and will, can form ideas upon his imagination—control his voice—and even wield his limbs;— twice my arm has been raised and moved suddenly, as by a galvanic force, without my having any intention to do so, that I was conscious of. This also is curious, that when I was eating my breakfast, the voice about me often said, "If you will do so and so, WE will ask for another piece of bread and butter for you;" and if I obeyed, without my needing to speak, the servant, after looking attentively at me, would come and offer me the bread and butter. I conceive now, that by my countenance or manner I was made to express the desire for more food; but it is a proof that the voices I fancied I heard were in some manner connected with my well-being and with the operations of my mind; or, rather that I was made to fancy that I heard those voices by a power in me, intimately acquainted with the operations of my mind.

On one occasion, shortly before I left Dr. Fox's, as I was leaving the house and walking through a back gate, I was desired by the spirit to "lift up my head and open my voice, and see what I should see"—and I looked up to heaven and yielded my voice to the power upon me, and forthwith I uttered horrible oaths and blasphemies, so that I was frightened and refused to speak. Again I was desired to lift up my head and open my mouth as before, and I did so, looking up into the sky, and forthwith I uttered the most gross and revolting obscenities, by the influence of a similar power, and I again chose to be silent, rather than to obey. I was thus cured of my folly that I was to yield my voice up to the control of any spirit at hap-hazard, without regard to circumstances, and without discrimination, and thus my mind was set at rest in great measure from another delusion; or rather, the superstitious belief that I was blindly to yield myself up to an extraordinary guidance was done away.*

* Three observations I have overlooked, which may be of importance. The first, to prove that there was a method in the mystery of my disorder; the second, in a scriptural; the third, in a medical point of view.

I. The voices gave the appellation of Herminet Herbert, only to the keepers; but several of the patients they called Fitzherbert.

II. One of the keepers they styled GOD ALMIGHTY, another JESUS, another the HOLY GHOST, whether on account of their several characters, or in good-humoured and innocent buffoonery, I do not know. One of the patients also, a stout, good-humoured old gentleman, was pointed out to me as the TRINITY in UNITY, and named also "Benevolence" and JEHOVAH.

III. My loss of all control over my will, and belief, and imagination, and even of certain muscles, was immediately preceded by three successive crepitations, like that of electrical sparks in the right temple, not on the same spot, but in a line, one after the other, from left to right.

CHAPTER XXXIV

BEFORE I left Dr. Fox's, I thought I observed that the cause of that delusion, whereby the stature of persons appeared to change, consisted in my comparing them in the agitation of my spirits, and in that weak state of health, solely with the objects around them, or in the distance, in the same way as I have often found when attempting to draw—I have made all the objects in the middle distance in fair proportion one with another, but much too large to sort with the size I was compelled to give to the objects in the foreground, on account of the dimensions of my paper. I will not, however, be too positive of the cause being rightly stated, though I think it was so; but this I know, I was aware before I left Dr. Fox's, that this delusion arose from a defective use of the visual organs. This weakness of sight giving also a kind of unsubstantiality to persons I saw,—for their forms seemed to dilate and contract,—did, I have no doubt, contribute to a delusion I was under, that I was surrounded by spiritual bodies—and myself in such a body—not of flesh and bone, and not needing sleep or food.

Let me observe, that the voices I so often speak of, were mostly heard in my head, though I often heard them in the air, or in different parts of the room. Every voice was different, and each beautiful, and, generally, speaking or singing in a different tone and measure, and resembling those of relations or friends. There appeared to be many in my head, I should say upwards of fourteen. I divide them, as they styled themselves, or one another, into voices of contrition and voices of joy and honour. Those of contrition were, I think all without any exception, on the left temple

and forehead; those of joy and honour on the right temple and
forehead; but on each side of the head, as it were over the middle
of the eyebrow, two spirits seemed always to sing or speak to a
measure more quick and more flaunty than the others—that on the
left was, I think, called the spirit of my eldest sister—that on the
right was the spirit of Herminet Herbert. I understood the use
of these spirits, which were spirits of humour and politeness, to be
necessary to a holy turn of thought, and that the world did not
like the use, or understand the use of them. My thoughts flowed
regularly from left to right, guided by these voices and their suggestions; and if I turned them from right to left, I was told that
I was playing the hypocrite. I think it right to mention this
because it was always so; and though it may appear fanciful, there
may, nevertheless, lie hid some truth in it connected with the
nervous system which I cannot venture to explain. Amongst the
names given to the spirits were those of Contrition, those of Joy,
of Gladness, of Joviality, of Mirth, Martha (by which I understood
over-anxiety), and Mockery, of Honesty, of Sincerity, and, amongst
others, "a spirit of honourable anxiety to do my duty to the best
of my own satisfaction," which I was told was the spirit of one of
my sisters—the use of such a phrase is evidently humourous, or
ironical, or satirical.

The following observation may also not be unworthy of attention. When I was confined in my straight waistcoat, with my
arms across my breast, and my feet fastened to the floor, and a strap
across my belly confining me to the wall, I used to get up, and sing,
and behave noisily. I used then to consider what was my stimulus
to action, for often I had no external motive or object, and I found
it was to get rid of two uneasy sensations in the roof of the mouth
—the one, at the back of the palate, consisted of a dull, heavy impression, as if made by a thick mucilaginous spittle—the other was
more painful, and about the top of the throat, as if the breath
came up very fiery, and impregnated with electrical matter. I conceive it probable, therefore, that nature prompted me to action to
relieve an over-heated system, and to purify a stagnated state of
the blood and humours. This was usually on days when I was not
taken out to walk after dinner. Then I was most boisterous—

bumping up and down upon my seat, and crying out or singing.

On one of these occasions I contrived to get out of my bands, and I undressed, and ran naked, by order of the voices I heard, into a small yard attached to our prison, singing, in Portuguese, the following lines, which were inspired to me at the moment. I transcribe them as one of the most singular specimens of that nature of inspirations that often came upon me.

> Meu amo, ti amo
> Com amore fedele;
> Mas nao posso senao
> Ser desobediente
> As teus ordems,
> Porque os meus amores
> Sao mais fortes
> Que os teus ardores
> Para mim, Para mim,
> Que os teus ardores
>   Para mim.

The translation of these words is as follows:

> My master, I love thee
> With a faithful love;
> But I cannot but be
> Disobedient
> To thy commands,
> Because my loves (or affections)
> Are stronger
> Than thy ardent love
> Towards me, towards me,
> Than thy ardent love
>   For me.

It was not till the year 1834 that I understood the purport of these lines. Since my restoration to liberty "I have pondered over many of these things in my heart"—with much bitterness of spirit, however, and not often in the humble and patient disposition of Mary. I did not know, in 1831, that the word *amo* was a Portuguese noun, signifying "master," but on referring to my dictionary, in 1834, when at Hampton Court, I found it was so. The accent, also, which I was obliged, in singing or chanting them, to lay on the word *desóbediente* struck my classical ear as incorrect, wherefore I questioned at the time if the Holy Spirit could prompt me to scan falsely—the jingle of words also, *nao posso senao,* was then unintelligible to me—but the word *"ardores"* I for a long time refused to recollect when thinking over the lines at Dr. Fox's. This is an instance of what I mean by the power of utterance leaving me puzzled how to proceed. When I came to the word *"ardores"* I could not proceed. The voices then taunted and jeered me, saying that I knew what the word was, but that I did not choose to pronounce it, or to admit the sense of it. I pleaded ignorance, and then the word *"arvores,"* which in Portuguese meant *trees* was suggested to me, and was interpreted to me in two childish ways—one that it meant the gallows trees, on which I was to be hung, according to delusions I had in a thousand bodies all over the world—the other, that it meant some "cherry-trees," which the Lord in his goodness had ordered to be planted for me at home.

Thus it would appear, that the Almighty has power to make a man utter sentences of a reasonable nature, and words which yet he does not comprehend; and therefore, that the gift of tongues mentioned in scripture may *not* be altogether false or unattainable to in these days: also, that what was a reasonable and consecutive speech or hymn, may have been turned to nonsense and folly, on account of the disingenuousness of the instrument made use of to utter it—at the same time I do not plead guilty to this disingenuousness, neither do I deny it, it is an accusation which was often made of me—in the spirit, and which I do not understand— but whenever I have been unable to comprehend the leadings of the spirits upon me, I have been told, that I did not choose to comprehend—which did not appear to me to be the case, but, that I *could* not comprehend. I was told also that I was insincere, and seeking my own glory instead of that of the Lord—or afraid to confess the glory upon me becomingly before man—that I was unsimple—and that therefore the Lord turned me to ridicule, and put me to confusion.

I recollect amongst other instances of my memory failing me, and of accusations being made of me in consequence, in a similar manner, that I one day heard, and was desired to sing, and to apply to myself these words:

> I'd be a butterfly born in a bower,
> Kissing all buds that are pretty and sweet.

Here I paused—I heard no more, I was desired to open my mouth in faith and go on—but I could not recollect the remainder of the song. Then different spirits suggested to me words, with which I was not satisfied, and amongst others—

> But I would not be a little idle thing,
> Sitting here all day to do nothing but sing.

I have to observe, that although I had heard the song "I'd be a butterfly" before my illness, I do not recollect ever having committed it to memory, or being very familiar with it; therefore to have remembered the concluding verses could not naturally be expected of me, but would in a manner have been a gift. I bought the song since my liberty to see what were the other verses. Many persons have the gift of an extraordinary memory—they will hear a sermon and go away and repeat it word by word. I question now whether this is not in consequence of the machinery of the mind being in this respect, in them, in perfect order, and whether this power is not latent in all men, but disturbed through passion— through the mind being ill regulated—perhaps through organic disease.

Now all or nearly all the phenomena which I have narrated, strange as they may appear, are to some degree or other familiar to all men*—and such, as I can in a certain degree recollect in myself during the whole course of my life. For instance, this power of a spirit to control the utterance is daily experienced, though not remarked, in what we call a slip of the tongue; where one

---

* Shyness is one very common species of LUNACY to which many are painfully subjected. A shy man will be quite annoyed, imagining the curtain in a window is a person looking at him; and often has not power to look up to ascertain his error. He is overcome by thinking that if he moves, every eye in a room, or a church, will be directed upon him: and though convinced by argument that it is not so, still he cannot overcome the impression. A good remedy is, to have an honest and serious occupation, and to determine quietly to observe others.

word is put for another, and one letter transposed with another, and as the mind by a positive law always thinks on contraries at the same time, it almost invariably happens that the word made use of by mistake is the contrary to that intended. The universal for the particular—the affirmative for the negative, and the like. (By the same law, voluptuousness and cruelty have been so often united in one person.) The degree of error is not the same, but the phenomenon is the same—the organs of speech are made use of without the volition or rather intention of the person speaking. This is remarkable, because it would prove the residence in the temple of the body, of two distinct powers, or agents, or wills.

In writing also, the phenomenon I have mentioned of the hands being controlled without the will or intention of the person writing, often takes place, when one word is written for another, and this we call inadvertence, but it is really the effect of the same cause not recognised, which became evident to me through the state of excitement and weakness I was in, and my faith that it was possible.

Many of the things I have spoken, and many of the things I have heard and written, and done in the spirit, I have not understood for a long time after: and yet, when my understanding has perceived their meaning, they have often been quite simple. It seems to me, that in the effort to understand, made by a deranged mind, the faculties become stupified and confused.

The following is another remarkable phenomenon, which I observed during my illness. When I was fastened down in my bed at Dr. Fox's, in the cruel manner I have elsewhere described—the voices I heard gave me to understand that I was not to sleep—that as a spiritual body I did not need sleep, and that if I slept, I ran a risk of increasing the dreadful lethargy, which rendered me unable to resist any degrading or mean thought or feeling presented to me. I was to lie awake, and to endeavour to understand the directions given to me. Weary at length, and unable to comprehend these commands, I sought for sleep, and recollecting what my mother had formerly told me of my father, that he used when he found himself unable to obtain rest, to keep continually counting to himself, I tried the same. But then the power of thinking numbers for myself was taken from me, and my mind or life lay in my body, like a being in a house unable to do any thing but listen to the sound of others talking around him, and voices like the voices of females or fairies—very beautiful—very small, and with a rapidity I cannot describe, began counting in me, and entirely without my control. First, one voice came and counted one, two, three, four, up to ten or twenty—then a second voice took up the word twenty, and kept repeating twenty—twenty—twenty—whilst another after each twenty called one—two—three—four, and so on till they came to thirty—then another voice took up the word thirty, and continued crying thirty—thirty—thirty, whilst a voice called out after each thirty—one—two—three—four, and so on till they came to forty, and thus the voices within me proceeded, dividing the labour between them, and so quickly, that I could not possibly pronounce the numbers.

I conceive from this and other experiences that the mind acts by beautiful and delicate machinery, which is disorganized in all men by sin and violence—by perverseness. That we have no idea of the beauty of diction and of conversation—of the grace and majesty of action—of the perfection of the mental faculties which might be attained to, if more liberty were given in early life to the fancy, and if mankind chose to obey the laws of nature, or the guidance of God. I hope and expect to see such a state arrive in this world, or in a future life—but now we will not suffer the glory of God to be manifested in us; we will not allow God to dwell with us.

But our whole system of education is wrong; the mind is over-tasked, overstrained, and cramped, or allowed to lie waste and run into riot; and healthy exercise and behaviour are not sufficiently studied and attended to.

I ought to remark before I leave this subject, that the voices I heard accused me of crimes I had never committed, "they laid to my charge things that I knew not"—I was terrified by the charge of having wilfully connived at the drowning of an old woman in London, and vilified by the supposition that, being not the son of my real mother, but the adopted son of a poor American woman, named Robinson, I had denied her on account of her poverty.

CHAPTER XXXV

When I came to Mr. Newington's, therefore, I had recovered to a great extent from many of my delusions, and whatever they were that remained, they no longer rendered me an object of alarm, or a person from whom any danger was to be apprehended. The back of my enemy was broken; that superstitious fear was done away with, which made me suppose that I was to act blindly according to the inspirations I received, without exercising my judgment; my readers will therefore understand the claim to liberty which I made before one of my brothers at that time, though still confessing myself lunatic. I knew I was still of unsound mind, because I did not comprehend the nature or the meaning of the voices I heard continually, or the visions which I saw; *and I had not resolution then entirely to disregard them.* But the intimations I then received were not of a violent kind; but set before me the actions and manners of a life beautiful and holy.

At this time I found on many occasions that I could not speak; I did not know why: I was compelled to write my wishes to my brothers, and a day or two after my arrival at Mr. Newington's, I was obliged to write, finding my voice fail me, and I wrote in the power of a spirit (I have the paper still by me), these two sentences:

"I intend to write to my mother for leave to go up to London, and to remain here afterwards if she think proper."

"It is for the sake of medical attestations, of persons who have known me formerly, to my actual state of mind and body."

But after I had been a few days enjoying the tranquility of

my private room at Mr. Newington's, (oh! how delightful that tranquility then was to my jaded and exhausted and feverish mind) I found on examining into the cause of this phenomenon, when I had more self-possession, that my voice was overwhelmed by my feelings; grief checked my utterance, and prevented me from speaking. I found then that I was choked, as it were, or suffocated; and that if I would discourse on the treatment I had suffered from, or on any subject connected with my misfortune, nature refused to do so, except by broken sentences, and with much broken speech; I might call it stuttering, only that it was not confused, but difficult, and repeated, articulation of syllables. This is still often the case when I think of those things; and now, as formerly, if in conversation with another, I have been hitherto obliged to force nature, and to speak with pain, not only because I am loath to show my feelings, but because my manner, my utterance, my diction might alarm, and cause a suspicion of my sanity. I consider this one of the cruellest trials of the lunatic—that on their recovery, by the formality of society, they are not allowed to utter their sentiments in the tone and manner becoming their situation; but if they do, they run a risk of having their dreadful and deleterious confinement protracted—the world, the magistrates, and physicians, who are their judges, considering *themselves* of sound mind, in expecting from such as have been insane, and are sensible of their misfortune, the same tone, gesture, cadence, and placidity, that meets them in persons who have not been through any extraordinary vicissitudes.

I was at this time very weak; my nerves had been very much shaken—inwardly I had been much exasperated; and the cold shower-bath, at that inclement season of the year in Dr. Fox's madhouse, had given me the most dreadful and acute pain I can remember having ever suffered from, and that in the head; and during the remainder of the day my head seemed to burn with fever as if pricked by a crown of thorns: in vain I lay down on my sofa, and covered my face with a handkerchief, for relief—restlessness and anxiety continually agitated me, and I began to fear for my life, or that I should be driven mad again; to entertain suspicions that Dr. Fox had a design to drive me mad again, that I might not be believed when I complained of what I had endured and seen. In this state it is not wonderful that when I came to Mr. C. Newington's, I found even the ticking of a watch painful to me. A fortnight's comparative peace, however, soon made me recover tone and strength.

To say that I am surprised at the ignorance of a lunatic doctor, would be to say that I am astonished the night should be dark. But how is it that that ignorance should so long have been allowed to dupe the world? They seem utterly ignorant of the sufferings of nervous patients; to whom although loud noises shake and terrify them, and make their pulses leap—slight noises, such as the creaking of shoes, the crackling of a newspaper, the hemming and coughing of a vulgar servant, and the like, are sources of real pain, and maddening excitement and irritation. They are exposed, however, without the slightest thought to all, and worse than these; and it is a hard case, when a man desires to better the circumstances in which he or a friend is placed, in order to effect a cure more speedily,—to find reasonable desires thwarted by the ignorance of these men—through the implicit confidence placed in them.

Having at length, with difficulty, succeeded in obtaining a private sitting-room, I soon reaped the advantage of my comparative quietness. Here it was that I discovered one day, when I thought I was attending to a voice that was speaking to me, that, my mind being suddenly directed to outward objects,—the sound remained but the voice was gone; the sound proceeded from a neighbouring room or from a draft of air through the window or doorway. I found, moreover, if I threw myself back into the same state of absence of mind, that the voice returned, and I subsequently observed that the style of address would appear to change according to the mood of mind I was in; still later, whilst continuing these observations, I found that although these voices usually came to me without thought on my part, I had sometimes a power, to a certain extent, to choose what I would hear. I had observed at Brisslington that the thunder, the bellowing of cattle, the sounds of a bell, and other noises, conveyed to me threats, or sentences of exhortation, and the like: but I had till now looked upon all these things as marvellous, and I had been afraid to examine into them. Now I was more bold; having discovered so many deceits that had been practised on me; and being more desperate, and even reckless of ever being able to attain to an understanding of the guidances which I had imagined that the Lord had sent to me.

I discovered, and I think very nearly in the manner I have stated above, the nature of this delusion; and, prosecuting my examinations still further, I found that the breathing of my nostrils also, particularly when I was agitated, had been and was clothed with words and sentences. I then closed my ears with my fingers, and I found that if I did not hear words—at least I heard a disagreeable singing or humming in the ears—and that those sounds, which were often used to convey distinct words and sentences, and which at other times seemed to the fancy like the earnest cries, or confused debating, or expostulations of many spirits, still remained audible; from which I concluded that they were really produced in the head or brain, though they appeared high in the air, or perhaps in the cornice of the ceiling of the room; and I recognised that all the voices I had heard *in* me, had been produced by the power of the Deity to give speech to sounds of this nature produced by the action of the pulses, or muscles, or humours, &c. in the body—and that in like manner all the voices I had been made to fancy outside of me, were either formed from or upon different casual sounds around me; or from and upon these internal sounds.

Strange as it may appear, I believe that there are few persons living who have not, during the course of their lives, been aware of this phenomenon; I suppose there is scarcely a child breathing that has not, at some time or other, imagined that he has been called by name when no one was present. Often, when a lad, sitting alone, by the side of a pond, with my rods and lines, I have heard my name loudly called from the surrounding trees, and, looking round, I have said, to myself, "I have mistaken another sound for the calling of my name;" or, I have said to one of my sisters, if she was by, "How like that was to my name." But the truth is, there is no mistake—the person called does really hear his name called by a power the Deity has of causing any sound to appear to articulate or speak. But when our blood is in healthy circulation, and the mind and body healthily occupied, we throw off the impression, and cast it aside, and take no further notice about it.

My readers will observe that I make mention of a power to clothe any sounds with articulation, as residing in man, not under his control, and actively developed in certain men. It is obvious, therefore, that as this power can give speech to sounds which have no shape, if I may so call it, so it may change the shape of speech, or make a man hear different words from those addressed to him. I suppose it to have been the double action of the secret power to control man's utterance mentioned in the last chapter, and of this power to change the nature of sound, that caused the miracle of the confusion of tongues, if there is any truth in that story. The Babylonians did not only speak differently to one another, but they heard other words than were spoken, according to the will of Him who made the ear, and can destroy that and man together. We often find now, in society, a young man will address another, and the person addressed will tell him he used such a word, which the other will deny, affirming that he used another; but all present will declare that he used the wrong word, and yet he will swear and protest and become angry, declaring that he used the word he intended. I have little doubt now, but that often this arises from a juggle upon the senses, such as I have described. That the young man has, indeed, used the word he intended, but that the ears of the bystanders have been made to hear another. It seems difficult to account for the obstinacy with which the mistake is, on many occasions, denied by any other supposition; for the very fact that it also repeatedly happens that the wrong word has been used in mistake, and that the person who spoke acknowledges his error, renders the stubbornness of denial at other times the more striking and inexplicable.

In a former volume* I have mentioned, that when an old lunatic patient came to lie down near me, in Dr. Fox's madhouse, upon some chairs, and began reading a newspaper, I heard not only the

---

* Page 167 of this edition. G.B.

news that he mumbled to himself, but other words from his lips, conveying spiritual advice or suggestions. The sounds formed by the opening and shutting of the lips, and by the action of the tongue and breath in thus reading low to himself, were the foundation of this speech whereby the Deity then caused me to be addressed. For I must observe, the sounds usually clothed with speech are not always loud sounds, but minute and intense, and generally so; but, by comparison and by resemblance, they suggest the ideas of shouting, crying out, laughing, bewailing, weeping, expostulation, and the like, and the effect is very beautiful, extremely delicate, and to a sensitive frame of mind enchanting; so that I would willingly be able to lead an idle life, to enjoy the delirium of happiness and joy produced by these sounds, which, however, are delightful only so long as the mind conceives itself an object of special favour and patronage from the Deity, but which still convey consolation, and strength, and confidence with them, when they are accompanied with the impression of fear and of suffering from the Almighty's wrath; or charged with his imprecations, and menaces, and threats of tortures.

I attribute the hearing and fancying that we speak with others in our dreams to the same causes as the above, and I dare say many of the ancient auguries are to be explained in the like manner; for instance, that of the beam of the ship Argo—I conjecture that the augur who consulted this oracle was made to hear directions of different kinds in the creakings and strainings of that beam. Perhaps, also, the many Eastern fables of birds talking, &c., &c., may be derived from a more repeated experience of these effects in Eastern climes, where not only the imagination is more vivid, but the population are more ignorant, timid, and superstitious, and exposed to greater vicissitudes.

During my stay at Ticehurst, one of the judges, who had been trying a case of highway robbery, in charging the jury, very wisely warned them against putting too much faith in the evidence of the prosecutor, who swore to the identity of the prisoner, and who had been very much terrified. The evidence of a person to identity, whose mind at the time of recognition is disturbed by fear, or any other excitement, is certainly not to be depended upon; for fear is a great unsettler of the understanding, and bodily trials predispose the mind to be unsettled. I have found that whenever my bodily health has been deranged, particularly whenever my stomach has been affected, I have been more than usually troubled by these fancies, particularly if at the same time, through sluggishness or through cold, I have not been breathing through my nostrils, or drawing deep breaths. The ancient prophets, also, and the first Christians, particularly the apostles, were men who went through severe exercises of fasting, watching, and prayer, by the latter of which the imagination is excited, and the mind fatigued and exhausted. St. Peter saw the vision which was to teach him to receive the Gentiles, whilst fasting on the top of a house, where, through weakness, he fell into a trance; such men being fishermen also, and therefore prone to superstition and to believe in wonders, were likely to see visions, and to hear warning voices. So, also, St. Paul, when terrified, being deprived of his sight by the lightning. The mind was prepared for receiving the commands supposed to be divine, by the castigation of the stomach, with which the nerves of the brain are so intimately connected, and by terror. In these days, and in this nation, probably all these inspired persons would have been consigned to the madhouse, as it is probable Ezekiel was by his nation, of which the Spirit forewarned him;* and in these days all these phenomena are actually classed by physicians in medical works under specific names, as diseases of the sight and of the hearing. Mr. C. Newington, I am shocked to say, did not hesitate to tell me, in a conversation that I had with him, in which I alluded to Ezekiel, that he should treat such a person as an insane patient; and, profane as his ideas were, I conclude he would have been justified in doing so by all sects but one, from the total neglect of any precautions against the power of such a man being abused, on the part of the Church of England and of all the Christian communities, except the Society of Friends. Let the clergy prove their consistency, I decline the task; but I see either that Faith must be made shipwreck of, or that FIDELITY must be much suspected.

Now I find that augury was a science *studied* by the Romans,

---

* Ezekiel iv. 8.

and that they sent their youth to acquire it of the Etruscans; I find also that the Jews had *a college of prophets*—I find also that the gifts of the primitive Christians caused at first confusion among them, and that they required much reproof to bring them to order. I find also that the Romans believed that lunatics were able to foretell future events—I am told that in the East, they are looked upon as inspired persons. In reference also to what I have above declared, that I have often spoken and written sentences the meaning of which I did not at the time comprehend and could not apply—I recollect having heard in 1829, from a gentleman of the name of Meyers, a converted Jew protestant, then a minister of the Church of England, that the Jews had a tradition that the prophets of old did not understand fully what they wrote. This is hard to understand by those who have not experienced it. Where is the boast of the Protestant religion—where is liberty of conscience, if the lunatic doctor is allowed to be supreme judge over his patients in these matters, when lunatic asylums supply the place of the Inquisition, and in a form so dreadful?

Here, where we boast so much of freedom,—in matters of religion, which is of all things the chief—we are really slaves. Slaves to opinion, slaves to custom, slaves to power. No church, truly free, could submit to the *reformed* system of bishop-making. The Church is deprived of her rights and privileges by the very authorities to which they are entrusted—and instead of Christians assembling together to be taught of God, as THEY profess to believe they might be, one or two clergymen are set above the whole congregation—they preach doctrines which are often contradictory to Scripture, and if any members of the church were to rise even to question the doctrine, they would be silenced, seized, ejected, and taken before the magistrate. They who gain a livelihood in the name of the Bible, by the exercise of commonplace natural abilities, and the display of a refined classical education, knowing no other authority than that of having been ordained by the bishop and presented by their patron, and confessing no other powers of mind or sources of enlightenment than other men enjoy, will necessarily put down those who have or lay claim to authority of another kind, and who possess an enlightening power within them, and faculties which they acknowledge are not of themselves, but gifts from above.

If, then, the Christian religion be true, and if the miraculous gifts formerly boasted of by the Church be yet at hand, for the faithful to lay hold of, how can we expect such faith to show itself, or such gifts to be exercised, when the ministers of the church themselves point, as it were, to the doors of the madhouse, and open wide those portals to receive them who too simply receive the word of the Scriptures, out of which they are taught. Single-hearted people, recollect this—whatever true religion may be—religion with the world is a play and a farce; and ye, who are the underlings, must not carry this play too far—outstripping the piety, and disturbing the interests of your superiors.

The tones of the voices I used to be made to fancy that I heard, were often like the tones of angels, very beautiful and honest, and usually musical, and singing rhymes or verses. In this respect my former habits were connected with my malady—for I am very fond of music—and even before my illness, I could sit and enjoy in my imagination the music of the most brilliant orchestra or bands. Since my illness I have once or twice dreamt airs of music, but I do not understand writing notes. These voices were also often very pathetic, sweetly persuasive and seducing, but I had at times a stubborn, perverse and spiteful will not to obey them. Sometimes they appeared to address me jocularly—sometimes joyfully—sometimes enigmatically. I will give a few of the forms of speech addressed to me and put into my mouth, below:—

> The will of Jehovah the Lord is supreme,
> He must be obey'd, and thou shalt worship Him;
> Come up to heavenly places, you, &c. &c. &c.

> Keep rising—keep rising to heavenly places,
> In the power of Louisa's glory.

> I am risen to heavenly places
> In the power of the Lord Jehovah.

I am the lost hope of a noble family—I am ruined—I am ruined—I am lost—I am undone—but I AM the redeemed of the Lord—I am the redeemed of the Lord Jehovah-gireth—who is true to His word, and His saints love it well.

> The time of the trial of the time of the trial,
> And the trial of the time of the trial of the time,
> And the trial of the time of the time of the trial.

These puzzling and intricate words, referring to the profitable use made of our time, by successive reflection and action, &c., I heard in Dublin, under horrible impressions of divine wrath and tortures, if I did not comprehend them or use my talents profitably.

I was threatened with many cruel punishments—"to be drowning—boiling alive—suffocating—in darkness for ever and ever and ever—to be dissected alive—to be crucified—"

> To be hacked and hewed,
> And manacled and brewed
> In a manner most distressing;

to have to submit to these and the like horrors from everlasting to everlasting, without hope or fortitude, or power to meet and endure them without shameful cowardice and terror, and dreadful cries and blasphemies.

> I am a lunatic, but not as I think.—
> I am a hypocrite, but not as you think.—

I was desired never to say,

> I would if I could, and I could if I would;
> I will if I can, and I can if I will;

that it was hypocrisy—but to think and speak thus:

> I could if I would, and I would if I could,
> I can if I will, and I will if I can.

And I was given to understand that all men's thoughts run in one of those two forms, distinguishing the dissembler from the resolute man; and also thus:

> It will be so, and it won't be so,
> It shall be so, and it shan't be so.

That is, that it depended on the state of a man's mind and dispositions, whether his deeds would be acceptable before God—

and he happy in contemplating the nature of the Deity in another world.

M—— ——'s spirit of honourable anxiety to do your duty to the best of your satisfaction, bids you to pause for a reply.

Obedience is better than sacrifice, and sacrifice than obedience.

I'm doing my duty, but not as I think.

Do your duty and have your greed taken from you.

Do your duty and have your greed too.

Do so-and-so,—but not if you think not proper.

Impenitent—hypocrite—who are you now?

Herminet Herbert, come to my room, and save me from my melancholy doom and destiny.

Bl—sted hypocrisy, go from my heart, And cleanse me from my melancholy doom.

Victoria, victoria, the victory's won!

> I am joyful, cheerful, happy, grave and gay,
> In the knowledge of the LORD my REDEEMER.
>
> Be simple and civil, and all shall be well,
> But be not an insolent whoreson rebel
> To the best of good masters—but
> Be sober, and silent, and vigilant too.
>
> CHRIST HALLELUJAH! is your cue—
> CHRIST HALLELUJAH! is for you—
> If you'll prove faithful to your cue—
> > Not otherwise.

Keep looking to Jesus, the author and finisher of your salvation—oh! keep looking to Jesus!

I will conclude this chapter with the lines of Byron, changing a few words to suit my ideas.

> OUR LIFE IS TWOFOLD. FANCY hath its own world,
> And a wide realm of wild REALITY,
> And dreams in their development have breath;
> And tears, and TORTURES, and the touch of joy.
> They leave a weight upon our waking thoughts,

They take a weight from off our waking toils;
———————— ——— they speak
Like Sibyls of the future; they have power—
The tyranny of pleasure and of pain.
They make us what we were not—what they will—
And shake us with the vision that's gone by,
The dread of vanish'd shadows—*are they so?*
Is the past NOT all shadow? WHAT ARE THEY?
Creations of A SPIRIT which can mould
Substance, and the soul's presence occupy
With creatures brighter than have been, and give
A grace to forms which doth outvie all flesh.

CHAPTER XXXVI

When I had been thus far freed from my delusions, and delivered from a blind and superstitious respect for the mental phenomena by which I had been hitherto influenced and misguided—the voices directed me to declare that I was of sound mind, and reproved me as acting with false humility if I did not do so; and in one sense I might have claimed to be considered of sound mind, inasmuch as whilst examining the phenomena I have here attempted to describe, I was on my guard against doing any thing that could endanger others or myself; and I desired to do nothing, which I had not a right to do, but to pursue strictly that course of life most likely to restore to me health of body, through freedom of exercise; and with health of body, freedom and health of mind. But I now no longer obeyed their word, and I was so scrupulous, that I could not seriously claim to be considered of sound mind so long as there was one phenomenon remaining, the faithfulness of which I had not tested, and the source of which I had not discovered. I have mentioned that I used to see visions; these visions were sent to me, as I imagined, to guide my conduct and that of others; and I was often put to great pain of mind, being invited to attend to these visions as a guidance and as a pleasure; which I found became broken and confused; by reason, as I was accused, of my want of ingenuousness, or of my presumption, or of other sinful dispositions in me; because I was a simpleton, or because, instead of being tranquil through faith, my mind was disturbed by anxiety. Had I been at liberty I might very soon have brought one of these visions to a test, but being confined I adopted this plan. My youngest brother lost a favourite terrier bitch, and when

I heard of it I was grieved; then being confined in a lunatic asylum, with no manly occupation, this like many other petty occurrences, took great possession of my thoughts; I wished my brother to recover the dog, and it was suggested to me that if it was lost or stolen, the place at which it was lost, stolen, or kept might be made known to me if I sincerely desired it, in a vision. Soon after this I saw a vision of an inn and a turnpike-gate, and I was made to understand, that such a place was connected with the loss of the dog; I wrote to my brother then a description of the places as seen in the vision; supposing that he would recognise them, having been there, or having seen them in his neighbourhood. He replied that he had no recollection of such a place. From this I knew that I had been deceived—and concluded that this species of mental phenomenon also was not to be considered as an unerring guide.

About the same time, moreover, I discovered the source of this kind of delusions—or rather the means by which they are presented to the spirit. One day I entered a dark closet in which there was opposite the door a small opening to give light, and in it two or three upright bars. I gazed a short time unconsciously at this, and turning to the left, I saw to my astonishment a window or opening in the dark wall which I had never observed before. Recovering from my surprise I found that what I saw was not real —but visionary, and then reflecting, I found that the image formed on the retina of the eye, by the light from the opening on which I had gazed upon entering this dark chamber, appeared by an ordinary law of nature, thrown out upon the wall which was in shadow, to which I afterwards turned. In the same way as if any person gazes on the sun—he will see several green and blue suns floating in the air around him. I drew from this the following inferences, that neither when I had seen persons or ghosts about me—neither when I saw visions of things—neither when I dreamt— were the objects really and truly outside of my body; but that ghosts, visions, and dreams are formed by the power of the Almighty, in reproducing figures as they have before been seen, on the retina of the eye—or otherwise to the mind—or by arranging minute particles in the visual organs, so as to form a resemblance or picture of these figures—or by combining the arrangement of internal particles and shades, with that of external lines and shades, &c., so as to produce such a resemblance—and then making the soul to conceive, by practising upon the visual organs, that what it perceived really within the body exists without side, throwing it in a manner out, as the spectre is thrown out of a magic lantern.

I have said that these visions are presented to the mind through the retina of the eye or otherwise, because it is the spirit that seeth; the eye is merely an organ for communicating impressions from without to the spirit. Often when observing objects around me in the room, I have at the same time seen miniatures of friends, or other small pictures, as it were, in my loins or other parts of my body; and any person of a lively imagination, if he chooses, may fancy horses, churches, houses, or children running with their hoops, behind him, whilst he is looking to the front. For these reasons I do not think the retina of the eye the necessary instrument for the perception of visions.

I have seen very beautiful visions both in my sleep and when awake, which I have alluded to in another volume, and in which figures, endowed with great majesty and decorum, and of exquisite grace and beauty, were combined in postures, easy, elegant, and delightful, and in actions of refined voluptuousness; were I to call it sensuality or debauchery, I should not convey the idea of holiness—of innocence, and of honest merriment, or which these forms were the expression. Neither do the works of any artist that I have yet seen, excepting a few of the ancient statues of Venus, Apollo, and busts of Jupiter, manifest their character. These phantasms of silvered and venerable age, and of youth of both sexes, *"odiosa multa delicaté jocoséque facere videbantur."**

I am not sure whether it is lawful to mention these things; and whilst I unveil them with reverence, I call to mind the verse of Orpheus,

Φθεγξομαι οἱς θέμις ἐστί, θύρας δ' επίθεσθε βέβηλοις;†

and the words of St. Paul: "I knew a man once—how that he was

---

* Cornel Nep. Alcibiades.
† To whom it is right I will speak. Close the doors against the profane. G.B.

caught up into paradise and heard unspeakable words, which it is not lawful for a man to utter."

There is a natural life and an eternal life—there are things carnal and things spiritual—it does not follow that things seen in the spirit are to be practised in the flesh. Nevertheless, it may be that we do not understand that liberty to which the Gospel professes to call us.

Had I been, or were I master of my own faculties, when I beheld these things, I might be ashamed to allude to them in a country where the worship of Juno and of Vesta, of Pallas and of Diana, so much prevails above that of other attributes of the Deity; but, although they may betray the natural temperament or disposition of a constitution which the severity of the religion and moral tone of my country curbed and extinguished, I had no choice or control but to see what was brought before me. That which I have before beheld, however, I can faintly and indistinctly recall, and I can refuse these ideas by turning to other occupations, though, at times, in spite of all my efforts, they will still haunt me. I think it probable that they are common to all men, but that the world generally reject them, being taught so to do, and fearing God, or the accuser.

At times these figures, thus grouped together, appeared white, like ghosts—at times, coloured, like the human flesh—the substance of them was as of flame, and such that they might be imagined capable of incorporation with those who gazed upon them. At the time that I first saw them, I was very desperate—overwhelmed by a sense of degradation—of degradation from the high calling of a Christian, and from the glories offered by the religion of Jesus Christ below the station of the beast of the field. I was beginning to awake from my delusions, and I was enraged and disgusted at having been deceived. I spoke to myself thus: "I am cast out of heaven, I have been disgraced by the Almighty—no temporal king has dishonoured me and turned me to ridicule; the King of kings—the Lord of Lords—the Ruler of the universe has despised me, from whose presence I cannot flee—to whose omnipresent court of Holy Spirits I have been exposed." Shameless from having been put to shame, out of revenge and out of despondency I almost ceased to endeavour to resist any temptation, and gave myself up to every low, grovelling, base, often savage feeling and thought that came upon me. I had no respect—no reverence. I attacked every subject, sacred and profane. I muttered, "I will burst into the sanctuary, and at any risk, at any loss, unveil this being whom we call God, and discover the nature of him we worship as the Divinity; till I know him I dare not attempt to serve him." In these days first, females came to me without attire; I speak of them as if they were, for so they seemed to be —spiritual beings—deities—perfect and lovely. My mind was silenced by their delicacy, their modesty, their winning beauty; and I slowly relinquished those resolutions, soothed by the persuasiveness of their appearance, in which appeals to my fears and to my honour often made me only the more stubborn. I braced up my mind also to courageous and virtuous efforts, in hopes of still being worthy of conversation with such as these who deigned to come to me. I recollect when one of these creatures of flame, the express image of a female of great beauty, married to one of my friends, appeared to descend from heaven unto me, when I was lying on the grassy bank in my wretched prison-yard, and uniting her spirit with my person, filled me with comfort. "Surely," I thought, "she is praying for me, and her prayers are heard, and her Spirit is living in me." I was then, perhaps, bordering upon phrensy or upon melancholy madness, and thus the Almighty condescended to heal by the imagination that which, by tricks on the imagination, he had wounded, broken and destroyed.

But to return to the physical causes of these beautiful illusions. Let me observe, that within the eye there is a phosphoric light which produces shades of more or less intensity, and which is sometimes white, sometimes of the colour of flame, sometimes, also, red. Besides this, there are often black spots in the eye, whether they arise from the bile, or from defective vision, I do not know. By the combination and methodical disposition of these regions of light and shade within the eye, those forms were produced to my mind which by illusion appeared to be outside of me. That this phosphoric light exists no one will doubt, who recollects that in dreams he sees day, and sunshine, and colours of every description—these could not be produced in the chamber of the imagination without the presence of light or fire of some kind. But when I was at Dr. Fox's, tied down in my bed, *in the dark,* and contentiously thinking within myself—replying to the voices about me—the motions of thoughts within me caused my eyes to flash frightfully with fire, and this often accompanied with sharp pain—I call this light or flame phosphoric, because it appears of a phosphoric nature, and I have been told that French surgeons have discovered phosphorus predominating in the brain of lunatic patients.

Thus I account for many of the pictures I have had shown to my mind—only cautioning my readers that whilst I venture to explain the means whereby these phenomena are produced, I do not question the presence of the intelligent power that made use of those means.

An example of this kind of vision occurred when I was at Brisslington, working in the garden among some currant-bushes —a female form, without habiliments, rose from the ground, her head enveloped in a black veil. I was told it was my eldest sister, and that if I chose she should rise up entirely, and address me unveiled. These propositions, depending on my choice, I never understood, *and they caused me great pain and anxiety of mind;* at length, recollecting how I had been deceived, and what I had suffered, I lost my temper, and replied, "she might come up if she would, or go down if she would—that I would not meddle with the matter;" but my mind was much disordered. At this rude reply the vision disappeared.

However, these phantasms are not always produced, merely by *internal* lines and shades artfully disposed together, neither are dreams. I recollect one morning awakening with a shout at Mr. C. Newington's, after dreaming that I was in an Irish village, with a lady and a friend, and that an Irish peasant pointed a musket at me, close before me. I found that I had been sleeping with my eyes partially open, and that part of the window, through which the sun shone upon me, had formed in my dream the muzzle of the musket. Thus, also, the ciphers which I have seen and copied on paper when writing, are, I conceive, partly caused by the internal arrangement of light and shade in the eye, partly by that of the lines and light and shade on the paper being combined with the other. If this is not the case with the writing, at least it is with sketches and figures, or parts of figures, which I often see on the paper, but now imperfectly; and which, I recollect, even many years before I was ill, often tempted me to use the pencil. Now of this phenomenon all people of any imagination are, I suspect, more or less conscious; for it is the same thing, when we look into the fire, and see our friends' faces, or picture to ourselves other forms in the glowing and ever-changing cinders, or trace out forms in the veins of a marble chimney; only I must distinguish between the mere notice of certain lines that are *like* a man, or *like* a face, or *like* a horse, or *like* a tower, and that pleasing apprehension of the very figure itself, caused by an internal operation of the mind, combined with the lines which are without.*

So it is—and so it was that I saw persons around me at Brisslington, clothed with the countenances of my relations and friends.

I observed also, during the slow progress of my recovery, which was made so unnecessarily cruel, by the state of exposure in which I was placed; that He who rules the imagination has the power, not only to produce written or printed words, and to throw them out upon *blank* paper; but to cover written or printed words or letters with other words or letters that are not there. This is also the case with larger objects—but not so usual. It takes place (I will not say *always*), when in reading, persons put one word for another, and it generally happens in little words that will derange the whole sense of a sentence; such as *no,* for *yes; from,* for *to; unlike,* for *like;* or in words similar, *humour,* for *honour; quack,* for *quick;* and *sample,* for *simple.* When persons make these blunders in reading, they immediately correct themselves and say, "Oh! I have made a mistake;" but generally speaking, I am persuaded, they make no mistake, but read the word which they saw —but being in good health, the operation of the mind, of the

* Mr. Charles Dickens will bear me testimony. "What do you mean, Phib?" asked Miss Squeers, looking in her own little glass, where like most of us she saw not herself, *but the reflection of some pleasant image in the brain*."— *Nicholas Nickleby,* chap. xii.

muscles, or of the pulses, which cleared the eye of the film, on which the Almighty produced the false word, which at the same time he threw out apparently upon the paper,—was so rapid that it was not perceived; but my pulses, and my circulation, and the operations of my mind being unusually slow, through disease and oppression, I saw and discovered the sleight that was played upon me. A trick which, until I became stronger in health, made me doubt that the objects around me were REAL: so that I threw myself against doors and walls, expecting to find that they were not there, as I have written more at large in a former volume.

If I may be allowed to hazard a few theories, or conjectures, or speculations on this subject, I should say,

1st. Is God a God of the sincere, the grave, the sober, and the chaste only? Is he not also the God of fun, of humour, of frolic, of merriment, and of joviality?

2d. May not humour and jocularity be NECESSARY for the healthful conduct of the understanding? and although excess of levity and of abandonment are injurious, and border on lunacy, yet, may not extreme starchness and severity, like a French tragedy, be equally unnatural, irksome, and ungrateful? I conjectured, long before I became ill, that the human mind, and the human constitution too is double. We have (what I call ignorantly, seeking for one to catch my meaning) a life in the bones and a life in the flesh—a life in the marrow and a life in the nerves —an inner health and an outer health. We have also, spiritually, a double nature. Self-love and the love of others—self-esteem and ambition—the desire to unite uprightness with grace. The two serpents that Mercury found contending together, and which, touched by his wand became united, are emblems of these. They are two principles of wisdom which sin makes to rack and rend the world and every man's bosom with discord and contentions; but which one like Mercury can reconcile by the word of salvation. Of these faculties, the weaker or more feminine should twine round the other, as a maiden round her lover—as a vine twines round an elm. But without pliability, without yielding, without elasticity, how can this be? Now humour, mirth, and merrymaking are necessary to the mind's pliability and elasticity, producing wit, and rendering instruction amusing, and learning healthful. But in this country every brow is overcast with melancholy. This nation is morose and religiously mad.

3d. In the exercise of any study, art, or occupation, may not the natural and healthy process of the mental machinery—may not the health or perfection of the very organs we are making use of require an alternation of toil and rest, exertion and relaxation, earnestness and humour; and this, if not always, at times, even as rapidly as the pulsations?

4th. That which God intended for my good—may not a perverse, unsimple, and suspicious disposition in me have turned to evil, or may I not have erred through impiety and hasty conceit.

Thus one man, through presumption, is misled by an oracle, like Pyrrhus, who thought he should conquer Rome, from want of modesty, not asking for an interpretation, when the spirit spoke ambiguously:

> Aio te Æacida Romanos vincere posse.
> Æacides the Romans conquer shall.

But another like Philip, through good sense, interprets the word rightly:

> Αργυρεαις λογχαισι μαχου, και παντα κρατησεις,

which may be rendered,

> With silver darts thy foes assail,
> And over all thou shalt prevail.

Which Philip found true, by sending bribes to the Greek orators and ministers.

I have observed that the power of sight has been often thus perverted in me, for a merciful purpose—showing, I may say, the fatherly and material, ay, marital love of that great and terrible, but benevolent Being, who has made us, and who protects us, and "who tempers the wind to the shorn lamb." Whose name be praised. I have in this manner been prevented from seeing objects and apprehending ideas too suddenly, which might have struck me rudely, and given me great pain, when my mind was not prepared to receive them.

We are fond, in my family, of observing old sayings and old customs, without any positive faith in them, from a respect to ancient traditions. I have often heard there, when any trifling article is missing, this expression—"I suppose 'Orthon' has taken it away," alluding to an old superstition. Now it is often the case, not that a power takes the article away, but that in the manner I have above described he prevents it being seen, casting a film over the visual organs; or, at the same time that the eye is resting upon the thing mislaid, covering it with the semblance of something else in the imagination.

If there is any truth in the story of the men of Sodom being blinded so that they could not see the door of Lot's house, I attribute that miracle to an illusion of this kind; likewise, when Jesus escaped from the violence of the Jewish mob—passing through the midst of the people; and when (the doors being closed) he came and stood in the midst of the disciples; and when he disappeared from the disciples at Emmaus, I conjecture, not that he was made invisible, but that the eyes of those around him were fascinated so that they could not recognise or see him. As, indeed, it is written, Luke xxiv. 16, "But their eyes were holden, so that they should not know him;" compare, also, the wisdom of Solomon, chap. xvii. and xix. Let me add, the experience I have had of these several phenomena explains to me many of the phrases and passages in the Bible in an extraordinary and satisfactory manner; I do, also, derive much more pleasure from those passages in ancient authors connected with the heathen worship of the Deity, and I find there is *a reason*, also, in much of what the wise and learned look upon as the credulous and superstitious antidotes of witchcraft and as foolish prognostications.

Thus I have brought this painful part of my work to a termination; and may He who made me a monument of his wrath in my destruction, and a monument of his mercy and loving kindness in my restoration, bless this work to the relief of those whom I have left behind me, and of those who may now be in, or who may hereafter come into like trouble.

CHAPTER XXXVII

In the manner I have above described, and by the successive steps above recorded, I became at length of sound mind; and I should think that very few persons who have read what I have written, and weighed my arguments, could doubt that I was entitled then to assert my claim to be considered so; or further, as I used to declare, extraordinary as it may appear, that I was the best judge of my own sanity. By soundness of mind, I do not mean any unerring powers of judgment, or any invincible moral strength: I know too well, as the wise man says, that madness is in the heart of all men. But I use the terms in the ordinary sense in which they are employed, to denote a man against whom there is no true ground for the charge of being unable to manage his own affairs, —unfit for liberty through mental *incapacity*. A man who knows who and what he is, his position in the world, and what the persons and things are around him; who judges according to known, or intelligible rules; and who, if he has singular ideas or singular habits, can give a reason for his opinions and his conduct; a man who, however wrong he may act, is not misled by any uncontrollable impulse or passion; who does not idly squander his means; who knows the legal consequences of his actions; who can distinguish between unseemly and seemly behaviour, who feels that which is proper and that which it is improper to utter, according to the circumstances in which he is placed; and who reverences the subject and the ministers of religion: a man who, if he cannot always regulate his thoughts and his temper and his actions, is not continually in the extremes, and if he errs, errs as much from benevolence and hesitation, as from passion and excitement, and more frequently: lastly, a man who can receive reproof, and acknowledge when he has needed correction.

To prove that I was unjustly dealt with by the doctors under whose detestable and un-English control I now was detained until the end of the year 1838;* to prove that I was grossly and timidly betrayed by the magistrates, to whom I was compelled to look for protection, I need only establish that, however much insane, I was not a dangerous person to be at large, or, as the act of Parliament so indelicately words it, "that I was not a proper person to be confined." But I do not hesitate to say that I was in good faith of sound mind, and much more fit to be at large than many others whose title to liberty and to uncontrolled freedom is unchallenged. There are persons who will say that after what I had gone through, I must have been weak in body and in mind. That I grant; and if I had not known and felt conscious of that weakness, if I had not desired to follow a plan calculated to compose and strengthen me, to arouse and cheer me—if I had not had resolution to adhere to such a plan, there might have been *a risk of the return* of illness, perhaps of insanity; but my insanity *was* then gone; the legal objection to my being at large was removed, and it was shameful to detain me on a medical hypothesis—doubly shameful in members of the medical profession. At that time, moreover, I used to assert that I never could, and I still question whether it is possible after the manner in which I have been undeceived, that I could ever possibly become an insane patient again. Other patients are cured, as it is called, that is to say, are taught to kiss the rod of the lunatic doctor; their delusions wear out, their impulses waste themselves, but they relapse, because they do not discover the secret of their disorder, they do not exercise the same scrutinizing spirit, or they are not taught by the same experiences which were given to me. My weakness should have pleaded *for* me, not against me; my necessities were rendered by that more urgent and more overpowering: I needed quiet, I needed tranquillity; I needed security, I needed even at times

* Probably a typographical error; see Introduction. G.B.

seclusion—I could not obtain them. At the same time I needed cheerful scenes and lively images, to be relieved from the sad sights and distressing associations of a madhouse; I required my mind and my body to be braced, the one by honest, virtuous, and correct conversation, the other by manly and free exercise; and above all, after the coarse and brutal fellowship I had been reduced to, I sighed for the delicacy and refinement of female society. But I was tried beyond my power to bear. The dull routine manner of thinking, or the sordid avarice of my doctors, thwarted me in my honest endeavours to obtain a reform of my situation; and the base treachery of the legislature, and of Englishmen towards their fellow-countrymen in this awful affliction, abandoned me to their frightful power.

> Around me, hark! the long and maniac cry
> Of minds and bodies in captivity:—
> And, hark! the struggle and the heavy fall,
> And the half-choked cry and blasphemy,
>   *   *   *   *   *
> Mid sounds and sights like these long time I've passed.
> Feel I not wroth with those who made me dwell
> In this vast lazar-house of many woes?
>   Where laughter is not mirth, nor thought the mind;
>   Nor words a language; nor even men mankind:
> And each is tortured in his separate hell!
> For we've no rest even in our solitudes,
>   Many; but each divided by a wall
> Which echoes madness in her babbling moods—
>   Whilst all can hear, none heed his neighbour's call—
> None, save that one, the veriest wretch of all,
>   Who was not meet to be the mate of these,
>   Reviving slow from anguish and disease—
> Feel I not wroth with those who placed me here?
>   BYRON.

If to resent neglect, insult, and ruffian-like violence, is a proof of madness, I was insane under Mr. Charles Newington. If to call by such terms the treatment I received under Dr. Fox, and to believe that it could not have been proper or wholesome for a nervous patient, was a delusion, I am still the puppet of a disordered fancy. If a desire and a determination to expose such a system, and to punish the conductors of it by lawful means, and a hope to be able to obtain their conviction for having compelled me to submit to a course of discipline contrary both to medical and surgical science, was an unjust, or even immoderate desire, I am still of unsound mind. If to postpone all selfish considerations, and to overcome the natural desire for avoiding publicity, in order to vindicate my rights, to uphold the law, to relieve the oppressed and to destroy the oppressor, and to set the Church up in proper authority in these matters, are symptoms of my being unfit to walk at large in my beloved country, hold up your hands, my readers, hold up your hands for Mr. C. Newington.

If my exasperation against my family, and even against my mother, caused by long ill treatment, and by my confinement needlessly protracted in improper circumstances, made it wholesome or reasonable, or necessary, to *continue the causes of that exasperation;* if my requiring of her to join me in prosecuting a man who had evidently deceived her, and my opinion, in consequence of her refusal, that I was *bound* to include her in my prosecution—if even that cool judgment degenerating at times into a desire to do so from vindictive motives, proved me to be of a disordered understanding—if my being unable to correspond in temperate language with those who in fact were mocking and oppressing me, whatever were their designs or intentions; if my sense of that inability which made me protest against being compelled to carry on direct correspondence, and to claim the interference of my friends—if my disinclination to meet my relations, until they acknowledged their errors, arising from a similar consciousness of the impropriety of doing so—if my refusal to see or to correspond with my brothers, who under these circumstances had referred me to the magistrates of a strange county—if my attempt to effect my escape, and the frank expression of my determination to do so at any risk, and without regard to the life of those robbing me of my liberty;—lastly, if my opinion, my desire, and my resolution to hold Mr. C. Newington responsible to me at law for acting upon these infamous pretences, and to try my cause with him also at law, proved me to be a madman, and justified him and the enlightened magistrates who visited the asylum, in the detention of my person—in prolonging my civil confinement—in excluding me from church, and in banishing me from society; then I have no right to be at large now, and I am still a dangerous and unworthy member of society.

These were, with the exception of one other, yet to be mentioned and explained, the only reasons ever given to me for refusing me my liberty; and these reasons I could not obtain until the middle of the subsequent year; for to add to the cruelty of my treatment, and to the dastardly nature of the conduct pursued towards me, I was left in dreadful suspense, almost entirely ignorant of the grounds my enemies—I beg pardon, *"my friends,"* were acting upon.

But there was one other reason, one plausible, one ostensible reason, one, in this country so custom-ridden and obsequious to fashion, perhaps convincing proof of the necessity of my confinement; and here I must beg Mr. C. Newington's pardon, and that of the three justices who came to *look* at me; having repeatedly told those respectable gentlemen, that no reason whatever had been given me for my detention. This was not correct, I had forgotten; but I found, on referring last year to a letter I received at Ticehurst from my family, that I had made notes on it in pencil, of a conversation with Mr. C. N—— [Newington], in which he had told me that he considered me insane, because I wore my beard and long hair. Whether the manner in which he mentioned it to me, had not struck me as very decided; or whether I considered it only as his opinion, and therefore it made no impression upon me; or whether I meant that I had no authority from my family (who Mr. C. Newington told me were responsible for confining me) for stating this as a cause of imprisonment, I do not know. But though I repeatedly declared my ignorance to the magistrates, and protested against being kept in the dark, and demanded information it was in vain; they had not the sense of justice, or humanity, and of common honesty, to procure for me any information. Neither did I obtain any until removed from under their jurisdiction.

I have stated, that I adopted the resolution of wearing my beard at Dr. Fox's, from a determination to reconsider all my opinions

and my habits, taking nature as my guide; and that I was directed
by the voices I heard to do so immediately out of love to my
Saviour, in consequence of the disgusting manner in which I was
often shaved. This command led to a violent scuffle, by which I
was immediately cured of the fancy that I had been specially required to commence wearing that costume; but the original
reason, and my objection to the recurrence of being shaved in a
room full of servants and patients, and of being washed in the
dirty water others had been using, and wiped with the servants'
begrimed towel, still remained. On these grounds, therefore, I
allowed my beard to grow when I came to Dr. Newington's, and
I also, shortly after, wore my hair in ringlets, from the same idea
of following nature, and from the desire to hide the deformity of
the ear, which the servants had disfigured by their blows at
Brisslington. In this latter respect I was pleased also with the idea
of concealing from observation, which might lead to inquiries,
the serious injury I had received through the neglect of my family.
At the end I preferred both these costumes as more natural and
comfortable, and together more manly, handsome, and becoming.
I had communicated to my family from Brisslington, all the circumstances attending the original attempt to wear my beard; for,
whatever may be said of the suspicious character of lunatics, I
had then no disguise. I learnt mistrust from having been repeatedly deceived.

That my family should make this costume a pretence for keeping me in confinement, scarcely entered into my thoughts. I
readily conceived that the doctors might be narrow-minded
enough to do so: but I felt confident in persons of a liberal education, that they would be above and smile at such trifles. Afterwards, when I began to suspect that I had deceived myself, I did
not attribute their wrong judgment to my wearing my beard
alone, but to their coupling it with the fancies which had accompanied my first attempt to do so; indeed I recollect one of
my sisters writing to me subsequently, "that my wearing my beard
and hair long, were a PROOF of the continuation of my delusions."
This made me very wroth. My word had been doubted, I had
been kept many tedious months in confinement, I had enquired

the reasons for their so doing, which were refused; and I found at last, that I had been condemned upon presumption, and without inquiry—and for delusions which, if true, were surely as harmless as any that a man could be influenced by. What injury could have happened to any person, for which I could have been accountable, by my wearing my beard and hair long, because I fondly supposed Jesus had so commanded me? But the fact was not so; my hair had never any connexion with any delusion; and those fancies connected with my wearing a beard were dissipated long ago. I am sick to make so much about a subject so personal; but I was very wroth. I conceived that it was the duty of those who doubted my word that I was of sound mind, and who abandoned me to a long and tedious and painful imprisonment, to which I saw no end —to have allowed me at least an early opportunity of knowing their reasons; to have taken care lest they condemned me un- justly; to have made inquiries, and to have stated candidly their reasons for suspecting my honour. I felt that my honour was suspected, my word being doubted; and I was wounded to think that my family should conceive it possible in me to desire to de- ceive my mother, and in a matter affecting her mind's peace; and that they should take the word of a common lunatic doctor, in preference to that of a son of my father. They pretended, it is true, not to doubt my honour; but I replied, that although it might not be impossible that a man restored so far to a sound state of mind, as my letters must give evidence to them, that I was, might be still insane; yet that it was impossible but that, if such was the case, I should know it when restored to my lucid intervals; and therefore that I could not in such a case assert my sanity without being conscious of a lie. I could not help, there- fore, feeling that my honour was questioned, and I was dis- gusted to think that I had been condemned on presumption. My heart became hardened and steeled against every gentle consider- ation.

I was shocked and *amazed* at the terrible system to which, in common with so many, I was subjected; without help, without hope. I resolved—I was necessitated—to pit my strength and abilities against that system, to fail in no duty to myself and to my country; but at the risk of my life, or my health, and even of my understanding, to become thoroughly acquainted with its windings, in order to expose and unravel the wickedness and the folly that maintained it, and to unmask the plausible villainy that carries it on. I do not think that I was wrong. The work that I am now writing may, I hope, *rescue* many wretched persons now ill treated and oppressed under it, and enlighten many generations.

I determined to give no man the slightest reason for having allowed my hair and beard to grow; I wrote to my family, taunting them, and daring them to come into court with me on such a ground. I said it was sufficient for others to know that I chose to do it. I thought myself of sound mind, in considering it an impertinence for any one not acquainted with me to make any observation upon it to me personally, and I do so think still. I may add, that it is indelicate for a man's family or friends to interfere in such a matter, except upon a certain footing; and that it is unjust to take an advantage of a man shut up as a lunatic. I determined, even if I came into court, to refuse to give a reason for wearing this costume, unless ordered by the judge, against whose decision I should have protested. "If," said I, "any one declares that I am actuated by delusions, I will reply;" but even then, such delusions could not justify my incarceration.

Persons will say, that although strict law and justice and argument were on my side, that I was not acting reasonably, that I was not guarded by moderation or by common sense; but I say that I was actuated not only by a strong sense of duty to the crown and to my country—and so much the more honourable, inasmuch as the crown and my country had neglected me—but by common sense. For how was I to act in the world, with any honesty, with any prudence, with any self-respect after I was restored to liberty, if I had betrayed my rights? and if I felt that I was only *connived* at for a man by those who *knew me*, what dignity, what spirit, what life could a man have under such an impression? I knew that my principles were different from those of my family and of the world in general. I was not fool enough to suppose that principles should not influence my conduct, for good or for evil; and was I to come out of prison, kissing the hands of men who had been spoiling me, and subject to have the meshes thrown over me again on any occasion, when my "friends" should be over-anxious about my doing myself some irreparable injury? Was I to be restored to society a milksop like this? Had I chosen the friendship of, and did I place confidence in honest men, thus to throw it away? No, gentlemen; those may be the terms on which lunatic doctors and visiting physicians may like to live in society, but I loved liberty, to live with an honest spirit and with honest men, I loved freedom to be free. I do not call a life of timid hypocrisy and servility liberty, any more than I call a madhouse, like Dr. Fox's, an asylum; but this was beyond the comprehension of the "bright" geniuses that came to *look* at me. Of whom more hereafter.

But if persons of that description should still affirm that my conduct was immoderate and unreasonable, and that my resolution to escape from imprisonment, even at the risk of being compelled to take another's life, was outrageous, to them I answer, that if I was conceited, obstinate, and violent, it did not prove me unnatural or insane. I had been provoked, and I had the right on my side. But to others whose judgment may be misled by such observations, I say that I regret extremely the division that took place between my family and myself; but I ask, was moderation to be only on one side? I put the question plainly; is any English-man to submit even to one month's confinement, purely out of complaisance to his family? and was I to submit to months and months, and interminable months of confinement, the end of which was shrouded in mist, whilst I was kept in cruel suspense, and refused any reason or any explanation? Was *I* to do this from deference to *my* family, who had abandoned me to the ill treat-ment I met with in Dr. Fox's madhouse, the recollection of which was fresh upon me? Was I to pander to others' curiosity, to ex-plain facts to those who made no sort of inquiry; to deal frankly with those who perverted what I said against me; admitting that it was *just* that I should be confined still, because *I had been* in-sane—when for THAT VERY CAUSE, it was most cruel and unnatural for my relations to detain me unnecessarily; when for that very reason they ought to have strained a point to improve my circumstances, and to make my situation more lively and more cheerful? No, no! Let not moderation be all on one side. Let there be a little thought for my feelings also.

Again, with regard to the respect I owe to society, and the deference due to the institutions of my country; I pray what does the lunatic owe to society? what does he owe to the institutions of his country? Society takes great care of itself—but not of them. The very refined, and *"religious"* state of society, make it ten times more revolting that they are so neglected. My countrymen wink with their eyes, whilst we are being murdered, in spirit and in body. If I had felt that I had been respected, as a lunatic, by the laws and institutions of my country—I would have given my own life, before I would have attempted the life of any man to recover my liberty. When I was informed, even falsely, that the legislature had provided for our defence, I gave up my resolution until I could obtain legal opinion. But was I to be mocked at, was I to be exposed to the brutal ruffianism of Dr. Fox's menials and system, without redress? was I to be imprisoned as mad for resenting that ruffianly treatment—was I to wait three months barred and locked in, and deprived of the exercise of every public act of devotion in this land of religious freedom, before I could see a soul to whom by the laws I could appeal for justice?—and then am I to be told that I was to respect my country; and the feelings of society? I consider that in such circumstances I respected my country and society best by standing by my rights—in throwing aside deference to a false, a morbid, and a hypocritical delicacy.

Should it be said, "You admit that you had been insane—it could not have been fair to expect that your liberty should be restored to you immediately—your friends and society required some security for your good behaviour?" I answer—"A man may be mad to-day, and yet perfectly sane to-morrow; and then his sense of the dreadful snare thrown around him may upset his reason again, in a more fearful manner. (If a man—how much rather a female, whose nature is more delicate, whose frame is more sensitive, whose situation is more defenceless?)" Nevertheless, I allow that society should have some security; but I was not to suffer with tameness and resignation, for the sake of society which had neglected their duty to themselves and to me; or rather which took such selfish care that I should not get out. Moreover, there is a difference between confinement and observation: observation, I desired to be placed under, and had my family respected me, I would have continued under observation, to relieve them of any reasonable anxiety, almost unto this day. But I could not submit for society, or for any body else, to be confined passively in a situation which *I could not bear*. Surely I am the best judge of my own experience.

Such was my position at the end of April, 1832.

I knew of no reasons for my continued confinement; and if any had been given me, I had forgotten them, or they had been communicated in a manner which made me think lightly of them. Mr. Newington also repeatedly assured me that I was NOT a lunatic but a NERVOUS patient, and that he was only afraid I should be made ill again by society! My mind looked forward then to a weary confinement in loathsome circumstances, and in a degrading position, until this man's conceit and vanity, or cupidity were satisfied. I could not imagine that honest and liberal minds, possessing such power of judgment, and such diversity of talent as belong to my family, could confine me as insane because I wore ringlets and a beard—or because I had certain views of instituting legal proceedings against Dr. Fox and Dr. Newington, or even against them. I cannot now conceive how any honest minds could come to such a resolution.* At the same time, I could not believe it possible that a family so just and truly amiable could confine me merely to compel me to relinquish my objects. To question my relations seemed to me to be a reflection upon myself. I had such faith in their simplicity and honesty, that I was rather driven to doubt my own self. Too great were the sufferings of mind I endured, watching continually over, and scrutinizing my own conduct and emotions to see if they betrayed any symptoms of insanity—I became so alive to cruel anxiety that I even walked

---

* It would be a short way to settle all causes, to have the appellant shut up as a madman.

about with a small pocket-glass—and if any one passing me or conversing with me, seemed to notice me, I stole on one side to examine what was the expression of my features. At other times, I feared that my mother might keep me confined—from the fear that I might expose my family, by my religious opinions—either as a member of the Row heresy—or as an unbeliever—according as I changed from one to the other; or from the fear that, my moral principles being gone, I might indulge in criminal excesses; or from fear of my attempting my own life, and to do injury to others. But of these, I have no ground to suppose that any but the latter had any influence over her conduct. My family have not much originality of idea, or independence of mind. They thought, with the world, that lunacy was an impenetrable mystery; that lunatic doctors were the only persons capable of meddling with it; that they were entitled to submission, if not to implicit confidence. They never thought to question these premises. They thought also that it was their duty to conceal the misfortune that had happened to me, and that *no one in his senses* could wish to have it exposed. Simple, faithful, and conscientious in their own dealings, and living retired, even my brothers not being aware of one half of what *I* now know goes on in the world around them, they were not prepared to guard against such a system of duplicity and chicanery—of revolting insult, and murderous violence—of racket and confusion, as I was subjected to. They could not believe it possible, or, if possible, so wholly unnecessary. They will not believe it true, nor how much they have wronged me; and therefore, even now, like many others, they may consider me, for publishing this work, yet scarcely of sound mind. But now these things are true—therefore I cannot keep silence. Necessity is laid upon me, and I must bear witness of these things. And yet who is on my side? where shall I find energy to reform these abuses? "Who hath believed our report, and to whom is the arm of the Lord revealed?" "I have trodden the wine-press alone, and of my people there were none with me." "My acquaintance and my friends stood afar off." "But I will tread them in my anger, and I will vex them in my sore displeasure."

In these pages I do not intentionally bear witness against the inspirations which came upon the godly men I knew at Row and Port Glasgow; indeed, I am not worthy to be compared with any righteous and virtuous man, therefore let the sufferings of each and the merits of each stand on their proper foundation; moreover, I was denied, I understand, by the church at Row; and they said, I am told, that I was possessed by a devil; therefore, I conceive, no inference is to be drawn from me to them. I thought that I loved them, but, since the inward cross-examination I have endured for so long a time, my mind is become exhausted and confused, and I hardly know what is life, or what is death—what is feeling, or what is affectation.

Neither do I pretend to determine what was the nature of the influences by which I was misguided. Others may expect, that as I profess to be of sound mind, I ought to be able to express a decided opinion; but I consider, on the contrary, that I should not be of sound mind if I did not hesitate to make up my own judgment. Having, therefore, minutely, and, as far as I am able, faithfully recorded what I have experienced, I leave it to others to determine. For myself, I am not able to say, whether those influences were or were not entirely the effect of derangement—whether they were altogether evil, and in no part divine.

Do I presume, then, to compare the broken or absurd sentences spoken by or inspired to me, with the compact and consistent body of prophecy and revelation contained in the holy Bible? I reply—That is not my present object. I compare only *the Power* which acted upon me with the Power which of old influenced the prophets and the apostles. I question if that Power was not physically the same, from the resemblance of the physical effects. Nevertheless, let me add, that though the inspirations or revelations, if I may so call them, which have come to me, were broken and confused, and in appearance contradictory, I can ascribe that confusion and irregularity to defects in my own disposition, and I think I can reconcile the apparent contradictions. I may also remark, that custom makes us dead to the extraordinary nature of the ancient prophecies. Absurd and horrible as have been my *delusions,* I have not, like Abraham, been commanded to slay my own child—I have not, like Ehud, been commanded to assassinate my king—I have not, like Samuel, or Elisha, been ordered to anoint a subject king, in the place of my sovereign's children—I have not, like Ezekiel, laid on my side thirteen months or eaten dung—I have not, like Adonijah, snatched my companion's cloak from him, and rent it in two. It is all very well to say now, after these signs have been fulfilled, that such acts were reasonable. Before the things signified came to pass what would my readers have thought of them?

I divide such mental experiences as we have described in the Scriptures, and as I was misled by, into three kinds—preternatural, supernatural, and miraculous. By preternatural, I mean such as are to be attributed to a defect of mental or physical power, to a diseased, a feverish and excited state of the organs of perception; by supernatural, I mean such as the seeing of ghosts—the visions or inspirations of the ancient sibyls and pagan priests, where we may conceive demons are permitted to exercise a power on the mind superior to nature; by miraculous, I understand such as are the work of God, for some special purpose—such as we suppose the prophecies and visions recorded in the Bible to be. I do not affirm that there are any properly belonging to these two latter denominations.

I argue this:—It does not follow, even in the case that the facts mentioned of the prophets and apostles were divine—that they were any thing more than preternatural. The apostles were, many of them, men of a superstitious class, and both prophets and apostles lived in an age of credulity and of superstition, and in an eastern clime; they were also subject to great privations and extraordinary trials,* and besides fasted long and often. These things try the constitution, and make the mind very susceptible:— they were predisposed then to see visions, and to hear voices addressing them, and to have singular feelings—in short, to all the experiences of persons of nervous temperament. We know also that by medicines, by opium, and by other drugs, many of these effects can be produced; that the ancient priestesses at Delphi and elsewhere inhaled a powerful gas before giving their oracles; and

* Daniel, Ezekiel, Elijah, &c.

I myself can bear witness that when my mind is most troubled with joy or anxiety, *and when my stomach is most disordered,* I am most liable to see visions and hear voices; or, as I conjecture now, my thoughts are most liable to float around me, or to buzz around me like bees. The nature of the visions I then see and of the words I hear may depend upon the state of my blood, of my dispositions, of my conscience; only that, as in dreams, sometimes, I conceive, they are suggested by contraries. I also must remark, when I say *my* thoughts, I do not speak as if I had control over them, and I feel doubtful if any sights or sounds so beautiful and singular can be *mine, in a proper sense,* being unconscious generally of any thing more than the usual humdrum method of thinking in which other people plod on; but this may be that my mind is ill regulated, hurried, vexed, distracted, so that I, like others, do not notice the operations of it; and latterly, I think I have observed that these visions at least, *are essential* to thought, and combined with it and with perception: so one person clothes all objects with a spirit of drollery, or, as we say, sees every thing in a droll light; another is always finding resemblances in persons and in objects—that is, his imagination clothes them with this resemblance; another sees every thing fretfully; another takes every thing in good humour—the imagination of the one clothes the lines and angles and figures presented to him, with irritating —the other with good-humoured representations or recollections.

The mind being thus preternaturally disposed to be influenced through the imagination, it is possible that the Almighty may make use of that faculty, in some to enlighten and instruct them, and to give them foreknowledge for the instruction of others; in others to amuse them; in others to deceive them; in others for all these purposes united. I would class, therefore, the *miraculous* relations of Scripture, and all others, under the one head of *preternatural phenomena.* And I would define them all—extraordinary impressions on the mind produced by the influence of the power which informs the imagination, working in a disordered or decayed frame. Thus, I conceive that such sensations may be only preternatural and yet divine. Neither do I mean that, when I declared that I was of sound mind, I had ceased altogether from hearing these voices, or from seeing visions, any more than that I have ceased from seeing and hearing persons speak in my dreams. I used the terms in good faith, as they are ordinarily used in society, not including necessarily an unerring judgment upon religious subjects, a positive knowledge, or a fixed faith in any particular sect or religion; all which a person may *profess* to have, and yet be very wrong, and yet be of unsound mind. Like Balaam, I can declare no further than what is permitted to me. My meaning, therefore, is, that though I still occasionally heard these voices, and saw visions, I did not heed them more than I would my own thoughts, or than I would dreams, or the ideas of others. Nay, more than that, I rather acted diametrically opposite to them, hating them for having deceived me. My organs of sight and of hearing may have been still disordered, but not my understanding.

As a proof of this, I recollect, when I was aware of my having been thoroughly duped, or mistaken; and was considering what course I should adopt to escape from my fearful captivity— whether to play the hypocrite, and secure the good opinion of Mr. Newington, which was foreign to my nature, or to look to the law and to the magistrates for my release;—when I had adopted the latter resolution, as a duty to myself and to others, these siren tongues and visions came to show me the semblance of a holy, godlike, and perfect patience and resignation; whereby I might put it into execution, manifesting, as they pretended, the life of the Holy Spirit in me, and imitating the manners and the behaviour, as I supposed, of the Lord; but I resolutely refused to listen to their suggestions, and I determined to carry out my resolutions, with all the defects, as well as all the sincerity of a natural man—a plain and very weak Englishman.

CHAPTER XXXVIII

As I regained health, I naturally desired to employ myself, and to recover lost time, by returning to keep my terms at the university. As Mr. Newington's refusal to allow me to do this, constituted one of my grounds of complaint against him, and for an action at law, to recover damages for loss of time, which I believe I should have been fully justified in undertaking; I will insert my first letter to Dr. M'Bride, which probably led to this resolution. I cannot mention his name without expressing my regret that my acquaintance with that amiable and talented gentleman was so soon severed.

Ticehurst, May 2, 1832.

My DEAR SIR,

It is with infinite regret that I take up my pen to make so late an apology to you, for having disappointed you in not returning to Oxford in 1830; as I had designed doing, and given you reason to expect. The overturning of my reason by the singular chastisement of the Lord, was the only thing that prevented me from either returning to Oxford, or excusing myself to you. This ruin took place in Dublin on the 15th or 16th of December, 1830, and I did not return to the possession of my faculties again till the latter end of November, 1831; since which time I have, as far as my affliction would permit me, been labouring against the prejudices of my physicians, and the misled judgments of my friends, to obtain more repose and quiet, by retirement in a private lodging, or in a private family; as I find an asylum a place of continual disturbance, and of disagreeable and indelicate exposure: it was not however till Monday that a dawn of hope broke in upon me.

It was not till within the last month or two that I had any decided idea of returning to Oxford, to prosecute my studies, for

I had no hopes of being able to resume them, owing to the extremely cruel tortures of soul and spirit which I was compelled to submit to, under pretence of healing my understanding, together with personal violence. This happened under the physician my mother intrusted me to at Brisslington in Somersetshire. I am now under the care of a gentleman named Newington, at Ticehurst in Sussex, a well-meaning and humane man, but on some points mistaken. Here, having had, for nine weeks, a private room to sit in—a luxury I had not enjoyed for THIRTEEN months before!—my nerves have begun to recover their original tone, and I have hopes of returning to Oxford soon, if the Lord permit.

I desire it—for I love it on account of its peace, freshness, and tranquillity; but I fear that I shall find some difficulty in persuading my friends and my physician, that I have strength of mind enough to avoid anxious subjects in conversation, or to leave society and my studies, when I find them pain me and hurtful, but I will endeavour to do so.

I shall be obliged to you if you will do me the favour of letting me know how my friend Cameron is, and whether he is still at Magdalene Hall, as I intend to write him a few lines. I request you also, to remember me kindly to Mr. Hill, and to his family, if you are acquainted with the principal of Edmund Hall; also to Mr. Buckley, of Merton, and Mr. Harrington, of Brazenose. I shall also be glad if you will mention my recovery to Kilbee, the person with whom I lodged, with whom I believe you are personally acquainted. I do not know if there is any one else at Oxford, that I can hope will have much recollection of me. Hoping that Mrs. M'Bride and your daughter are well,

Believe me, dear Sir, &c., &c.